THE REAL STORY OF THE LIBYAN UPRISING

ALEX CRAWFORD

COLONEL GADDAFI'S HAT

Collins

To Rick, Nat, Frankie, Maddy and Flo,
without whom I can do nothing

First published in 2012 by Collins
an imprint of HarperCollins*Publishers*
77–85 Fulham Palace Road,
London W6 8JB

www.harpercollins.co.uk

1 3 5 7 9 10 8 6 4 2

A catalogue record of this book is
available from the British Library

HB ISBN 978-0-00-746730-3
TPB ISBN 978-0-00-746739-6

Printed and bound in Great Britain by
Clays Ltd, St Ives plc

MIX
Paper from
responsible sources
FSC
www.fsc.org   FSC C007454

CONTENTS

PROLOGUE

Saturday, 5 March 2011

I look over at Martin and catch his eye and I know instantly he is thinking the same as me. We're going to die.

We actually can't get out of this. The tanks are outside. Right outside where we are sitting. Gaddafi's soldiers seem to be all around us. This is it. I had often wondered how I would go, what the end would be like. I hoped it would be after my four children had had their own children. But no. We are actually going to die alongside strangers in this mosque in Zawiya, a long, long way from home.

Martin's face is shiny with sweat. His big eyes seem even bigger than normal. He's looking at me from across this small room. We stare at each other without saying anything for several seconds. I can see my own fear reflected in his face. He looks terrified. I think I must look the same. I know I feel it.

Oh God. I don't want to die. My youngest child is only 8. Nat is my oldest and he hasn't even finished school yet. I haven't said goodbye to any of them. I haven't seen them grow up. I haven't seen how they'll do at school, who they'll marry, what jobs they will choose, where they will live. I glance over to Tim. He has his head in his hands, looking at the floor. He has three sons. He's thinking all these things too. Christ, this is bad.

Quick, awful, selfish thoughts hurtle through my mind. Will it be quick? Will it hurt? But these are quickly replaced by regrets. Regrets at all the love I am about to say farewell to. All the children's hugs I will miss out on. All the things I won't be able to do now. All the places I won't be able to see. All the adventures I planned with my family but never did. Oh God.

And then there's all those special occasions I've missed because of reporting far, far away – birthdays, school plays, anniversaries, friends' dinner parties, holidays cut short. How will my children cope? How will Richard, my husband, cope? Will my friends miss me?

Then I stop myself. Shit, I think, if we're going to die I'm bloody well going to let everyone know what happened to us, what's happening to these people around us. My phone still has a signal. Unbelievable. I ring the office in London and ask to be put on air.

Chapter One

LIBYA BOUND

Tuesday, 1 March

Four days earlier, I'm in bed in my home in Dubai, where I have been posted for Sky News as a Special Correspondent and where my family and I now live. A buzz sounds on my phone and wakes me. It's late and I'm disturbed but that's all. I had been hoping for this message, and when the text comes I feel a rush of adrenalin.

'Can you go to Libya? John.'

John Ryley, the head of Sky News, never wastes words (or letters for that matter). But this is all I want to hear from him anyway. Great. We are off. Martin Smith, who is my cameraman, and I have already been on a whirlwind of Arab Spring stories, our feet barely touching the ground as we rush from one revolution to another – Tunisia, Egypt, Bahrain, and Egypt again. Now it's Libya. And Libya could be the hardest, most brutal regime to be taken on so far. Colonel Gaddafi has been in power for forty-two years. He and his sons run the country like a personal fiefdom and he shows no sign of giving up despite the huge protest demonstrations calling for him to end his rule. Libya is also important to the rest of the

1

world for another, particularly significant, reason. It is one of the world's top ten energy-producing countries – accounting for nearly 2 per cent of total oil production. The unrest has led to a sharp increase in global oil prices. It is a hugely exciting time to be a journalist, exhilarating to be at the centre of these huge events with big implications for the world. We all want to be there.

Recently, Martin and I haven't even had time to unpack before we're off again – to another country where the regime would rather shoot or arrest us than let us report or film what's going on.

This time, though, it's different. We are going in legitimately. The Libyan government is issuing visas and 'invitations' so journalists can travel to the country and 'see the truth for themselves'. But it is already becoming clear that the regime intends to manipulate the journalists as much as possible. They want to get their message out. And that message is that Colonel Muammar Gaddafi is still popular, still powerful and still very much in control. But, before tackling the Libyan regime, I have to manage my own domestic revolt.

Telling my four children I am off again and going away from them is definitely the very worst part of my job. My youngest child, Flo, who is 8, is looking up at me and her brown eyes are filling with tears. 'But for how long, Mum? How long are you going away for? Will you be back in time for my parent–teacher conference?' I say the same thing every time. 'I'll try, baby. I'll try really hard. I'll be back as soon as I can.' She's clinging to me, sobbing into my stomach. I am feeling rotten. 'Please don't go, Mum. Pleeeease? Why can't you be like other mums? If you love me, you wouldn't go. Will you be back by next week? Will you? Will you?' I hate having to disappoint them but I know in my mind the revolution probably isn't going to be all over by next Thursday. That's not a revolution timetable. But I just can't find the courage to break her heart by telling her this harsh truth. I hope I'm braver in Libya.

Florence is not yet in double figures but is more than adept at pulling the heartstrings and deploying a fearsome array of emotional blackmail tactics. 'You know what would really help when you go away? (pause for effect) ... A puppy.'

'Hmmm, let me think about it,' I say, playing for time.

Sometimes I don't even have the chance to say goodbye. They might be at school, on a play-date, or it could be I leave in the middle of the night to catch a flight or make a connection. If I can, I try to leave little notes hidden around their rooms. They don't say much. Maybe 'I love you' or 'Remember when you are reading this, I am thinking of you and missing you loads.' Sometimes – much to their irritation – the notes will have more functional messages, such as, 'Have you brushed your teeth yet? I will know if you haven't!' and 'Remember to do *all* your homework, even the reading for twenty minutes a night bit.' I'm not sure it helps fill the yawning gap of an absent mother, but they tell me they enjoy trying to find the notes under their pillows, hidden in their school books, tucked away in their underwear drawers.

My eldest, Nat, who is 15, gives the outward appearance of being the most stoic about it all. He'll just anxiously ask how long I'll be away and where I am going. He's not happy in Dubai, where we're living now. He doesn't much like the new school. He doesn't much like the students. He misses India (where we were previously posted) and all his friends there. He's still sore at us for taking him away from his old life and he's constantly asking to go back. Oh dear Nat, no, my love, there's no going back. My heart is hurting for him. I loved India too and I desperately want him to be happy. But the job is here now. In Dubai, in the Gulf. And the Middle East and North Africa are bubbling with discontent. And not just Nat's either.

The dynamics of the family change when one of us is absent. I notice, when one of them has a sleepover elsewhere, the noise levels dip, there are different family allegiances, different sparring matches. When Mum disappears for weeks it must alter considerably. Frankie is the second eldest (just 13) but far more mature than all of us put together. She used to be terribly upset when I disappeared for work before, now she becomes very angry. And she doesn't seem to get used to it either. She just gets angrier.

'Mum, you really have to sort out your priorities,' she tells me. 'Why do you have to go? Can't someone else do it? Why *you*? Just tell your news desk you have children, Mum. Don't they realize that? You know what, Mum, when I grow up I am going to do a job where I actually see my children.' Wow, the volleys are coming in thick and fast. Frankie gives me the hardest time out of all the children but also bombards me with affectionate text messages while I am away. But she has one final warning: 'And you better not miss my birthday, Mum.' It's coming up in less than three weeks. Yet another deadline to meet. Oh, my gosh, I'd forgotten all about that. That's going to be tight.

Maddy, at 11 years old, is the least outwardly perturbed of the three girls and probably the most interested in news events and what's going on in the world. She records her own little news diaries on her mobile phone and always signs them off: 'This is Maddy Edmondson for Sky News.' She has an audience of one – Maddy Edmondson – and occasionally Maddy Edmondson's mother. She has her own Twitter account too – long before her mother was encouraged by her office to get one. I think she had three followers – her two sisters and her mum. She's more a Facebook girl. But Facebook doesn't replace a mum who is away working. She doesn't like me going away either. They all – Nat apart – cry when I leave, and as soon as the door shuts they start counting down the days until I am back.

And then there's Richard – a hugely successful and decorated racing and sports journalist who is now largely responsible for keeping the Crawford–Edmondson household afloat. Sometimes even close friends ponder: 'And what's old Rick doing these days?' What? You mean apart from looking after the four children, doing the homework, the cooking, the ironing and the school drop-offs? Well, yes, in between he's also trying to do some freelance writing and keep a foothold in the business he loves while his wife is off racing round the world. Yeah, not up to much really.

Richard gave up his job on the *Independent* newspaper after more than twenty years so I could become a foreign correspondent, which involved us all moving to India so I could take up the post of Asia correspondent at the end of 2005. It was a lot harder than either of us imagined. For a start, I'm sure you know, the world is still very sexist, one which remains largely divided on gender lines. And it's emphasized particularly when you are an expat living abroad. Richard will quite often be the only man doing the daily drop-offs at the international school gates, the only man at the parent 'get-to-know-you' lunches, the only man solely organizing his children's birthday parties, the only man at the school coffee mornings. It is hard for him and I have no doubt it is also very lonely.

There's also a crushing loss of status which many women will be all too familiar with after having children and stepping off the career ladder. I wouldn't say Richard is used to it by now. Does anyone ever get used to it? My former Foreign Editor, Adrian Wells, used to say he should be canonized. 'How does he put up with you? How does he put up with *it*? How on earth does he do it?' are the common questions. And if Richard is viewed as a saint by some, I often feel the opposite about my own status.

Most of the time I feel I am failing – failing as a mother, failing as a wife, failing as a foreign correspondent – because I can't give any of my roles the time I want to. A foreign correspondent's job requires 150 per cent commitment. I have waited so long to be a foreign correspondent based abroad and came to it that much later in life. I feel I have a lot of catching up to do. It's a 24/7 job and to do it well you have to put in so much time and effort. The necessary skills of being a mother of four often seem to involve having the organizational and diplomatic qualities of a CEO cum banker cum chef cum sergeant major. I constantly feel torn between all of my roles and feel like I am not succeeding at any of them.

Now I'm the main breadwinner and, for all the pain caused by constantly leaving the family, the work has to be worth it. I can't afford to do a bad job. It has to be good. Well, more than good. Otherwise why put everyone through all of this? I love the job, the places it takes me to, the people I get to meet, the stories just waiting to be uncovered. To be honest, I love the thrill and the adventure – so much so, it often feels terribly selfish. I don't enjoy being shot at. It's not the danger I love. Often I am terrified. Rather it's the opportunity of going to corners of the world I wouldn't get to if it wasn't for my job. It's the chance to make a difference somewhere to someone. Along with many foreign correspondents I realize how damn lucky I am to be doing this job and frankly I don't want to screw it up. I want them – my family – to be proud of me. I want them to feel like it's worth it. For all our sakes, I must try to do my best in Libya.

This particular departure coincides with a visit by the in-laws – or it is about to. This will ease the pain for all considerably, particularly Richard. His parents, June and Bill, have arrived in the region for a holiday. They are going on a mini cruise which was booked months ago and – unbeknown to them at the time of booking – seems to take in all the Middle East revolution hotspots – Bahrain, Oman, the Gulf of Aden. Half the itinerary has been adjusted, with many of the hotspots crossed off owing to 'uprisings'. So now it's just the pirates they have to watch out for. After the cruise, they will stay at our home in Dubai for the rest of their break. Good. The children will be distracted by loving grandparents. Richard will be distracted by being run off his feet as the host.

Right now, though, I have got to pack. The goodbyes are always horrendous and, to be honest, I want them over as soon as possible. They're just too hurtful for everyone.

Wednesday, 2 March

Martin and I fly from Dubai to Tunis and meet Tim Miller, Sky's Deputy Foreign Editor. He is a hugely popular figure in the newsroom – easy-going, sensible, always pleasant to deal with. '*Bonjour, mes amis*,' he says with a broad smile. '*Allez, Libya!*' We're pleased to see him. We're all pleased to be on the trail of the story. For now, all we can see is the future.

The plan is that the three of us will enter the country legitimately but try to shake off Gaddafi's 'minders' as soon as possible.
Their remit is to ensure the 'right' Gaddafi version of events is
broadcast. Our remit is to try to report on what is really going on
inside Libya.

At least that's the plan. The three of us relocate to a small café
in the airport where we have the first of many *croque-monsieurs*
waiting for the Tunis Air check-in desk to open. But when it does,
the answer is a firm '*Non!*'

We are still waiting for the official letters from Tripoli cordially
inviting our attendance and, as far as the airline is concerned,
they do not exist. We beg, we plead, we rant with the elderly Tunis
Air official, who is Libyan. We get letters faxed and emailed from
Sky and show him our journalist press passes. *Non, non* and *non*
again.

He asks if I can talk Arabic. I say: '*Kafah halak*' ('How are
you?') Somehow he recognizes I'm not a professor of the language.
'How can you go into Libya if you don't speak Arabic?' He's smiling
a smile which indicates he's not smiling much inside. I'm thinking,
can you please just let us on the plane? What difference does it
make to you? But he won't be persuaded. In fact I think he's enjoy-
ing our discomfort and our pleading. 'I am so sorry, ma'am.' He
doesn't look sorry at all to me. I think he's a Gaddafi loyalist. He
doesn't want to make this easy for us. We don't give up until the
plane actually takes off.

Then it is time for Plan B. Tim has heard Air Afrique is letting
people on without visas. That's the good news. The bad news is the
planes are leaving from Paris. We get the next plane to France. We
book a hotel near to the airport, and by now we're all becoming

very twitchy about our complete lack of success in getting into Libya. We're actually moving further away.

Still, optimism never dies. We have to hold on to that. I ask the foreign desk in London whether our colleagues in Tripoli need us to bring anything out for them. Lisa Holland has been reporting from the capital 'under the restrictions of the Libyan government', helped by producer Lorna Ward. We're given a huge long list of items to bring out which includes coffee, tea bags, energy bars, sun cream, snacks and odour-eaters (no one owns up to asking for these). Tim gets up really early to rush round a supermarket close to the airport to fill a rucksack full of these various 'essentials'. He rings up at one point as Martin and I are checking out of the airport hotel to ask for the French word for 'odour-eaters'. Oddly, neither of us knows. Then we all set off for the airport.

We get as far as the check-in desk and, again, an airline official stops us. No visa? Hmmm. But she is a Libyan who has lived and worked in Paris for years now and is much more sympathetic. She has the personal number of one of the Gaddafi officials in Tripoli and rings him up in front of us. Somehow our names are on a list and she agrees to let us on. Hurdle one crossed.

It's a short flight to Tripoli – only a few hours – and we are bursting with anticipation and suppressed excitement. What will it be like? How will we be treated? Will we get through the airport security OK?

When we land we are immediately segregated from the other passengers, the ones who all look like Libyans and have Libyan passports. We're taken to a small room where there is already a European crew. They say they have been waiting for hours. We sit down. Within a very short time, the other crew is led away. They have their permissions to enter the country.

The BBC's Wyre Davies is on our flight and he joins us in the room. There is a large picture of Colonel Gaddafi in the corner and I get Tim to take a picture of me with it. It's the closest I ever get to the leader. So we sit and wait and wait and wait. All of us are tired already and we use the time to sleep. There's plenty of time.

Wyre is told he has his visa within half an hour, but we are there for another three and a half hours. Finally we are allowed through immigration. As we walk out we see Wyre. He's still here. He hasn't been able to get any transport and he joins us. The airport is very busy. There are people milling around everywhere trying to get flights out. Many governments are evacuating their nationals out of Libya and those people who haven't got help from their government are still trying to leave. Even though it's dark and already night-time, it's still pleasant temperature-wise – around the early thirties – typical Mediterranean weather, very balmy. We're on the coast of North Africa but somehow it feels undeniably Arabic here, with a number of women wearing the *hijab* (Muslim headscarf). We walk out of the airport, following a Libyan official who says he will take us to the media hotel. We're led onto a government bus and notice – even through the darkness – there are lots of people waiting outside the airport's front entrance. We're told not to film and none of us wants to do anything to irritate the official who has just let us into the country. So we don't.

It feels tense. Everyone seems tense – the workers, the would-be flyers, the newly arrived, the armed guards who are standing both inside and outside the airport. Everyone seems edgy. Several towns in eastern Libya have already erupted in fighting – Tobruk and Benghazi are the two most notable. It began on 17 February, just over two weeks ago, when a general call for uprising was answered in several towns. It is the date the Libyans are calling the start of their revolution. They've seen their neighbours in Egypt (to the east) and Tunisia (to the west) rise up and defeat their dictators. Now it's their turn. The fighting has already spread to Tripoli, with heavy gunfire heard in the capital and reports that the airport itself was taken by the rebels in the last week of February. Several planeloads of African mercenaries from neighbouring Sudan, Chad, Algeria and Niger have been seen being flown into Tripoli to help the Colonel fight his own people. Already there have been some defections from the Colonel's own military: he needs to find other soldiers to help him stay in power.

The People's Hall in Tripoli (banned to the actual people), which was the meeting place of the Libyan General People's Congress, has been set on fire about a week before our arrival. Several police stations have been set alight, as well as the Justice Ministry in the capital.

We've seen pictures uploaded onto YouTube of Libyans burning the *Green Book* in Tobruk. This is Gaddafi's book of 'rules' and ideas – his political and economic philosophy for Libya. It is compulsory reading for every Libyan, a sort of Libyan answer to Chairman Mao's *Little Red Book*. It is both hated and scorned. In it, the Brother Leader, as the Colonel has renamed himself, teaches that the wage system should be abolished, that people should earn just what they need to and no more, that they should not own more than one house, that private enterprise is 'exploitation' and should be abolished. For the past twenty years, Libyans have told me,

Gaddafi's state machinery has even attempted to restrict access to private bank accounts so the regime can draw on those funds for government projects. He has set up People's Supermarkets where prices are controlled. He says often that he wants to ban money and schools. As the American commentator Michael J. Totten put it, he 'treats his country, communist-style, like a mad scientist's laboratory'.

Despite some liberalization over the past couple of decades, there is huge discontent and many of the educated and wealthy Libyans have long fled abroad to neighbouring Egypt or farther afield to Britain and America. Now there are large street protests, the Brother Leader has responded with bizarre and eccentric speeches on state television, threatening to slaughter protesters and promising the death penalty for numerous crimes. In one speech he addresses his discontented nation from underneath an umbrella. 'We will fight to every last man, woman and bullet,' he says.

We were hoping to see here in the capital some of the seething discontent of forty-two years of built-up repression. We know it's happening; finally Libyans are saying, 'No more!' But this seems to be contained in the east – in Benghazi and Tobruk. The fighting in Tripoli seems to have been quashed so far, with forces loyal to Gaddafi tightening their grip here. Certainly there's no obvious sign of rebellion right now, not here anyway. I had expected more evidence of fighting somehow, but there's none. Mind you, it's dark. I half wonder whether that's why we have been held in the airport for so long – to ensure we can't see very much on the journey to our accommodation. And if that is the case, it has worked. The streets seem clean and quiet from what we can make out on the way to the hotel.

The bus journey is swift. The Rixos Hotel, our destination, is already full to overflowing, not just with journalists but also with Gaddafi officials and minders. Lorna has said there is no room for Martin and me, so we say we'll go to stay at the Corinthia Hotel. This is the second media hotel, selected for us by the regime, but it's some distance away and virtually unoccupied. Many journalists feel the place to be is the Rixos, as the news conferences are held there and any information to be gleaned from the Libyan authorities is probably going to come from this location. Martin and I are fine with being away from the media pack. We prefer it that way.

We get off the bus at the Rixos only to say a brief hello and goodbye to our colleagues. We're famished, even more so when we notice that the hotel is serving the most wonderful five-star buffet. I look at Tim's rucksack laden with snacks, tea bags and the vital odour-eaters and think, why did we bring all of that?

Martin and I guzzle down a quick meal. Lorna and Lisa have spent the day driving around Tripoli with Saif al-Islam Gaddafi (the Colonel's second son but considered his heir apparent). They are very pleased with their journalistic coup. Lorna tells us: 'You know, I'm almost beginning to believe them [the regime]. He got a very good reception out on the streets whenever we stopped.' It sounds like quite a story and they have done well to persuade Gaddafi's son to be filmed and interviewed in this way. It gives us all an insight into just how deluded and controlling the regime is. But this is a country where Saif and his father have outlawed all political opposition, where there is no freedom of speech or media, where people 'disappear' and are routinely tortured during interrogation or as a punishment.

I am extremely doubtful that Saif is really that popular and conclude – as all the journalists at the Rixos have already worked out – that this regime is bent on attempting to manipulate journalists and, for that matter, politicians too.

The hotel is extremely comfy and the food excellent. You wouldn't find much better in many other cities around the world. It's far superior to the fare offered at our Paris airport hotel the night before. It's all very cleverly aimed at making the recipients feel well looked after and catered for. It is, unfortunately, a necessary evil for the journalistic fraternity to stay here. It's the only way to get any access at all to the regime. I am certain it must take an especially strong type of person to remain untainted or unaffected by the twenty-four-hour-a-day brainwashing which must be going on around here. But many of the journalists present are the most senior from all the international channels around the world. If they can't remain immune, then no one can.

Martin and I are desperate not to fall into the regime's clutches in the first place. By staying at the Rixos we might find out how the mind of the regime operates (but our colleagues are doing that already). We want to find out for ourselves what ordinary Libyan people are thinking and what life is like for those outside these walls. We're not going to be able to do that if we are escorted by Gaddafi minders, that's for sure. Martin and I quickly adjourn to the Corinthia. We don't want to be spotted by too many of the minders who are also staying at the Rixos. Tim will stay with the Sky team in the Rixos and we arrange to meet him first thing the next morning to work out a plan.

The Corinthia is a large, five-star hotel with two huge skyscraping towers set just a little back from the Mediterranean coast.

It has three impressive arches contained under a giant one at its entrance and looks incredibly plush – perhaps even more so than the Rixos. We step into a large, open-plan lobby with gold or gold-coloured furnishings and decoration everywhere. There are gold-coloured pillars, gold-coloured walls, wood floors with a sort of dark-gold sheen about them and a gold-coloured dome where the reception is. Set to the left of the reception is an odd-looking large silver bowl with water pouring out of it down some ornamental steps. Plush indeed, but there's a big difference from the Rixos. The Corinthia seems to be deserted, with only about six guests in it – and they are all journalists. We see them sitting round a table the next morning. We go over to say hello. One of them is Richard Spencer from the *Daily Telegraph*, who is also based in Dubai but with whom I have spoken only on the telephone until now. There's a guy from the *Guardian* and Anita McNaught from Al Jazeera. They are all very friendly and they give us a quick briefing about how difficult it is to get out without the minders. But occasionally they have managed to escape, mainly because they are away from the main media gang in the Rixos. I exchange telephone numbers with them and say we will try to keep in touch.

We go over to the Rixos and walk into the breakfast room, which is packed with journalists from around the world. Bill Neely from ITN comes up and says hello, friendly as ever. He is a fierce competitor but that doesn't stop him from being approachable and good company. Then Paul Danahar, the BBC's Middle East Bureau Chief, greets us. 'They're trying to get everyone to go to Sirte,' he says. 'They're expecting trouble in Tripoli after Friday prayers today, so they're doing their best to get as many of us out of the capital as possible.' It's generous information from a rival given to the new guys in town. There are different rules among competitors in a hostile environment, and he is being very helpful.

We have travelled light, carrying just two rucksacks with 'day' equipment. We've been told there's a trip somewhere – by helicopter maybe, or by bus – and so we are just taking what we need for a day's filming. After breakfast the journalists are causing a bit of a rumpus outside the front of the hotel. The minders are trying to persuade them to board a bus and no one much wants to go. There's a row developing. Martin starts filming as a few of the journalists – led by Paul Danahar – start remonstrating with the officials, primarily Moussa Ibrahim, who is the Gaddafi regime's spokesperson at the Rixos.

Ibrahim has a body language which reeks of hostility. He has prematurely thinning hair and a fairly stout figure which is clothed in the European 'uniform' of open-necked shirt and jacket. He is also staying at the Rixos – a fellow 'prisoner' – and we've seen him earlier having breakfast with his young German wife and very young child. He speaks impeccable English, having studied in Britain at Exeter University and afterwards taken a PhD at Royal Holloway College, London. He's a very well-educated and adept arguer of the Gaddafi point of view. Right now he is walking in large circles in the hotel car park, trying to avoid answering Paul's rather persistent points about leaving the hotel. Ibrahim is insisting he cannot let any of us out because our presence could trigger violence among what he calls the 'affiliates of Al Qaeda' who are on the streets outside. In the confusion, Bill Neely and his crew make a break for the hotel car park's gate, which has armed men guarding it. The three of us just happen to be watching this all unfold. Yep, good idea, Bill, I think. We follow in their wake. We manage to gct out before the guards are alerted and try to stop any more of us. Most of the other journalists are prevented from leaving.

Outside the Rixos is strange, uncharted territory for the foreign journalists. Few have been able to leave the five-star luxury of the hotel without a government chaperone. The regime has been insisting Tripoli is a city packed with Gaddafi supporters, any number of whom could turn us in or report us to the authorities, not necessarily out of loyalty but maybe out of fear. We're not expecting to meet many friends out here.

Now some of us are outside the confines of the Rixos and out of the control of minders. We have escaped their gilded cage. We run straight away into a traffic roundabout which seems fairly busy with cars. There don't seem to be many, if any, people walking around here. It is a built-up area and I can't see much above the walls which have been erected around what look like residential properties next to the hotel. It's just an intersection with about three or four roads leading off the circle and we're all anxious to get as far away as possible from the Rixos as quickly as possible before the minders come out and find us.

Bill tries to jump into a taxi but the driver refuses to take him and his team. We head off in another direction, leaving them behind, and flag down a man who has his family in the car. The three of us cram ourselves in, apologizing and thanking him in equal measure. He has a Gaddafi poster on the front of his dashboard.

We ask if he can take us to Tjoura, where we have heard there has been some protesting by anti-regime people the evening before. He raises his eyebrows. 'No, no, it's dangerous. Too danger-ous.' OK, then maybe just to catch a taxi? He drops us off a few streets away and we manage to find a taxi. The man in control of the wheels appears to be the most grumpy cab driver in all of Libya but, crucially, he agrees to take us to Tjoura. Tim has photocopied a piece of paper written in Arabic which has been given to him by the Sky team in the Rixos. It is a letter-headed document from the regime saying we are journalists and should be looked after as we are travelling with the government's permission and are accompanied by a Libyan representative (minder). This will be our get-out-of-jail card many times over.

We pass army tanks positioned at the entrance to Tjoura, a city on the south-east flank of Tripoli. But they don't stop us. Tjoura is important to us for two reasons: it is the site of a nuclear research facility (Gaddafi has long harboured ambitions to build a nuclear weapon) and it is home to a considerable body of the Opposition, known to be the most anti-Gaddafi district in Tripoli. We are expecting there will be a large turnout today after Friday prayers to express this discontent once again. But it's very quiet. Too quiet. The streets are empty. There are some smouldering piles of ash outside the mosque, but, even though it's Friday and the time for midday prayers, the doors are shut and there's no one around. We circle for a while but the taxi driver is not comfortable being here and so we head off towards the port.

In this vast country – the fourth largest in Africa – most of its 1.76 million square kilometres of land mass is consumed by the Sahara desert. Libya is around seven times larger than the UK but has only a tenth of the population and not a single permanent waterway throughout the country. The significance of Tripoli's port is therefore huge. But, instead of the trading which is its hallmark, there we see thousands of migrant workers all waiting to be rescued from Libya. Some are from Côte d'Ivoire, which itself is suffering violent upheaval. But to them even Côte d'Ivoire seems preferable to Tripoli. These foreign workers are castigated by the Libyan revolutionaries, who think they may be Gaddafi mercenaries, while also being victimized by the indigenous population, who resent them for taking their jobs (there is 30 per cent unemployment). We film and interview many of them. Our grumpy taxi driver is anxious to go. He wants to get to the mosque, or anywhere else for that matter. What he doesn't want to do is hang around for some foreign television crew. For a start, what he is doing will be viewed very dimly by the authorities and he runs the risk of jail or torture or worse. We pay him and he leaves, relieved.

Another man approaches us offering to take his place. He is rotund and middle-aged, with greasy hair, and looks decidedly untrustworthy. 'Come, I will take you. Where do you want to go?' he says. He's seen our interaction with the grumpy cabbie and heard me talking to Martin. 'Christ, what are we going to do now?' or something along those lines. I hesitate. There's something I just don't like about the man. I can't put my finger on it and it may well be unfounded but here I don't want to give anyone the benefit of the doubt. I thank him and move away.

Another gentleman, in his late sixties, is also watching us. He says in an aside to me that the rotund, persistent man begging to be our driver is an undercover Gaddafi agent. I notice he is weaving in and out of the crowd but never going very far away from us. I have no idea whether he is telling me the truth or not but I instantly like the cut of this older, more calmly reassuring man. My instincts tell me he is OK and right now I have nothing else but instinct to guide me. There appear to be very few taxis and certainly none here. We are outside of the official set-up at the Rixos so we are very much on our own. Our office in London can't help us either. It's not like you can call up a minicab company or flag down a black cab.

Martin likes this man too, and I reckon if Martin and I think the same of someone it's usually the right impression. 'Will *you* drive us?' I ask him. 'We need help.' It's his turn to hesitate, but only very fractionally, and it's immediately more reassuring still. He's not doing this for the cash or because he's the real Gaddafi agent. 'Yes, yes,' he says. We ask to go to Green Square. (This is one of Tripoli's most notable landmarks, originally called Piazza Italia, or Italy Square, when constructed by the country's colonial rulers. Then, during the Libyan monarchy, it became Independence Square, only to be renamed Green Square by Gaddafi, to reflect the political philosophy set out in his *Green Book*.) The elderly gent is a lovely man, very kind and constantly saying: 'No problem, no problem. Everything good.'

When we arrive at the Square, there is a demonstration all right but not the type we expected. About half a dozen demonstrators are moving down the middle of the road. Just a week ago – according to witnesses – this square was filled with rebels who were then fired on by government snipers in crow's nest positions on buildings. It was here that soldiers opened up with live ammunition on those calling for change. But today the small group is waving the green flag of Gaddafi supporters, chanting their love and support for the Brother Leader. We're disappointed and wonder whether this is going to be the end of our streak for freedom from outside the Rixos. Still, we get out – a little hesitantly – to see what's going on and film. We realize instantly the marchers are clearly being organized and directed by soldiers on the side-lines. A big banner denouncing the BBC is pinned up on a building. As soon as the small group see Martin's camera they start chanting enthusiastically. A short time later, a van pulls up in front of the soldiers and it is full of pro-Gaddafi placards and flags, which are handed out to the growing number of his supporters who are gathering or being corralled. The soldiers are more concerned with marshalling the pro-Gaddafi supporters than worrying about whether we have permission or not to be there. And besides we are doing just what the regime wants us to do – filming the support for the Colonel.

I try to do a piece-to-camera – with Martin filming me walking along – and the small group follows me everywhere, filling the background so the 'crowd' looks plump and heaving. Even when I keep fluffing my lines and retrace my steps, they too stop and come back with me as I start my walk-and-talk again. It's almost hilarious, but also frustrating. I am racking my brains as to how we can show this farce in one of our television reports. I notice a soldier approaching our taxi driver and taking down the old boy's mobile phone number. We leave shortly afterwards. We have some material for a report, but we're all thinking the same thing. Are we missing something? Where are the rebel protests? Are they too scared to come out? We want to carry on looking. If there are none, then there are none. They can't be invented. But we don't want to be embarrassed by simply not finding them.

'Why don't we check out Zawiya?' says Tim, out of nowhere. Zawiya is fundamentally important to the regime because it's not only home to one of the two most important oil refineries in the country, but it also straddles the road between the capital and the

Tunisian border to the west. It is right on a vital supply route – so retaining control of Zawiya is imperative. (The city has been in the news recently because the media group at the Rixos had been taken there on a chaperoned trip about a week earlier.)

Zawiya was supposed to be an example of a city which had been 'retaken' by the Gaddafi loyalists; where a small group of rebels had fought but lost. But when the media bus arrived in the centre they were met by flag-waving, protesting rebels. It was a bit of an embarrassment for the Gaddafi PR team. I agree with Tim. Let's go to Zawiya. I haven't got a better plan. We've now been in Libya and working on this story for about eighteen hours and got precisely diddly squat from the Opposition. So far we haven't seen a single rebel or anyone who will call themselves an Opposition fighter or supporter in public.

Zawiya is only about thirty miles away – a relatively short distance if it wasn't for the many checkpoints, which become more and more frequent the closer we get. At one stage we get a call from the foreign desk saying there's been tear-gassing of rebel protesters back in Tjoura. Damn. How did we miss that? We were only just there. Should we go back? The taxi driver sighs. 'We're nearly there now,' he says, rolling his eyes. So we carry on.

We breeze through the first few checkpoints. The taxi driver cannily puts all over his dashboard a huge Gaddafi poster which he'd been handed by the green-flag-waving people in Green Square. Tim pulls out his photocopied permission at each enforced stop and the driver indicates he is our minder. He has a natural authority which comes with age and living life, and the soldiers believe him. We get waved through. The driver gets a call on his mobile. I hear him saying, 'Zawiya.' When he puts the phone down,

I ask: 'That was the soldier from Green Square, wasn't it?' He laughs slightly nervously and nods but carries on regardless. The soldier is checking where the foreigners are going.

Then, as we get to the town's perimeter, the atmosphere and mood at the checkpoints change. The checkpoints are much more heavy-duty, there are many more military personnel and there's much more military hardware on show around the outskirts of the city. 'No problem, no problem,' says our driver. 'Everything good.' He takes us a circuitous route round the back, round the west, then the south. I like this man. He reminds me of my grandfather. He is gentle and wise and always charmingly polite, but he's not going to be pushed around.

We're stopped each time and asked several questions by the soldiers guarding the checkpoints. We explain we are guests of the government and the driver is questioned over and over again. Each time we have our hearts in our mouths, trying not to look anxious but desperately trying to work out the body language and the nuance of the conversations. I can hear the driver saying 'Sky News' a lot and 'British' and waving the permission letter. Whatever he says, he is convincing and we are allowed through. Martin notices we are one of the few vehicles heading *into* Zawiya. Most of the traffic is heading out of the city. And those who are fleeing are being given what looks like a pretty hard time. One family with young children is standing outside their vehicle looking on while the soldiers tear their belongings off the roof where they've been loaded, and throw them all over the ground as part of the 'checking' process.

*　　*　　*

Finally, we are inside Zawiya. The streets are empty but Martin still reminds the driver to remove his pro-Gaddafi poster. We are in rebel territory now, or so we believe. No point taking chances. The driver nods appreciatively and stuffs it into his footwell. We can hear the distant rumble of shouting. We hear the sound just a few seconds before we see a wave of people marching over the brow in the distance. Our driver stops. They are so far away I can't quite work out what it is they are waving. Are they flags or weapons? And what flags are they marching under? Who are they?

Then, we see the rebels' tricolour, the Libyan flag before Colonel Gaddafi's coup in 1969, before he toppled King Idris and replaced it with his own all-green version. I jump out of the car at the same time as Martin is unravelling his legs and grabbing his camera gear. 'Shall I stay with the taxi?' says Tim. 'No, take everything,' I say. By this time the old man is very agitated. 'No, no, come back. Danger, danger!' he's shouting. 'It's OK, don't worry, we're just going to see what's happening. Wait for us, please,' I reply.

We walk quickly towards the crowd of advancing protesters, wondering how they're going to react to us. This is the city filled with youngsters who have been duped into 'destruction and sabotage with drugs and alcohol', according to Gaddafi. I look back and I see the driver doing a panicky, fast three-point turn to get out of the way of these rowdy rebels. I hope he's finding somewhere round the corner to park.

And then the crowd is upon us. There's a few seconds of nervousness as we wait to see how they react. But straight away they are welcoming. 'Thank you, thank you,' a few of them say in broken English. 'Come, come.' They are loud, they are angry and there are lots and lots of them. At first we think there are just a few hundred but soon we see, as the crowd snakes round corners and along streets, there are many more, running into thousands. We're walking very quickly to keep up with them. It is steaming hot and within minutes we are sweating and puffing. The temperature has got to be in the high thirties now. The protesters are mostly on foot and the bulk of them are unarmed. In fact, they keep coming up and saying to us: 'Look, Gaddafi said we had weapons. Where are the weapons?'

I spot a man holding a rifle and make a point of interviewing him, asking him why he has a weapon. 'Defence,' he says. There is a van driving very slowly in the middle of the crowd with men hanging out of it. We jump on – partly so Martin can film as we're moving along, partly to have a breather. One of the men clinging onto the frame of the open door is holding a small pistol. But these are exceptions in a sea of marchers. The rest of them don't even have sticks or stones, nothing at all.

They are mourning the loss of one of the rebel leaders, whom they have just buried in the city's Martyrs' Square. He has been shot by a Gaddafi sniper. They're terrified of the snipers – of all the Gaddafi men who are inside the town – but they're also furious.

'Tell the world,' one man says as we're filming. 'Please tell the world. We need help.' 'What help?' I ask. 'What do you want anyone to do?' 'We need the international community to help.' Young boys are jumping up and down rather annoyingly in front of Martin's camera lens. It's an occupational hazard. There are children too here on this march but no women, no females at all except for me.

They are heading towards the Gaddafi tanks, which are parked beneath the underpass and blocking the exit to Tripoli. We drop back a little. We don't want to be right at the front when they meet up with Gaddafi's army. Several hundred marchers go past us. I notice an anti-aircraft gun mounted on the back of a pick-up truck which is driving along with us. 'It's one of ours,' one of the men tells me. 'We have had defections from the Gaddafi army and they brought some weapons.'

Then, suddenly, there is the familiar crackle of machine-gun fire. It's coming from the direction of the Gaddafi tanks. At first the crowd don't really react but, as the shooting continues, all of a sudden men are running back, running away from the firing which just keeps on going on and on. Men are being shot in the back as they're scrambling to get away. They're collapsing on the intersection; they're dropping as bullets hit them on the concrete flyover which straddles the tanks underneath. There are so many of them sprinting away that we are in danger of being knocked down in this bull-run stampede.

We duck behind a wall which offers us a little protection as the crowds run past and the bullets follow. 'Crawfie, we've got to get the fuck out of here,' says Martin. He's thinking, the tanks will be on us next, on us all. The soldiers will be coming on down this road, charging after the protesters. Then we have no chance. 'Stay here, stay behind this wall.' I'm panting. 'We'll just get caught up with the crowd if we run with them.'

We're cowering behind our wall but Martin can see through his camera that the people on the bridge who are trying to recover their injured friends are being shot at. He's giving me a running commentary. I can see several figures lying on the ground ahead but they are too far away to make out exactly what's going on. 'They've been hit,' Martin says. 'Other guys are trying to bring them here.' There's still so much shooting that they are crawling along the road to reach their friends, too scared to stand upright. Several times they are driven back by the shooting but they keep edging farther on their stomachs, determined to reach the still bodies. A car reverses at speed up the embankment to reach one of them and bundles him into the back and then tears down the road again towards us, bullets flying past it. Ambulances scream down the road to pick up more of the wounded and they are fired on as well. This is a massacre.

All over the place people are falling and being hit. The firing is indiscriminate and relentless, so relentless. Men are running for their lives, shoes scattering as they frantically try to escape the shooting. A few shout to us as they pass: 'This is Gaddafi!' and 'Look what he does to us!' Several are furious, yelling at us, anyone who will listen. Others seem to be in shock, scurrying past but with no real direction, constantly glancing over their shoulders at the tanks and soldiers behind, still firing. The rebel anti-aircraft weapon is driven up and fires towards the tanks. We're both startled it's actually shooting. It makes a tremendous noise because it's so close. It fires off a volley of shots, but that almost immediately backfires dramatically. It just draws more fire from the Gaddafi lines. People are still running past us. We're just watching, clinging to our wall, tucked in close to each other as this scene of mad, terrified panic goes on. With this amount of shooting, there must be many more casualties than those actually right in front of us. We can see several, but the flyover is obscuring our view and we don't want to venture out into the middle of the road where the bullets are spitting.

Yet more cars are driving past, screeching past, bundling the injured inside and driving off. We have to get to the hospital. A man is staggering towards us, a bullet wound in his chest. He's being held up and helped by two friends, one either side. They're half dragging, half carrying him. An ambulance pulls up and Martin just follows the injured man, who is muttering, 'Allahu Akbar' (God is great). He climbs in and I pile in after him. I look back and see Tim on the pavement. 'I'll see you at the hospital,' he shouts.

This is the first time we have seen any first-hand evidence of Gaddafi forces firing on predominantly unarmed civilians, the first time we have ourselves witnessed the cruelty of the regime. And it is cruel. It feels ugly and evil and very one-sided. I feel reluctant to mention (although I am duty-bound to do so) the very small number of weapons we have seen in a crowd of several thousand protesters because it seems to give the wrong impression. These were almost all unarmed, defenceless people, just marching, just shouting. What sort of a man, what sort of a leader, what sort of a regime orders the shooting of hundreds of his own countrymen, even children? This isn't crowd control. This isn't anything but shooting to kill and maim and injure and terrify. It's difficult to feel anything but sympathy and fear for these defenceless people.

Once the ambulance doors shut, it's quiet. All we can hear is the sound of the injured man's harsh breathing and his gasps of 'Allahu Akbar'. His friend is crouched over him, trying to lift his clothes to see the wound. We can all see a round, bloody hole where the bullet has entered his chest. There are no medics in the ambulance, only two or three protesters who are trying to calm the man and urging the driver to go faster, faster.

The doors are flung open and there is a wave of noise. We tumble out of the back of the ambulance into a big crowd outside the hospital entrance. Among them are medics who pull the man onto a stretcher and he is whisked along inside to the emergency room. I'm surprised at how many people are in the hospital, how they have managed to get here so quickly. It is packed, packed with the injured, packed with mourners. Everywhere Martin points his camera, there are men with bullet wounds, wounds all down their backs, bullet holes in their arms, in their chests. Some of them look like pellets. One man lying on his stomach has dozens of pellet holes all over his shoulders and his back. A nurse comes up to us. Another woman at last. 'This is Gaddafi. Look how he treats his people. This is Gaddafi!' she is shouting.

Men are crying, hugging each other. There is no room to move anywhere. There are so many people, either injured or tending to the injured, but also worried friends and relatives and volunteers who just want to help in whatever way they can. Everyone is in a state of shock. One doctor in particular starts talking to us, taking us from ward to ward, helping us communicate with the patients. 'Look at these wounds,' he says. He is furious. 'This is a shoot-to-kill policy. They are not trying to frighten people. They are trying to kill them.'

It looks like that to us too. We're taken all around the hospital to see the random casualties – a man who was going to work, a woman out shopping, a child sitting on the doorstep of his home – all sprayed with bullets, shot by snipers, hit by Gaddafi troops. The intensive care unit is full too. Many of the injured have been shot through the head.

The doctor who has been taking a keen interest in us asks where we are going to stay. He is reluctant to give us his full name and asks us to call him Dr M. He is not alone in feeling wary about being seen on television and being tracked down by the Libyan secret police or the military at some later date. 'It's too late to try to leave Zawiya now,' he says. 'Even I am not going to my home. You'll never get through the checkpoints. Do you have transport?' Oh my God, the taxi driver! Where is he? Tim has joined us at the hospital by now and has been asking around for the taxi driver. No one has seen him. There aren't any taxis at all in town right now.

Everything is not good.

The doctor says there is a hotel where we can stay. A hotel? Really? 'Yes, it's quite good. It is four-star. You will be safe there.' He tells us the Gaddafi forces sometimes come into the hospital to fetch their wounded and dead. We don't like the sound of that. The hotel it is, then. He says we'll be taken by some of the fighters. It sounds unbelievably appealing. By now a few of the rebel fighters have heard about the foreign journalists in the hospital and have made themselves known to us. One is a big lad who talks with a slight American accent but who is half Irish. He is only 19 but seems to be well connected with the rebel 'leadership'. He says his name is Tareg. His father is Libyan and his mother Irish. He is Muslim and has been schooled at the International School of Martyrs in Tripoli. His family also has a home in Wales. He tells us they have set up a ten-man council in Zawiya, headed by men from the military who have defected. But so far I have not seen any soldiers. They all seem to be civilians, all ordinary people from Zawiya who have found themselves caught up in a civil war.

'We will arrange an escort,' says Dr M. He tells us he lives in Canada, works as a surgeon there and only came back to Libya for a break. He has a family home here just outside the centre of Zawiya but he came to the hospital to help out when he heard there were lots of casualties. Now he seems to be running the place and looking after us to boot. For him it has become the most intense of working holidays. He seems alert but mellow, very at ease here and totally unfazed. He is with his young son, who is about 17 and wants to be a doctor too.

We're taken outside. In the hospital car park, for the first time, we see regulation soldiers. They are wearing uniforms – filthy dirty uniforms admittedly – and they're carrying weapons. There are about three or four of them. OK, I'm thinking, now this looks like the rebel 'army' we've been hearing about. With our new escorts, we suddenly feel emboldened. They have vehicles arranged and we set off in convoy through the city centre towards Martyrs' Square. The doctor is following with his son in their car. I am asking them how much control they have of Zawiya. 'We control virtually the whole city,' the driver says. 'They [Gaddafi forces] are mostly on the outskirts.'

As we near the Square, we can see roadblocks have been built by the rebels. There are military vehicles being used as obstacles along the road. There are a few armed men manning the check-points but, as soon as they see the rebel soldiers, we are waved through. In the Square there are many more men, some of them chanting. There are a few soldiers among them. The crowd we were with earlier must have retreated here. There is also a small mosque in the Square and the mosque's loudspeakers are being used to rally the crowd and fill them with courage. Some people are holding hand-written messages scribbled on cardboard which say: 'No Al Kayda here.' It is in response to Gaddafi's claim that the rebellion is promoted by Al Qaeda fighters high on what he called hallucinogenic drugs.

At the far corner of the Square there is an eight-storey building with barricades around it and armed men at the two side entrances. 'The hotel?' I ask with a sinking feeling. Yes, it's the hotel. But the Zawiya Jewel Hotel has been taken over by the rebels and now it's not so much a hotel as the rebels' military headquarters. This is not good. We might not have been all that safe at the hospital but we're going to be staying in the one place that Gaddafi's soldiers will be pointing their tanks and guns at.

The hotel feels largely empty. There are lots of dark corridors and there seems to be very little electricity. We're taken up to the seventh floor. They've opened up all the interconnecting doors so the rooms melt into one. The balcony overlooks the Square, with the mosque on the left. One of the soldiers closes the curtains and tells us to keep them closed if we are going to use any lights at all. 'Snipers,' he says. Tim and I decide we have to find out where the exits are. We need to know how to get out in a hurry if the Gaddafi forces attack. We need to know where to run to, how to disappear if we have to; that's if we get a chance.

It's dark now and even Dr M is looking worried. 'I think we go as soon as it is light in the morning. You can come with me,' he says. 'I will take you to my house.' Thank you. Thank you, good doctor. That sounds like the only plan.

Tim and I go downstairs to familiarize ourselves with the layout of the hotel. When we get to the basement we find the only back door is locked and, worse still, in the room next to the exit there is a man lying on a stretcher. He is attached to a drip but is being guarded by another man who is armed with an AK-47. The man lying down is wearing the green fatigues of the Gaddafi military. I think this is what they call the worst-case scenario: we are not only in the rebels' headquarters but they have prisoners here too, prisoners whom the Gaddafi regime may well want to try to rescue. Or eliminate. The captive is not responding to questions anyway. I ask where he is from, how he came to be taken prisoner and what he was doing. But no, he will only reply there has been a mistake, he is not a sniper, he was only trying to defend himself. The rebel guarding him is pretty exasperated with the answers too. 'He just keeps saying the same thing over and over,' he tells me. 'He is a liar.' I quickly take a picture of him on my BlackBerry but the rebels are unhappy at this so I stop.

We go back upstairs and tell Martin the news. Little fazes Martin. He is a six-foot-three Irishman from a large family, brought up in County Down during the quaintly titled 'Troubles' in Northern Ireland. He grew up in a mixed area where Protestants and Catholics jostled each other and even children were accustomed to the place being mortared and were not surprised by the attempts to blow up the British Army stationed there. Martin is bursting with natural charm and has a keen sense of humour. He's a seasoned cameraman who has been to a host of war zones, including Sudan, Zimbabwe, Iraq, Bosnia, Georgia, Afghanistan, Pakistan and many others. At this very moment he's more worried about power. He has a limited amount of juice in his camera's battery, and we haven't brought chargers for our 'day' trip. No batteries mean no camera and no pictures – and we don't want that. But he downloads the pictures he has already taken onto the laptop we have brought with us. His memory cards are now ready to be refilled with fresh pictures.

The doctor tells us the rebels are organizing food for us. Great. We haven't eaten all day. We sit talking to them. It is difficult to get a sense of how many rebels there are as we stay in one room and people keep coming in and out – mostly to rubberneck the foreign journalists. They express their gratitude to us for being with them and talk about the battle. The men are all defectors, and most have been in the Gaddafi army for at least ten years. They seem to be around early to mid-thirties. I ask to see ID just out of interest and they produce their army identification cards with photos. They are Libyans and an example of the defectors we've heard about. I take pictures of them on my BlackBerry as we don't want to run down our camera batteries. Also there is very little light and Martin doesn't think any pictures he takes on his camera will be very clear. At this stage we are just thinking 'conserve energy'. We have no idea what's around the corner. The men seem friendly enough. Their clothes are grubby and worn, though. Most are wearing what look like very old army uniforms which haven't seen a decent wash in quite some time. Their hair is straggly and, over-all, they look like they have been living rough for a while. But they're chirpy enough, answering my questions with good humour.

For them the turning point, they tell us, was when they were ordered to fire on civilians, fellow Libyans. They have little love for Gaddafi, whom they seem to think is quite mad, deranged. They ask about us, about Sky News. They assume I must be married to either Tim or Martin and are a little shocked when I say neither. But what does your husband think? How on earth does he feel about you working with men who are not even relatives? This would raise eyebrows among much of the Muslim population. Does he mind you going away so much? Have you children? Who looks after them? It is all a foreign world to them.

The food is taking so long and we are shattered. I think I am going to try to get some sleep because I know we will be up in a few hours and on the move again. I excuse myself and take off to the adjoining room and the big, double bed waiting there. I say to Martin and Tim: 'There's plenty of room. Please don't sleep on the floor.' Tim has absolutely no intention of sleeping on the floor, but it's going to be very cosy with three of us on the bed. Martin decides to bite the bullet and take his chances with the rebels. He ends up in another room with a bed all to himself. Lucky devil. What our hosts make of this arrangement is anybody's guess.

Later the doctor wakes us up when the food arrives. It's past midnight. None of us feels much like eating now but the doctor is insistent. The rebels have gone to a lot of trouble. No is not an option. We struggle up and sleepily eat our way through a bowl full of rice and a red mixture with chunks of meat and pasta floating in it. It's actually quite delicious. I never really got a clear explanation how they managed to rustle this up but it seemed to involve a bit of a journey and a fair amount of preparation given the time it took. We flop back to sleep as soon as we have bolted our food.

The rebels fire rockets throughout the night. It seems to be a message to the Gaddafi forces sitting outside the town – we're not asleep and we're not going anywhere. Don't even think about attacking us.

Chapter Two

DAWN ATTACK

We're woken before first light. The doctor is anxious to go. 'We should start to make a move,' he says. I am standing on the balcony of our room just waiting for the others when I see the red tracers of machine-gun fire on the horizon. I call Martin to get the camera. We're all watching as there's more – and then the explosion of a tanker. We see huge clouds of smoke rising from the resultant fire. The cloud is only about two to three miles away. 'That's near the hospital,' the doctor says. 'They are coming inside the town.'

I ring the office in London. 'The Gaddafi forces are beginning an attack on Zawiya,' I tell Kasia, the young news desk editor on duty. 'Are you all right?' she asks. Her voice is very concerned.

We need to get to ground level and out of here. We are fair-ground ducks here on the hotel's seventh floor. We all run down-stairs. In the foyer, we can see there is barely controlled panic. There are all sorts of men here. Some look like soldiers. Others are obviously civilians, wearing jeans and T-shirts.

We watch aghast as they rush around desperately preparing for battle. One offers me a flak jacket and a helmet. I put the helmet on, then realize it isn't a spare one. It is his. I give it back. I can't take his only protection and, besides, I don't want to be mistaken for a rebel. The men are busy getting out weapons, unwrapping them and putting them together. There is such pandemonium that grenades are being dropped and rockets are rolling across the floor.

One man is busy giving a quick demonstration on how to fire an RPG (rocket-propelled grenade). He is bending down on one knee, holding the RPG launcher on his shoulder. He moves it around, then shows how to pull the trigger. The youngster who has been listening intently has straggly, curly hair and glasses. He is one of many who look like university students. It's a lads' army. The pupil says, 'Allahu Akbar', takes hold of the weapon and runs off to fight.

There is already firing outside and we can hear the tanks getting closer and closer. Some men are dragging anti-aircraft guns away, others are positioning machine-guns on the corner of the hotel. 'Do you want to go to the mosque?' one fighter asks us. I turn to Martin. 'What do you think?' He says: 'Crawfie, Gaddafi's troops aren't going to respect a mosque.' I know he's right. We have reported on the Pakistan army storming a mosque and killing militants inside the Pakistani capital, Islamabad. 'But we are definitely going to be hit if we stay here,' I reply. It seems like the least worst option.

The man has a small combi van outside ready and waiting. We all pile in. It is just a short drive around the Square to the opposite end, where the small mosque is situated, but bullets are whistling around the van. We can see fires are already alight around the Square where rockets have landed. There are freshly dug graves of those rebels who have already died in the fighting on the grassy patch in the centre of the Square. The mosque is blaring out anti-Gaddafi rhetoric in between religious exhortations. It doesn't look much like a safe haven. Outside there is a gaggle of people shouting, chanting, praying, calling on others to join them in the fight.

As we sprint out from the van into the mosque, I see straight away that they have turned one of the two small rooms inside into a field hospital. There are about three doctors dressed in green medical gowns waiting for casualties. They have three mobile beds already set up. That's pretty much all they can fit inside the room.

The mosque is really small, one of the smallest I have ever been in. There is an open courtyard roughly four metres square. There is another small room about the same size opposite the medical room. We open the metal door and see there are already a couple of people inside sheltering – young boys, barely men. Bags of flour and sacks of wheat are propped up against the walls and cooking utensils piled up on top of them. It's a storeroom. Right at the rear end of the courtyard, beyond these two rooms, is the praying area.

We don't even have time to find a seat inside the storeroom before the first injured are brought into the mosque and, within minutes, more and more. The tiny clinic is very soon overwhelmed. The doctors have little equipment or medicines to treat the injured – saline drips, morphine, bandages seem to be all that is available. And the injuries are horrendous. There are men with the backs of their heads blown away, but they're still conscious, muttering 'Allahu Akbar' as they are carried by friends. How does that happen? How can they still talk when their brains are exposed? How are they still conscious when I can see inside their skulls?

Martin and I are rushing around filming what we can, each with one camera, but it is becoming increasingly difficult to even cross the small courtyard. Bullets are pinging off the floor. We can see machine-guns firing just outside the mosque. We can hear the tanks so, so close now. The sound is deafening. The noise of battle is everywhere – above us, to the sides of us, behind us. And it's all sorts of noises – the big, thundering boom of the tanks, the crackle of machine-gun fire, the whistle of single shots, the whoosh of rockets. An incredible, terrifying cacophony. It is loud and threatening and very, very frightening. We're not on the front line. We are in the middle of the battle.

The casualties are getting worse. I am sitting in the corner of the clinic watching as the doctors are seeing injuries no medic in any state-of-the-art hospital with all the latest equipment could save. They certainly can't be saved here with these meagre medical supplies. I am quite sure the doctors cannot have seen injuries like it. I certainly haven't. They are battlefield injuries – arms blown off, legs half off, skulls smashed open. One man is so peppered with wounds I can't actually see anywhere he is *not* hit. His clothes are deep red. The smell is strong. Blood has a particular smell. Death has another. They are both in my nostrils and all over my skin. I am feeling useless, utterly useless. I can't help these people. I can't tend to them. All I can do is watch these people dying in front of me.

A large man comes in carrying another of about the same size over his shoulder. He must be more than six foot tall. He's big and strong. He puts the very limp, badly injured man down on the floor of the clinic as the doctors try to plug holes and wipe whatever they can. One of the medics is screaming: 'Saline! Saline!' It's constant and repetitive and takes me a while to work out what he is saying because the pitch is so high. He sounds absolutely panic-stricken. I'm thinking saline is not going to even start helping this guy. I look outside and the big man who has brought the casualty in is bent over a chair standing on its own in the courtyard. He's retching and vomiting. Is it exertion? Fear? Pain? Maybe a combination of all three?

I go back into the storeroom. I feel like crying. Am I the only one? I can't be. I'm sure we all do, but something stops us. Tim and Martin are sitting there with about half a dozen other people. One young man is sitting in a motorcycle helmet reading the Koran. Others are just staring blankly ahead. Everyone has this sweat of fear on their face.

I look over at Martin and see he's returning my gaze. He's thinking: Is she thinking what I'm thinking? I am. We know each other so well that I'm positive the same dreadful thoughts are coursing through his mind too right now. This is as hopeless a situation as we've ever been in. We're going to die.

I can't see a way out, and Martin – who has been in so many wars in so many countries – can't see a way out either. Boom, boom, boom. I can feel the presence of the monstrous Gaddafi tanks right outside where we are sitting, crouching, cowering. And the stone walls feel terribly thin and flimsy, more like raffia paper. They are no defence, no cover at all. Gaddafi's soldiers seem to be all around us. We feel cornered, hemmed in, and utterly defenceless.

The blasts from the tanks are so loud they are damaging my ears. The noise is crashing and thunderous and vibrates through us. Please don't turn that tank into this wall, please, I'm pleading.

The rebels outside are fighting for their lives – and ours. Their city is under violent, barbarous attack from Colonel Gaddafi's forces and, frankly, they have no choice. They fight or they are crushed.

In the storeroom there are people just like us, about half a dozen who have just been caught up in the fighting or who have fled here to shelter. We don't have a single recognizable weapon between us. There is a young boy next to me. He's probably the youngest – about 15 years old, the same age as my son, Nat. He's crying, his hands gripping his ears to try to stifle the noise. The oldest is a man of about 55. He is staring ahead into space, clutching a briefcase which has his laptop in it. The laptop has saved his life already, taking a bullet which then ricocheted past his thigh. It took a chunk of his skin with it and he's bleeding, but it's only a surface wound. That's not what he's going to die of.

Martin and I are just staring at each other across the room, not saying anything, but we're reading each other's thoughts. He looks terrified. Just like I feel.

I suddenly want my family. I want to be near them, to know they are safe. I miss them and their love in this well of hate in which we have found ourselves. Christ, I have got too much to live for to die here in a foreign country away from them all. I look over to Tim and see he's looking down at the floor. He's a picture of despair.

We're all thinking the same thing, but we're all too frightened to voice it aloud right now. We're not going to get out of this alive. I see Martin very definitely put down his camera. No point. Shit, he has given up, I'm thinking. Tim is telling me to stay inside, stay in the storeroom, stay still, stay with him and Martin, conserve my energy. He's holding his BlackBerry. We've both got pictures of our children on our phones. But we know if we look at them there'll be no holding back the emotions.

Is Tim saying goodbye to them in his head, saying goodbye to those he loves? Oh God, I'm scared to my very core. Am I ever going to see my children again? Am I going to die here in this grubby little storeroom frightened out of my wits?

I pull myself back from this dangerous frame of mind. It's the only way I can function. The only way I can carry on. I want people to know what's happening. I want people to know what it's like to be under attack from this massive military machine. Shit, I think, I've got to tell people about this. I've got to tell whoever will listen how no one here had a chance. My phone is still working. I'm clutching it, gripping it in my hand. They've got their weapons. This is mine. I've got to get this news on air.

I make continuous phone calls to London. They can hear the explosions in the background throughout but I don't think they realize just how close everything is, how much danger we are in. Sometimes the explosions are so loud I can barely hear the questions from the presenter.

'Where are they from?' Mark Longhurst asks. 'Are the soldiers from the Khamis Brigade?' I realize I have no idea. I can't get out. Most of the time I can't get out of this storeroom. There are bullets flying everywhere. Everyone in the storeroom is in a state of frozen fear. We're just waiting for what feels inevitable.

Suddenly the metal door of the storeroom is flung open and there's shouting as a man in Gaddafi uniform is dragged in. He is screaming in agony. He can't walk. His ankles have been blown apart. He's dropped in front of us. There is no more room. We are all perching on the grain sacks and some of us are on the floor and he is lying there taking up the rest of the space. A doctor is trying to calm the crowd outside, trying to shut the door on them. They're furious and frightened too. They want to lynch the prisoner. The soldier knows it and the doctor is the one person who can save him from an immediate and violent death. The doctor calls me to stand at the door. 'Show them your face,' he says. Then he says to the men clamouring outside: 'Look, we have a woman in here and other foreigners. Stop this.' There's a bit of angry discussion, but they go away, back to battle. There's still much to be done. Fighting is still raging outside.

The Gaddafi soldier is sobbing, making an awful noise as the medics rig up a drip and start injecting him with painkillers. They are trying to wipe his ankles. There are just holes where once there used to be bone and they are pouring liquid on the wounds to clean off the mess. He screams from the pain as they do it. They keep telling him to be quiet, to be brave. We are all just looking at this man writhing in agony in front of us, this man who until a few minutes ago was part of an army which is still trying to kill us all. I ask the doctors if they will put a few questions to him on my behalf, and they agree. The soldier has Khamis Brigade ID and says he came in with fifty tanks from different directions to attack the town. They have surrounded Zawiya, he says. 'We were told there was Al Qaeda here,' he adds, 'but I can see you are Libyans and good people.' He is Libyan too and pleading for his life now. He knows his only chance of survival is within the control of these people treating him.

The young lad next to me is sitting on his haunches, his head in his hands. He is still sobbing quietly. He looks just like the child he is now. I start filming him and then am immediately disgusted at my actions. Jesus, have you no heart, Alex? I reach out and touch him, hug him. I think how my own son would feel. What is he thinking now? Does he know what is happening out here to his mum? The young lad doesn't know me but responds. He seems comforted by this human touch, calmer straight away. One of the men spots this interaction and comes up to the boy, attempting, I think, to help lift him out of his misery. He jostles him affection-ately, like an uncle might. 'What are you crying for?' he says, slap-ping the boy on the back. 'Everything will be fine, *inshallah* [God willing].' It is utterly unconvincing to the adults watching, but everyone smiles and nods gratefully at this optimism. It's all we have.

I try to wrestle Martin out of his mood dip, Martin who is always so brave, always so fearless but also a realist. 'Come on, Martin, show me how to get the light on this camera. It's so dark.' He shrugs. What's the point? he seems to be saying. The boom of tanks is still so loud. But he shows me how to switch the light on in the camera. Come on, Martin. Come on, mate, hold on. I can't do this on my own. He is rallying, and that gives me some more courage.

I am getting texts now from worried friends and colleagues, and from Richard, who has been watching my reports back home in Dubai. 'For God's sake, keep your head down,' he writes. I don't want to talk to anyone. I know my voice will give away my true feelings and I am terrified and feeling utterly trapped. We can't run away anywhere. All we can do is sit and wait. Wait for what we all believe to be the inescapable. I write back: 'We are in the mosque. It's the best place to be.' He writes back: 'Keep going, it's riveting stuff.' He seems strong and supportive.

44

From Sky's London head office I am getting messages telling me not to mention the mosque or where we are, in case we become a target. For the same reason, I am not to say there is a Gaddafi soldier with us in case we become a target, nor to give away who we are with. I'm thinking, but we're targets already! We are all targets. They are trying to kill us all.

I look across at Martin and Tim and I know they sense this as much as I do. The Gaddafi men will be in here soon. It can only be a matter of time and then that's it. Over.

It's hard to judge how long this will go on. It feels like for ever. I think it's roughly three hours. Then the door opens and a young man comes in. 'They've gone,' he says. 'It's over. Come and see.' I put my head outside the storeroom first and see people streaming out of the front door of the mosque complex. Cautiously, I look outside. There's a tank immediately outside the front door, half on the green verge of the Square's central grass embankment. There's smoke coming out of the turret. I think the rebels must have managed to fire a grenade inside it. Jesus, that's close. It's just outside. I haven't stepped far from the mosque's entrance when firing begins again. I turn and run back into the sanctuary of the storeroom. 'Not over yet,' I say breathlessly to the others. The fighting goes on for at least another hour or so.

I keep broadcasting and keep hearing my colleague in Tripoli giving a rather different, regime-approved version. 'The authorities here say there is no fighting in Zawiya. They have regained control. It is once again in the hands of the government,' she is saying. Then the director in the London studio cuts to me in Zawiya and there is the sound of firing once again. 'I can tell you the fighting is still going on quite fiercely,' I say. It very definitely nails the lies being put out by the Gaddafi regime.

Then the same young man comes in. 'It's over, it's over, I promise you this time, it is over. We have beaten them back.' This time no one believes him. But I cautiously step out and now it feels very different. There are a lot more people outside. They are falling to their knees, weeping and praying and giving thanks. I run back inside to tell the others. Martin is immediately up and out, camera in hand, with me following in his wake. Outside the feeling is euphoric. They are hugging one another, crying and gasping in joy and relief. We feel the same. Have they really beaten back Gaddafi's army? How the hell have we all survived? Oh my God, we *have* survived. Some of us are still alive.

We spot tanks at either end of the Square. We're being dragged, pulled, coaxed by everybody around us to see what's gone on. They want us to see the dead Gaddafi soldiers round this tank and that tank. They're not Libyans. They're mercenaries – from Chad, from Niger, from Algeria. There are more here. And more here. The bodies are lying around, on the ground and outside the tanks, half in, half out. Look at this tank on fire. Look how we fought and beat them. See this other tank we destroyed. See what they had inside the tanks – drugs.

Martin tells them they aren't drugs. It's Nutella. No, it's drugs, they insist. I tell you, it's chocolate spread, Martin says, then gives up and continues filming the 'drugs'. I am on the phone to London describing the scene when there's more firing. People scatter. Everyone is very jittery. My phone cuts out at that point. I don't know where the shots have come from but they have stopped. Maybe someone fired off a couple in fear or by accident, but it doesn't seem to be an attack. I am punching the office number into the phone. I know they will be thinking the worst. Bad timing. I get through to the news desk and can hear the producer in the gallery saying: 'We just lost Crawfie and she said there was firing starting again.'

'She's here,' the news desk editor Jules Morrison updates. 'Just putting her through.'

The presenter, Andrew Wilson, says: 'You gave us quite a scare there, Alex.' His voice sounds comforting amid all this turmoil and fear. I have known him for two decades and he has been in many, many close scrapes himself. He's covered many wars, knows what we are going through, and I can sense his genuine awareness. I feel like he is sending me messages despite the official strictures of our on-air conversation. 'Are you all right? Take cover and get to safety,' he says. We decide that is sound advice. Our good doctor is still with us. 'Let's get an ambulance and get to the hospital,' he suggests.

Yes, let's get away from here. It still seems too volatile, victory or no victory.

An ambulance appears. This doctor has connections. We clamber into the front, him still in his green gown, while another doctor, also wearing a medical gown, drives. The doctor's son is in the back. Martin is filming through the ambulance's rear window. As we drive along we can see the citizens of Zawiya coming out of their homes, filling the streets. I am surprised. I didn't think there were so many people still left in the town. I turn and look through the windscreen and see Gaddafi soldiers in a row across the width of the street. The driver heads fast towards them. One soldier raises his gun and shoots at the ambulance. We can hear the scream of the bullet. But the driver keeps his nerve, swerves and turns into the hospital. Tanks are parked just outside the complex.

We bolt out of the ambulance and into the hospital and a strange tranquillity. Oh my gosh, it feels quiet. My ears are tingling and feel like they have cotton wool stuffed in them. Is this what they mean by shell-shocked? My ears are still bristling from all the percussive noises they have been subjected to.

We move into one of the doctors' offices. Everyone is still reeling from what has happened. But we are in survival mode now. Tim says: 'Have you rung home? You should.' I say no, but I have sent a text to Richard: 'We're out of the mosque. In hospital now.' It's short and doesn't say we're safe – a point not lost on Richard. It feels better here but we are not out of trouble yet and I wouldn't be able to reassure him of very much at this point. But we're in a different place and temporarily out of the firing line.

Chapter Three

UNDER SIEGE

We have no idea how we are going to get out of Zawiya but we know we have to – and with the pictures. If we don't make it out with the pictorial hard evidence, then this really has all been for nothing. The pain of the people of Zawiya – and our pain – will have been for nothing. That is not an option.

The medics and the people at the hospital – some fighters, mostly civilians – are worried, too, about the destiny of our film which shows the true fight for their city. We keep having to disappoint them by saying no, we haven't got any of the pictures out yet. No one has seen what is happening here but I keep reassuring them that I *am* telling the outside world but only by telephone right now. They look crestfallen, let down. We haven't brought a Began or any other way of transmitting pictures. (A Began is a small portable transmitter, about the size of a laptop, which transports images via satellite.) There's no Internet in the town, so that form of transmitting pictures is also out. We have to either smuggle the pictures out, or preferably ourselves *and* the pictures. The question is: how?

We are offered medical gowns as a disguise. There is a fear in the hospital that the army is not beyond storming this place to look for us or recover its injured or dead soldiers. We take the gowns gratefully and greedily – grasping at anything which might offer us some protection, however slight. We rush to put them on, but we feel odd and look faintly ridiculous.

The doctors have even given us medical facemasks in an attempt to hide our European look. Martin and I try these on with the rest of the new kit while Tim is outside making a call on the satellite phone. And then we take them off again. Deep down we realize that if it gets to the stage of the army entering the hospital it's probably curtains for us all anyway.

Some of the Opposition fighters are already wearing medical gowns and many of them don't inspire us with confidence. One in particular, we think, is trying to persuade us to hand over our precious pictures. Is he just masquerading as a rebel? Is he really a government stooge? Are we becoming paranoid? A few of the rebel fighters appear to be staying in the hospital because they feel a little bit safer. But, to be honest, everyone is a 'rebel' here.

There isn't a single person we talk to who doesn't castigate Gaddafi, his forces or his sons. They are coping with the consequences of his heartlessness. They are patching up the broken bones, torn ligaments and cracked skulls of their neighbours in Zawiya, their relatives and their friends. If they were rabidly or even slightly pro-Gaddafi before this onslaught, it isn't hard to understand why they have done a handbrake turn, changing their minds and attitudes.

We are repeatedly urged by those in the hospital to see and film the growing number of injured – in the Intensive Care Unit and in the general wards. Martin and I are taken to the basement to see a row of dead Gaddafi soldiers. The bodies are in a quite horrible state but the medics want to show us they are not Libyan. 'These are not Libyan faces,' one tells us. 'See, they are from Chad or Niger – mercenaries.'

I'm not sure how they are so certain about their nationalities, but there's no question they do look very different from the Libyan faces we see all around us. The medics keep on stressing this point to us – that these people are not from Libya. It is important to them. Fellow Libyans would find it much harder, find it abhorrent to fire on their own. At least that seems to be their thinking. But, in their minds, Gaddafi is showing his utter contempt for Libyan life, demonstrating his savagery and confirming his madness by buying in mercenaries to kill his own people. They insist Gaddafi forces have entered the hospital in the past and taken away their injured and dead. It sounds preposterous. I am ashamed to say I write this off as paranoia. I don't quite believe it. But again I note the growing feelings of paranoia inside myself at the same time. I have been in Libya for a little over two days. These people have lived with the dictator for forty-two years.

We go about our various tasks. Tim is urgently trying to find someone who can drive us out of Zawiya and is in constant communication with the London office. Martin is still being taken round the wards to see the range of horrible injuries. I go down to the front entrance, where the accident and emergency department is. I just want to see what's going on there.

There's a crowd at the hospital entrance, gatherings of doctors and nurses and plenty of other people too. The hospital has turned into the main meeting area aside from Martyrs' Square. The entrance is also packed with hospital beds on wheels – ready for the next round of casualties. Martin has joined me by now. Then we hear the rumble of traffic. We see a convoy of military vehicles driving along the road running parallel to the A&E's entrance. The army is heading back into Zawiya to give the people in the Square another pounding. Within minutes we hear the sound of shelling and rockets firing. All those people we left behind – in the mosque, in the Square, in the hotel – are under attack again. We can't have been here in the hospital for much more than half an hour. It crosses my mind that if we hadn't jumped in that ambulance when we did, we would still be in the thick of it.

Now, as we're making our way through the hospital corridors, the staff are greeting us, nodding appreciatively, catching our eyes and occasionally saying things like: 'Welcome, welcome,' and 'Thank you, Sky News.' Everyone seems to know who we are.

The doctor's tiny room has turned into our 'office'. We're brought thick, strong coffee, bread and butter, some juice in cartons. It sounds bland, but to us it's a feast. A stream of doctors come in to say hello, talk, give us their views on the regime and offer advice on how to get the pictures out. Martin is getting increasingly concerned about battery power and about filling up his memory cards. Once they are full of pictures he has recorded, he will have to decide whether to record over earlier material – so erasing it for ever. The alternative is not filming anything further. But that's no choice at all really. We aren't there yet, though. Still, he has to be very selective now about what he films. We can't afford to waste either battery power or space on our cards.

The 'rebel' we don't trust is in the little room a lot too. He is doing much of the talking and handing out advice on what to do with our film cards. 'Give the cards to me and I will try to smuggle them out,' he tells us. 'You are going to get stopped at the checkpoints because you are Westerners. I will find a way to get them out.' My instant reaction is: 'No way.' I don't want to hand over our cards – our gold dust – to anyone and certainly not to this young guy that we don't know, who may or may not be a rebel. But I don't say anything and neither does Martin. We just nod and listen to what he is saying.

We are constantly discussing what route we can use to get out. We still have no transport but we're just investigating how, where, when – all prefaced by a very big if. It's best to accentuate the positive. We just need some sort of plan, and planning means we have less time to think about how we don't have a vehicle or anyone to take us anywhere just yet. Right now we are well and truly stuck in Zawiya. Everyone here is. And there's no paddle.

I suggest trying to go out westwards through the Tunisian border – a long and difficult journey as the government still has control of the route. There have been constant battles between the Opposition fighters and the Gaddafi troops. The rebels are having sporadic success at best in securing control of the southern border post, only to lose it to the regime days – sometimes hours – later.

Tim is vehement that this is not a goer. He has just returned from covering the mass exodus of refugees streaming out of Libya via Tunisia. 'It's too difficult a journey and once we get to the border – *if* we get to the border – there are thousands and thousands of people trying to cross. I'm telling you, it's a bad idea.'

The other way is to try to make our way out through the desert scrub towards the oil refinery just outside Zawiya. There's been fighting there too but one of the doctors says he has a house nearby that we can stay in. No, no, I'm thinking, surely that area is going to be crawling with military, and even if we make it there, then what?

What about heading east towards Tripoli? It's the shortest route and there is an airport, but Plan C is also fraught with problems. For a start there's the headquarters of the Khamis Brigade to negotiate, the most notorious wing of the Libyan military regime. The 32nd Brigade is colloquially named after Gaddafi's favoured son and the Colonel has made sure it has been well funded over the years. Its barracks are just outside Zawiya on the road to Tripoli. The brigade is feared throughout Libya for its ferocity and interrogation methods.

We're also worried that the regime and its minders at the Rixos Hotel will be on the lookout for us. They know by now that there are three foreign journalists in Zawiya and they won't like what we have to say about what's being going on inside the city. They are already mounting a campaign of denial about my telephone reporting, saying it is lies and now out of date. But we have the first independent evidence that Gaddafi is attacking unarmed civilians. The regime knows it and will want to suppress it.

I am getting lots of texts now. A number of people and several news teams are urgently trying to get us out, help us or at the very least offer some moral support. The experienced journalists inside and outside Sky News realize we are in a desperately difficult position. Sky's chief correspondent, Stuart Ramsay, who is a veteran of many wars and has been on the receiving end of attacks from a multitude of vicious military regimes, probably realizes the seriousness of our situation more than most. He is on the Tunisian border trying to smuggle himself and his team into Libya with the rebels, via the Nefusa mountains.

'We are working on a plan,' he writes. 'Don't worry, we'll get you all out.' It's just what we want to hear, need to hear. It makes us all feel less isolated, and I, for one, have reason to feel cheered by what on the face of it appears to be wildly optimistic reassurance.

Stuart and I have worked together regularly on several joint ventures and investigations for Sky over many years, interviewing the Taliban in Afghanistan, exposing the militant insurgency in Pakistan, covering huge natural disasters such as the Burmese cyclone. He has got me out of some pretty tricky spots before, not least when cameraman Phil Hooper and I were illegally held and interrogated by Afghan intelligence agents in the country's Laghman Province in May 2010.

We'd spent some days studying a militant insurgency group in the area, filming their training camp, living with them, observing their methods and finding out about their motives. We had finished our assignment and were travelling out of the militants' territory when we were stopped by several car-loads of armed men. They bundled us into their vehicles at gunpoint and took us to the offices of the NDS, Afghan intelligence. Just before we were stripped of all our equipment and mobile phones, I managed to sneak out an emergency text to Stuart and Neville Lazarus, Sky's Asia producer. The two of them were on their way to pick us up at a nearby safe house when they got my alert. At first they made their own preliminary enquiries, checking out the safe house, asking locals if they'd seen us. But both of them knew time was critical. The longer we were incommunicado, the longer we were away, the less chance there would be of finding us.

Stuart has done countless embeds with the British and American militaries and has pretty solid contacts with both, so, without hesitation, he and Neville walked onto the nearby US army base and raised the alarm. The Americans put out feelers, talking first to their local informants on the ground about whether they had seen any foreigners. The answer came back positive. Yes, two foreigners had been taken into the NDS offices and one was a woman. But when they contacted the NDS offices officially, they were told there were no foreigners there. No, the official insisted, no one had been arrested, no one had been taken in.

The Americans went further, asking their informants inside the NDS offices to locate and identify us after passing on descriptions of us from Stuart and Neville. Yes, came back the information from the NDS. There are two foreigners being interrogated right now. Then came the news that we were to be taken elsewhere. Not good. The Americans believed we were to be sold to the Taliban. We would fetch a hefty ransom for the corrupt officials and become a keen bargaining chip for the militants in any negotiations with the Karzai government in Afghanistan and maybe even the British government. They had to move quickly.

Just before we were due to be shifted, about four or five armoured personnel carriers full of armed US soldiers arrived at the NDS offices. Again they asked officially for the return of the two journalists they were convinced were there. Again, the officials denied everything: no foreigners and no journalists here, they said. The Americans refused to accept this, cocking their guns and eventually bursting into the room where Phil and I and our Afghan translator were being held. The first we knew of their arrival was when this huge, six-foot-plus soldier carrying a gun battered open the door. 'Phil, Alex,' he said, 'you're coming with us.'

I dread to think what might have happened had it not been for the quick reactions of Stuart and Neville. Their swift actions certainly saved at least the day for us.

Stuart and I work well together. We are good friends though fierce competitors, repeatedly trying to outwit and outthink each other on stories. Our rivalry is a standing joke in the newsroom. But there is no one who has more war experience or who has better journalistic nous and resourcefulness in extremely hostile environments than Ramsay. Knowing he is in the vicinity is some sort of comfort blanket.

Right now Stuart is on the Tunisian border with cameraman Richie Mockler and Martin Vowles, who is security for the team. I have worked with both in Pakistan. Martin is one of a very small number who have already slipped over the border under the eyes of the Libyan guards and back into Tunisia again. Richie and Martin are both former marines. Together with Stuart they are thinking through the options with military precision and planning. They are negotiating with their rebel contacts, appealing to them for help and discussing sending in a team of Opposition fighters who understand the area and know the back roads to try to smuggle us all out of Zawiya. They are also investigating a sea rescue – lining up a boat to enter Libyan waters and then transport us out of the country that way – again with the help of the rebels.

We don't realize at this point we are relatively close to the sea. Stuart, Richie and Martin V have the benefit of maps and satellite photographs showing our location. The only trouble is we have to somehow get to the port and at present we can't even get out of the hospital. In between the plotting and planning, Stuart still finds time to text us some schoolboy jokes: 'Have you heard the one about the bloke who walks into the doctor's with a steering wheel around his dick? The doctor says: "What on earth is that?" The guy says: "I don't know, but it's driving me nuts."' It is stupendously incongruous, but it breaks the tension. And the doctors in the hospital roar with laughter. Tim writes back: 'That's the first time I have laughed in days!'

Bill Neely from ITN is also texting from Tripoli. 'I am in contact with a doctor in the Square,' he tells us. 'He says if you can get to him, he will help you, try to drive you out.' Bill says the regime at the hotel is talking about taking the media based at the Rixos on a chaperoned trip to Zawiya to show how it is 'liberated' and under their control. That is extremely unlikely right now, I am thinking. There's still fighting here and nothing has been either 'liberated' or captured.

Getting to Bill's doctor contact should be easier for us, but even getting to the Square a few miles away is off limits right now and trawling around for an unknown medic just isn't feasible when the sky is raining bullets. Besides – unknown to Bill – we are now out of the mosque and in a hospital full of people trying to help us.

Bill himself is desperately trying to get into Zawiya. He is a formidable rival too. A lot of the journalists realize this is a story which needs covering. But getting inside Zawiya, which is now firmly under siege, is at least as difficult as getting out.

Those in Tripoli, however, have the best chance of getting to the story as they are the closest to the area geographically. And Bill is generous with his information. He gets repeatedly arrested at the checkpoints trying to enter Zawiya and his equipment is repeatedly confiscated. At the same time, he continues to send snippets of vital information to us. 'There is a string of tanks outside Zawiya on the east side,' he texts, giving us locations and positions of the military vehicles he has seen. 'They are from the Khamis Brigade.' It helps us build a mental picture of what is going on outside the city in which we are trapped.

The BBC's Arabic Service team is another crew trying to get around the government restrictions and get inside Zawiya to find out just what is going on. We hear that they too are arrested but, instead of letting the three-man team go, the Gaddafi soldiers take them to a military barracks in Tripoli, blindfold them, handcuff them and beat them. They are hit with fists, knees and rifles and then subjected to mock executions. They also witness the torture of others who are being held with them. Many of those detained, whom they see likewise handcuffed and blindfolded, are from Zawiya. The three of them: correspondent Fera Killani, camera-man Goktay Koraltan, and Chris Cobb-Smith – who is there as the security expert – are held for twenty-one hours in total. It is a frightening, horrific experience. Once out of Libya, they tell how their interrogators questioned them about us, the Sky News team. The army wants to know how we got into Zawiya, who helped us and is continuing to help us, and where we are now.

Tim tells me that John Ryley, my head of news at Sky, wants to talk. Tim has been on the telephone regularly with London, updating them on the situation and talking to them about options. I am reluctant to speak because I don't really know how to reassure John and I know he must be very worried. We're in peril on his watch. 'Hi, Alex,' he starts, 'how are you all coping? Are you getting enough food and water?' I tell him the doctors are looking after us and we couldn't be in better hands. It's true. In a city which is now coming under almost constant attack, the hospital has got to be the safest place, relatively speaking.

It's late now. Dr M and his son have been constantly looking out for us. Dr M has been in and out of theatre, performing surgery. He is looking very, very tired. The man was just on a holiday visit to see family in Libya and didn't even work here, yet right now he seems to be indispensable in the hospital. 'Let's get some sleep,' he says. We are taken up to the children's ward, which is now empty of patients. We have no luggage, no change of clothes, no toiletries, nothing. But we have a hospital bed to sleep on and a bathroom close by. It doesn't take long before we are all asleep, exhausted by our experiences over the past twenty-four hours.

Sunday, 6 March

I wake early, before the others. In the few seconds before I really come to, all I can see is hospital paraphernalia – the beds lined up opposite mine in the ward, the emergency masks hanging above them, the oxygen tanks standing by. Where am I again? Then I turn over and see Martin and Tim curled up on the adjacent beds. OK, now I remember. I creep out quietly trying not to wake them. I go to the bathroom. There are already a few young medics up and working. One stops me. He's friendly and curious and wants to talk – and I want to hear what he has to say about Libya and the Gaddafi family. He introduces himself as Dr Salah and tells me that although many of his age (he's in his twenties) have long despaired of the Colonel, they had until very recently a lot of respect and much hope about Saif al-Islam, his most high-profile son. Until the start of the Libyan uprising, Saif had also been viewed by Western politicians as a possible successor to his father. He was educated at the London School of Economics, speaks English fluently, and was considered forward-thinking, almost liberal, and, most importantly, part of Muammar Gaddafi's inner circle. A man the West could do business with.

However, all those hopes disappeared at the end of February this year when Saif made a rambling television address as the protests first spread to Tripoli. The protests were brutally crushed with live ammunition, but there were few independent witnesses, with journalists having to rely on accounts from protesters who described indiscriminate firing into the crowd from snipers on rooftops around Green Square. One said he thought the snipers were using what sounded like machine-guns.

'Libya is not Tunisia or Egypt,' Saif al-Islam said in his television address, denouncing the protesters as 'drunkards and thugs'. Troops had opened fire on the crowds because they were not trained to handle civil unrest, he said, and the casualties were not as many as was being reported. He finally lost swaths of supporters by declaring that the country was on the brink of civil war and this was being stoked by international media reports which were exaggerating the demonstrations and discontent.

'We are so disappointed in Saif,' says Dr Salah. This doctor is so young, I am thinking, young enough to be my child, but he is so brave, so strong emotionally. He continues: 'I thought maybe, just maybe, he could lead us out of this, but not now.' He talks about his hopes for his country, talks about the inequalities, the natural resources which most Libyans never see. He talks about how he has not known any other ruler than Colonel Gaddafi, how Zawiya was known previously for being exceptionally boring and conservative. 'This was a very, very quiet town before,' he says. 'The most exciting, unexpected thing was a traffic accident. Now we have tanks all around attacking us. To us, this is unbelievable. It's not happening to us. We cannot even believe it now.'

Dr Salah is young but articulate and strikingly frank. 'You don't know the fear, Alex,' he says. 'People have been so afraid, too frightened to speak out, to disagree, to protest. But now there is a strong feeling. They won't put up with it for any longer. Everyone wants Gaddafi to go.' He wonders why the West is not helping. 'How can we do this on our own?' It's a question I can't answer.

He knows all about Lockerbie and the bombing of the Pan Am jet which ended up killing all on board and landing fatally on the Scottish town. He is ashamed at the link with Libya. 'Do they all hate us where you come from?' he asks. 'What do they think of Libya in the UK?' I can't tell him anything too heart-warming and say most of our perceptions are based on Colonel Gaddafi and he has given the world a fairly solid impression of himself as an erratic dictator who is both crazed with power and with keeping it.

Dr Salah is both charming and determined. He was diagnosed with leukaemia a short while ago but has had treatment and believes he is in remission. Now this young doctor is facing down Gaddafi and his military machine and he isn't afraid. He has already beaten worse than them.

Young female nurses come up to us while we are chatting and offer us tea or coffee. I accept the coffee gratefully. Tim and Martin are stirring now and come and join the chat. It's still early and we have another day of trying to escape from Zawiya. We need to start, and the earlier the better. It's only when we try to make our early-morning call to London that we realize we have no mobile phone signal. At first I think it's just my phone or maybe we are in an area of the hospital where there is poor reception. But it's more serious than that. The network has been cut. The regime is turning the screw.

One of the kindly nurses turns to me. 'Don't worry, my friend,' she says, 'it will be OK, *inshallah.*' I haven't said anything to her. She has just read the look on my face. 'Do you want to come into our room, maybe get a coffee?' I accept, slightly embarrassed by my unguarded expression. She leads me down the corridor with wards on either side to a door which is locked. She knocks. 'Nabila, open up, it's just me.' It takes several knocks and much coaxing before the door is opened by a younger woman. She looks as though she has been crying and she is wiping her eyes with the *hijab* she is wearing over her head. 'Come in,' the first woman says while she hugs her teary friend. 'You can take off your *hijab* here,' she says to me.

There are just three other women in the room. I have been wearing a scarf over my head as I go through the hospital. I don't want to upset any of these people by appearing to be disrespectful of their religion or their feelings.

When I enter, the mood lifts. I can feel it. Now they have a foreigner in their midst and I am their guest. There's a rush to find coffee grains and milk powder and, oh my goodness, the foreigner wants sugar. Please don't worry, I will take it as it is, I say, but they will hear none of it. The wish appears to be to maintain a very Libyan stiff upper lip, but all the same they are friendly and curious.

We're all worried, all scared, but in this room, just for a few minutes, we can talk and get to know each other a little. It's brief but we talk about families and our children, exchanging names and ages and anecdotes. We're not so different after all. I remember Martin and Tim and feel guilty about sipping a much-needed coffee without them.

'I don't suppose you have two other cups of coffee for my colleagues, do you?' I ask timidly. Of course, of course, is the answer. I am just walking out with cups in hand when Martin comes into view. A couple of the women seem to physically withdraw. To them he's a stranger and a non-Muslim one at that. But Martin is soon getting them to giggle and laugh over their coffee-making abilities.

I find Dr Salah again and tell him I need to go and see the Square. I want to know what is happening there, if anyone has survived. I have to know if the rebels have been beaten into submission or not. I just don't know what is happening there this morning and we have no communication with anyone. Remarkably, he agrees to take us. His car is in the hospital car park. He knows the routes through the rebel checkpoints and the safest way.

The doctor takes us along several small roads and through a number of barricades manned by rebels who recognize him as someone from Zawiya. Then we can go no farther. Opposition fighters stop us, there's a small discussion, and we are asked to get into a small, battered people carrier. It takes us down one of the main roads leading to the Square. As we get closer there are signs of battle everywhere, smouldering ashes, broken barricades, burnt-out cars, debris littering the streets. There are holes punched into the walls from shells and rockets and the buildings are peppered with machine-gun pock-marks. We are all stunned. What a battle. What destruction.

As we enter the Square the tanks we had seen the day before have been removed and so have the dead bodies of the Gaddafi soldiers lying close to the caterpillar tracks. Where have they gone? Who has taken them? The military convoy we saw entering the Square repeatedly on Saturday afternoon has been in and retrieved its dead, its injured, and its broken military machinery. It wants to leave no evidence of this one-sided battle, this pitiless massacre.

I am stunned, reeling from this news. There is a small crowd still in the Square and they greet us noisily but wearily as they see us pull up. I fire questions at them. Where did the tanks go? Where are the injured soldiers? What happened the afternoon before, after we left the Square? They reply quickly – the army kept coming back, there was more fighting, more bloodshed, they took their people and their machines and they left.

Dr Salah has gone into the mosque to try to find out the where-abouts of someone he knows, when another doctor approaches our vehicle. 'You must leave,' he says. 'Leave now. We have word the army is coming back. It is dangerous for you here. Go. Go now.' We don't need telling twice. We bolt back into the vehicle. 'Let's go, let's go.' But we are a man down. Dr Salah is still in the mosque. We can't leave without him.

We shout for him: 'Come on! Come on!' I am filled with fear at the thought of being caught here in the Square again by the regime's army but appalled at the idea of leaving behind our lovely new young friend to the mercy of the Gaddafi security forces. He only drove us here because I asked him and now we might be aban-doning him. No. We can't go. But, for God's sake, Dr Salah, hurry up, please hurry up. We're screaming now. We're all anxious, very anxious. We don't want to get caught in the middle of the fighting here again. As the seconds go by, I wonder what we will decide to do if he doesn't come back soon. Will we be brave enough to stay or will we leave him? He has no way out of here if we go.

But the decision is taken for us. Dr Salah appears. Relief. Huge relief. He jumps in and we rush to his car and head back to the hospital, hearts pumping.

I am not sure how long it takes, but it feels like a horribly short time. We are hardly back in the hospital when we hear the noises we have become so familiar with. It's the dreaded rumble of a large convoy of military vehicles and tanks heading back towards the Square. There are a lot of them – about fifteen or twenty vehicles. Some are trucks just packed with soldiers and, as they are driving along, some are shooting their weapons, spraying bullets along the side of the road. We can't see what they are shooting at but we soon see the results of the indiscriminate firing. I think about the people still there that we saw just a short time ago and how they will be fighting for their lives now – again. And I think how accurate their warning was to us. How lucky we have been once again. How did they know? Spotters? A tip-off? Instinct?

We know that many of the rebels have been worried about Gaddafi agents being in their midst, worried about informers posing as Opposition fighters so they can better glean information about battle plans and insurrection which they can then pass on to the regime. If the rebels have been infiltrated, could the Gaddafi military machine also have sympathizers inside its ranks who might be doing some tipping off too? It has certainly worked that way in other conflicts. In Afghanistan the newly trained army and police are constantly being infiltrated by Taliban and militants who use their positions – and training – to turn on their trainers, mentors and 'colleagues'.

Cars and ambulances are soon screeching up to the front entrance of the hospital, loaded with casualties. One man is brought in lying on his stomach with a large anti-tank bomb sticking up into the air, having lodged grotesquely in the back of his thigh. It is unexploded and he is still conscious, muttering 'Allahu Akbar' repeatedly as the medics run with him on a mobile stretcher straight into the lift so he can be taken up to the operating theatre. 'He will be all right,' one doctor tells me as he sees my horrified face.

A young boy is brought in screaming, writhing around a stretcher as adults try to hold him still to tend to the wound on his head. The doctors say he was shot as he sat on his front doorstep playing with his friends. Was that the indiscriminate spraying we saw earlier? The hospital staff show us at least two ambulances which have been strafed with bullets, through the windscreens, along the sides and through the rear windows.

While we are watching the injured being unloaded from one of the wrecked ambulances, with crowds of hospital staff around them all wearing white coats, there is more firing. Some of the bullets seem to land in the centre of the crowd of doctors. They scatter, leaving the injured man at the entrance marooned on his stretcher. It is a knee-jerk reaction and, within moments, a few return and drag the casualty to relative safety inside. Nowhere seems safe any more.

Tim and I go outside to make a satellite phone call. We have to be outside for the signal to work. But while we are trying to make the connection a Gaddafi jet roars overhead, sweeping low over the hospital. Christ! Is he going to start dropping bombs on his people from the skies now? When we get through to London – while we are telling them the news of the latest attack – there is firing above us. It seems to be coming from the hospital roof. Is there someone up there? Who is shooting, and are they shooting at us? Have they seen us? Are we being targeted or is this shooting, so close by, just coincidence? We run back inside.

There are tanks firing now and the noises sound very close to the hospital. The shelling is making the windows rattle. Nurses are busy trying to barricade the windows and give themselves more protection by leaning stretchers up against them.

Martin has gone to try to find a window higher up so he can get a better view of the area. He hopes to spot some of the military vehicles and get a clearer idea about what they are doing. There are clouds of smoke coming from the direction of the Square. Those poor, poor people. I can barely stop myself weeping for them. And I am scared for us too, very scared. I hate being apart from Martin or Tim now. I am constantly wondering and worrying about where they are. The doctors occasionally see me wandering around on my own and without prompting they say: 'He's gone upstairs to film' – talking about Martin, or 'He's in the office' – referring to Tim. I must look terribly lost and worried. I certainly feel it.

Dr M is still with us, popping in and out of surgery to find us and check on us. He is still working hard at trying to find someone to drive us out. Still no joy at all. He has been back to the Square himself to try to locate his own car and shows us pictures of it on his mobile phone. It has been blown up or incinerated by some sort of bomb. We don't know what destroyed it but we do know it's probably not going to pass an MOT test again.

Like us, the doctor and his son are stuck. I am constantly amazed, we all are, by his composure. He is here in the most horrible of circumstances with his young son. It's bad enough being here as an adult, looking after yourself and hoping. But to also have the worry of making sure your child is OK too? Yet he is calm and charming and constantly worrying about us.

I find myself down one of the corridors trying to get back to our 'office' and the others when I turn a corner and see the formation of about twenty doctors all in their white coats kneeling down in the corner praying. They are praying for help. I stop, sensing I am intruding. But this feels like a public demonstration, an affirmation of faith. This is *INSHALLAH* in big, capital letters. It is in God's hands.

Chapter Four

ESCAPE FROM ZAWIYA

Most people can't and aren't leaving Zawiya even if they do have their own transport. Most wouldn't get through the first checkpoint anyway, if they got that far. The shooting and firing seems frighteningly constant, with few lulls. But it's the lulls we are beginning to notice. There *are* some. Dr Salah says he cannot leave. He has too much work to do here and he doesn't believe his car is good enough to make the journey. It's old. Having been in it for the short journey to the Square, I respect his judgement. Besides, it's not an option. He says no and has solid reasons. We don't even try to persuade him. The trip is considered far too dangerous and those few who are making the journey – usually out of desperation – just won't consider taking three foreign journalists who are probably on the regime's Most Wanted list by now.

But Dr Salah comes back. 'I have found someone,' he says. It is one of his closest friends – Zacharia, Dr Mohammed – another medic, who is in his mid-twenties. He trained in Tripoli so he has a Tripoli ID card and therefore the perfect cover story when he is stopped by the military. He is returning to see his family who live in the capital. He also has a car – and one which might not break down. He is trustworthy by dint of being Dr Salah's close friend. And crucially he is ready to take us. This is our ticket out of here. God, this could be it.

We haven't even had a whisper of help before now and suddenly everything seems right, *inshallah*.

My heart hits the floor as I hear Tim reasoning with our get-away driver. He is pointing out the dangers to him. 'Are you aware of what might happen? Are you sure you want to do this? We need your help but we will completely understand if you decide against. We are asking an awful lot of you.' And so it goes on. What, Tim? Are you mad? He is our hope. Our only hope.

Dr Mohammed listens intently to Tim. But he is ready to take this enormous risk, ready to help total strangers. He has made up his mind. I hear the determination in his voice and feel tremendous, shuddering relief. Thank God. But it's also coupled with enormous respect for Tim. He must be desperate to leave too. Of course he is. Yet he still found it in him to make sure this young Samaritan was aware of just what he was being asked to do. What a man. What men.

We are in a larger room now to the rear of the hospital. It's about thirty feet by twenty, roughly the size of a squash court. It looks like it might have been a doctors' common room. It has seats up against all four walls and a coffee table in the middle. We are brought here because the fighting and shooting appear to be getting closer, with rounds landing in the hospital car park. There is a real fear that the military will soon try to enter the hospital. The 'rebel' is showing us how to get out of the rear room, through the window, into the small garden outside, then over the hospital perimeter wall and through the back gardens of the adjacent homes and away. Just get away from the hospital, he says, as far as you can.

Maybe he is a rebel after all, I am thinking, but I still don't want to hand our memory cards over to him. I am also worrying how I'm going to get over the wall. It looks impossibly high, maybe more than six feet. Christ, I wish I was fitter. The guys take one look at it and walk back in. Maybe they are thinking the same as me. I hope it doesn't come to that, hope it doesn't come to us having to crawl out of windows and clamber over walls to flee for our lives.

We go back into the common room. There are quite a few doctors here now, including the 'rebel', just sitting, chatting, waiting for the next bout of fighting to produce another load of injured. It has an awful predictability about it. But then there's a lull. The sound of firing stops for a bit. Maybe this is our chance.

Tim, Martin and I have all already spoken to Dr M of our suspicions about the 'rebel'. We all have our doubts about him and just don't want to jeopardize anything at this stage. At first Dr M is surprised. But something changes his mind. He's not sure either and, more to the point, he doesn't want us taking any unnecessary chances. He is absolutely certain about Dr Mohammed, his fellow doctor, though. And he insists we should all go now while there is a break in the fighting. We don't know how long the hiatus will last, but our recent experience shows the lulls are never long, so we must move quickly.

We are advised to leave the common room separately. As far as the general group knows, we aren't leaving. We are just moving around, doing more filming in the hospital, going to the bathroom, checking out what's happening at the entrance. We come up with a variety of entirely plausible reasons for our exit from the lounge.

I leave first, saying I am going to the bathroom. I meet Dr Mohammed at the side of the hospital beside his car, as arranged. I wait for what seems like ages for the others. Using the sat phone, I tell the London office we are on the move and trying to get out. I give them the numbers of the doctors here even though there is no way of getting in touch with them because the mobile phone network is still severed. I haven't even finished my call before Martin and Tim are in the car too.

There's an urgency now. Dr M is out beside the car too. We have no idea if we will ever see him again but we have so much to be grateful to him for. He shakes our hands and seems genuinely sorry to see us go. He's also anxious on our behalf. It feels like we are saying goodbye to an old trusted friend, a close relative. He has come to mean so much to us over these past few days. Yet another great man.

We have been working on different ways of smuggling out the tapes. We know that as a woman I am probably the best option for carrying anything about my person as the male Muslim guards may hesitate to frisk me. But we also reason that if we do get arrested by the security forces, then the gloves will be off and I will be no more off limits than the men. So we decide to split our treasured cargo between us.

We've used one of the loaves of bread to hide one film card, slicing it open and pushing the card inside. It's then been put in a plastic bag with bottles of juice and biscuits. We've put another card in the medical kit we brought with us, again making a cut in a bandage wrapped in plastic and pushing it in. Martin has wrapped medical tape round the camera and smeared it with muck and coffee juice to dirty it up. Our story will be that it got broken during the fighting so we didn't manage to film anything. We've acquired a blank DVD to hand over to substantiate our tale. The real gear will go in our shoes, in my bra with the memory cards from my phones, spread around our bags and rucksacks in hidden pockets.

We are all excited but very nervous too. At last we have got action. At last we're being proactive. It feels far better than sitting and waiting and being repetitively attacked, but none of us knows what is out there and what will greet us as we set off. We are all aware, though, it is almost certainly going to be hostile. Can we do it? Can we get through this all in one piece and with our pictures? It's down to this young man now, this twenty-something doctor at the start of his life. He is risking all to save us, three strangers he has only just met. I am in the front passenger seat. Dr Mohammed says it will look better if the soldiers see a woman in the front. They will assume I am his mother, wife or sister. The image will be less aggressive, less confrontational, less suspicious. He is wearing his green medical gown. Tim and Martin are in the back. They haven't shaved or washed properly in days and we've all been sleeping in the same clothes we set out in on Friday. That is only three days ago. It feels like a lifetime. The two of them are understandably dishevelled and grubby-looking. We all are. We're banking on this resulting in our not standing out too much.

We drive off out of the gates, but Dr Mohammed has been in the hospital for days now and isn't aware of the changing scenery and landscape outside. He is confused by the barricades and doesn't know which road is safe or which road is even passable. We hear the crackle of firing very close by in front of us. It's far too close. I don't know if the shooter is aiming at us, but I am wired up enough, scared enough, to think he might be.

'Stop! Stop!' I say, just a little too loudly and little too sharply. There are some guys on the street corner. 'Ask them,' I suggest, pointing. I sound snappy and terse. That's probably because I am. But I can see four or five young men on the corner half peeping out and sneaking a look down the road we are heading onto. The road ahead isn't safe and that's where Dr Mohammed is taking us.

Tim is telling me to let Dr Mohammed do the driving, not to be so bossy, to listen to him. In other circumstances I would be a back-seat driver. He's right, of course. This man is risking his life for us and does not deserve to be shouted at, by me or anyone. Everyone is unbelievably tense. We have hardly left the hospital but we've driven straight into firing. Christ. It's the first time since the three of us met in Tunisia that there has been a cross or irritable word between any of us. It's also the last. I rein in my bossiness (at least for a bit). Dr Mohammed brakes and stops the car almost immediately, talks to the boys on the corner. Yes, there are snipers ahead.

Dr Mohammed veers off the road and down a back street. I put my scarf, which has been curled around my neck, over my head, covering my hair. Dr Mohammed tells me I don't need to. 'No, no, I want to,' I say to him. I feel safer somehow. I don't know why. But I don't want to attract stares when the soldiers see a Western woman in the front. If their first glance into our car is of a doctor and his sister (OK, who am I kidding?) or more likely a mother or other female relative, then that might buy us some time – for thinking, if nothing else.

We make our way slowly round the back roads, mindful that we could turn a corner straight into a tank or twitchy rebel fighters. We don't want to alarm anyone from either side.

The first checkpoint is under a clump of trees. It's shaded and dark and seems busy. There are military vehicles around and I get the impression there are lots of people, but I'm trying not to look up too much. Just staring at my lap, trying to look unthreatening, trying to make myself look small.

The checkpoint is manned by Gaddafi soldiers who look as grubby and scared and sweaty as we feel. No one in the car is saying anything. The soldier is gruff and brusque. He glances at me, glances in the back, doesn't linger on any of us. Dr Mohammed is talking a lot and his tone is quite authoritative. They are roughly the same age, the soldier and the doctor, but our confederate is a highly qualified medic and the other guy is a far less educated man, albeit one with a gun.

There is a lot of military activity around the perimeter of Zawiya. The soldier seems anxious to get rid of us. Perhaps that's why he doesn't ask too many questions. He barks a few words and Dr Mohammed barks back, as if saying: 'Listen, how dare you question me. I'm a doctor after all.' We are waved on.

What did he say? I am desperate to know. 'He wanted to know why we are leaving,' Dr Mohammed explains to us. 'I said you had got caught up in the violence by accident and wanted to get away to safety and, as I was leaving to see my family in Tripoli, I agreed to take you out.'

Our first hurdle is crossed. It's an important psychological success. We are all feeling much better already. Even the doctor is. He might even forgive my bossiness in time.

We get through the next two checkpoints without raising much interest either. We are stopped each time and Dr Mohammed trots out the same lines. But these guards seem busy and preoccupied.

They are either anticipating being part of another attack on Zawiya, or expecting to be attacked themselves. These are the squaddies on the ground, the first in line to be fired at by the rebels, the first in line to be shouted at by their superiors in the Gaddafi army.

We don't travel very far before we reach another checkpoint. The soldiers here are more questioning. They ask us to get out. They want to check over the car. And us. They see the 'broken' camera. They start looking through our equipment. They even unzip the medical kit. We are all fighting not to show our obvious concern, trying not to look as they peer inside the first aid bag and then zip it up. They look at the plastic bag full of snacks, but move on. I'm really worried they are going to search us. I can't walk very well with two of the camera cards jammed down the ankle of my boots and I'm terrified they are going to order me to take them off. We talk nonsense to each other – amateur dramatics – as we are standing by the side of the road while they look through everything. Dr Mohammed appears to be making small talk with them, chatting away easily in a very unconcerned way, deliberately distracting them from their task. Then, curtly, almost absent-mindedly, they tell us to drive on. It just takes a slight wave of the hand.

We clamber back into the car enthusiastically. A massive surge of relief goes through me. My heart has been pumping so fast and hard I feel giddy with the adrenalin rush. Then there's another emotion. At first I think it's just sheer pleasure. But it's more than that. It's smugness, real, confident, raw smugness. Yes! We are doing this. We are not there yet but it feels like we are winning. We're going to get past these tough bastards. The feeling lasts only until the next checkpoint.

Now we change our story. We have made it out of Zawiya, but the road to Tripoli is crowded with checkpoints, all at regular intervals. The soldiers seem to be getting older, more intelligent, more sophisticated, more questioning, especially around the Khamis Brigade headquarters. Here the man who stops us is armed, but not in military clothing. He is older too, probably in his mid-thirties. He is worrying me. He looks too smart, too young, too cocky, too much in charge. I can sense Dr Mohammed's trepidation over the man's authority too, or what authority he believes he has.

We tell the soldier that we have been trying to get into Zawiya, really trying, but we have failed and are giving up. I lean over Dr Mohammed to look through the driver's window and say to the soldier: 'I heard that Tripoli is having a pro-Gaddafi rally today and we wanted to go and film that instead.' He nods slowly. He's not sure but he's giving us the benefit of the doubt. After all, they have successfully managed to keep all the media away from Zawiya so far, although those damned international journalists do still keep trying. It sounds about right to him. Besides, he has lots of work to do today. He waves us on.

There are cars now with green Gaddafi flags being waved out of almost every window, all heading for Tripoli. So there must be some sort of rally going on after all. From now on it gets busier and busier. The road is crowded, but we are well on the way. As we near Tripoli we notice the mobile phone network is beginning to flicker. Our phones spring into life. My main worry is how to get the pictures out and where to go. We have to get to a safe house. I don't want to go to the Rixos. I feel nervous and worried about what will happen to the cards and to us. I don't want to ruin it all now by walking into the place where we know for certain that representatives of the regime are prowling.

Dr Mohammed says he has a brother who will meet us. His brother has an empty house in Tripoli and we can use that. It sounds perfect. The house has power, so we can recharge everything, do the edit there, and then work out how to get ourselves out of Libya as soon as possible.

Tim is already on the phone, telling Foreign Editor Sarah Whitehead, the head of Sky's International News, that we are out of Zawiya. She is most concerned about getting all the rushes back to London so they have a copy of everything we have done before we even begin editing. She doesn't want to take the chance of our being arrested and our film being confiscated and disappearing for ever. The pictures are our evidence. Exhibit A. At this time they are the only independent evidence of Gaddafi's callousness towards his own, unarmed people.

Sarah is frantically worried about getting us safely out of Libya too – in fact definitely more worried about that – but *our* focus is on the report. We are all so committed to airing the pictures, doing the report. I allow myself to think, my God, we have made it. We have actually made it out alive and in one piece. But now we have to make it pay. I feel our responsibility, our duty, is to make sure that what we have seen, what we have been witness to, is shared with as much of the world as possible. I want it to make a difference. I want it to change things. I want people to sit up and notice what is happening to the people of Zawiya.

Martin and Tim feel the same. Both are very passionate journalists with a keen sense of right and wrong. Both are very private people, confident but not showy, solid and dependable but never boastful. It's just not in their natures.

Sarah hasn't seen the pictures yet, but she has a fair idea based on my telephone reports and based on Tim's conversations with her about what to expect. But I'm sure there must be a part of her, a part also of John Ryley, maybe a part of the news editors with whom we work every day, which must have wondered if we'd been exaggerating. Surely that would be just human nature. But Sarah understands we have been through a pretty traumatic few days and she's experienced enough to know the toll this will take on all of us. She knows she is now dealing with three colleagues who are stressed, exhausted beyond comprehension, and possibly highly emotional.

Sarah joined Sky from the BBC only at the start of the year. She had already had a very successful career at the BBC in its Foreign News department before being lured away to Sky. It was considered one of the top 'transfers' in the television news industry. She arrived at the Sky HQ in London and was immediately thrust into overseeing the coverage of the 'Arab Spring'. She has had to learn how to work with a new boss and instantly manage a whole new team of people she didn't know before as well as a team of correspondents out in the field, most of whom she didn't personally know either. All this right in the middle of one of the most busy, most exciting and most dangerous news periods of our generation. It has been a fairly full-on two months or so for her – and for the whole newsroom.

Sarah wants us to go and deliver the cards to Lorna Ward, the producer, at the Rixos Hotel, where the Sky team has a satellite dish. This will make it easy to 'feed' the pictures back via the dish.

But I am very reluctant to do this because I feel the one place the regime will have its eyes on will be our Sky office at the Rixos. I don't know how close the minders stick to the journalists, even if I can make phone calls to them without being detected. Instead, I telephone Richard Spencer from the *Daily Telegraph* because I know he is based in the other hotel, the Corinthia. I think he might be a bit more independent of minders and also there is no connection between him and Sky. Although he doesn't know me at all really, he is instantly concerned and says straight away: 'Are you OK? Do your team know you are OK?' I say yes, but I am worried about the security situation regarding the guards at the Rixos and about any of us being spotted. 'They are looking for you,' Richard says. 'They know you have been there [Zawiya] and I wouldn't advise going to the Rixos. I think it might be better if you went to the Corinthia.'

We mull it over while we try to find a meeting place down a back street away from crowds so we can link up with Dr Mohammed's brother. It takes a seeming eternity. There just appear to be too many people around. But, finally, we find a more deserted side street, dusty and potholed, in which to meet him. By this time the doctor has had a rethink about the loan of his house. He realizes the house will be traced back to him. If any of his neighbours or anyone at all sees us – the three foreigners – going in or out, his life will be in danger as well as those of his entire family.

OK, OK, that's fine, we say, our hearts sinking. It is so not fine for us. What are we going to do now? But, of course, we smile and tell him not to worry. What choice do we have? We know he is right. These people, this regime, will be out to get him and his family if they ever find out. We would never inform on him but there is every chance we will be spotted however hard we try to be invisible.

The doctor has an alternative plan already. He will take us to a small hotel where we can pay cash and there will be no questions asked. 'It will be OK,' he says. The plan is for Martin and me to pose as a couple, while Tim will be our travelling companion. It sounds risky but the best we have so far. We set off.

Richard Spencer rings back. He has been back to the Corinthia to check out how many guards are standing around and whether we would be noticed if we turned up. It is amazingly good of him. He suggests going in the rear entrance, to be really safe, but says there are very few people around and very few hotel staff. He says he will wait there, take the tapes from Tim, and then carry them to the Rixos, where he will hand them over to the Sky team.

The hotel is remarkably close to Green Square. Oh my gosh, I am thinking, how can this be safe? It has the impressive-sounding name of The Four Seasons, but looks like it is approaching the winter of its life. It is small – unassuming, I think they might call it in the tourist guides. It is nondescript, basic, unnoticeable. In another word, perfect.

The hotel's owners are welcoming and businesslike. Dr Mohammed's brother was right. They were waiting for us, happy enough for us to stay and super-swift checking us in, so we are off and out of sight, away from the reception, as soon as possible. We take two rooms. For the hotel's purposes Martin and I are in one room and Tim is in the other. In reality we all pile into a single room, set up the edit equipment, and Martin starts downloading pictures from the cards so we have our own full copy of everything on his laptop before the cards are taken away to be 'fed' to London. It takes a while.

As we are waiting, we take a moment – our first moment – to talk briefly about the past three days. 'Shit,' I say, 'I really thought we were going to die in that mosque. It was so loud, so near. Was I the only one?' I look at them both. I know the answer but I want to talk about it. I want them to talk about it to me. Now I can let them know how scared I was.

'Christ, yes,' says Martin with feeling.

Tim puts his head in his hands again. 'I said goodbye to my boys,' he says. 'I don't want to think about it.' He's shaking his head, looking at us.

I hear their admissions with huge relief. So it wasn't just me then. This interaction is brief. Important, but brief. There's far too much to do right now. We simply don't have the time to dwell on our great escape. We just get on with it. But I needed to voice it. I am still jangling, still emotionally drunk and quivering. Surely the guys must be too? We're also starving and thirsty and anxious to get this done and for it to be good, more than good. We want it to be the best report we have ever done. It has to be. We want it to make an impact.

A quick sandwich, a shower, calls home to say we're OK. They all go by in a flash and a blur. Our energy is all going on making this report. I get a text from Bill Neely saying: 'Where are you? Where are you? We're in the Square. We're looking for you. We have a car.' It doesn't make any sense. He's in the Square? What? Zawiya? I ring him.

He picks up. He has been to Zawiya and is back in Tripoli again. The messages have been massively delayed. I can't understand how he did it. We know there was fighting starting up again in Zawiya as we were leaving. Bill and I work out we must have missed each other by minutes. He has been into the hospital asking for us, ready to give us a lift out of the city. But at that time people in the hospital hadn't even realized we had gone. Bill has managed to get inside the besieged town and has his own shocking pictures showing the aftermath of a major battle. Somehow he has been lucky enough to do so in a very rare lull and timed it perfectly. Well, lucky unless you are a top-rate journalist like Bill and keen to be in the middle of it all.

Bill warns us too not to go near the Rixos and offers the use of ITN's satellite dish if we decide to avoid the Sky office altogether so we can to get the footage back to London. Now this is an extraordinary gesture from a competitor, but Bill too believes the story needs to be told. This is no longer about rivalry between opposing networks. This is about human rights.

We are still not safe and we all know it. We don't go out of our room and there's a long discussion about what Tim should do. He decides he is the least likely to be spotted. As a producer, he will be known only to those inside the industry. As we had only just arrived in Tripoli the morning we ended up in Zawiya, Tim is not known to any of the regime minders. He sets off with the cards to meet Richard Spencer at the Corinthia.

Martin and I get down to editing. I am stunned at some of the pictures Martin has taken. They are so evocative and capture the chaos, the fear, the desperation just perfectly. We want people to feel this. If they don't feel anything, how is anyone going to care about the people of Zawiya?

We finally edit a report which shows what happened when we first arrived in Zawiya and goes through to Sunday – fifteen minutes' worth of material in total. We still don't feel it quite covers what happened. There's so much we have left out, so much we can't show because it is just too gory, too unpalatable. But, on a news channel, fifteen minutes is a massive amount of time to devote to one story. We are hoping the pictures will persuade them it is worth it.

John Ryley and Sarah Whitehead are very enthusiastic about the project. They have set aside an experienced team to deal with the rushes and go through every frame – producer Stephanie De Groot and picture editor Armin Ruude. The two of them will polish and buff the material and make sure we have used the very best of what Martin has filmed. The decision is taken not to air it until we are off Libyan soil.

Tim meets Richard Spencer and the first drop is made to the Rixos and the Sky satellite dish. The pictures are relayed to London. Phew! Another element ticked off the list.

We finish the edit but it is very late and by now we are almost on our knees with exhaustion. Tim has already made a quick visit himself to the Rixos to check what it is like there so he doesn't have to trouble Richard for the next drop-off, our fifteen-minute edit. No one even looks up when Tim walks into the Rixos, admittedly from the rear garden. He has decided to take the edited version back there himself. He will stay the night there, then come and pick us up in the morning and we will go to the airport together.

That night Sarah Whitehead rings me. I realize she has been terrifically worried about us all. I feel selfish. I've just been thinking about myself, Martin, Tim, just us. But knowing what we were going through must have been awful for our colleagues, for those who love us, for our friends, and especially for our families.

Chapter Five

'WHY DO I KEEP CRYING?'

I wake up in my hotel bed exhausted, feeling like I haven't slept at all. My room is almost bare, with just the few belongings I brought with me all still unpacked in my bag. It is clean and functional but has that lonely, sterile feeling of a room you don't know, in a place you don't know. The furnishings are dated and worn. I have kept the curtains drawn since we arrived because my room looks out onto the street and I just want to hide behind everything right now. Martin's room feels more welcoming. It is strewn with all our equipment, cables, edit pack, camera kit – items which feel familiar. But I still don't feel safe. I start writing a piece for online. It turns into pages and pages and pages of scrawling longhand. When Martin knocks on the door to see if I want to have breakfast, I can't hold back the tears. I feel embarrassed and I don't want him to see how upset I am, but there's no hiding it either.

'Sorry, Martin,' I say. 'I just can't stop crying. How come you are so together?' He's understanding and comforting. 'Crawfie, we all deal with it differently, in our own way.' He makes me feel a lot better. I feel I don't have to actually explain to him why I am crying because he knows. He probably knows because he's feeling it too.

I'm reading my online report over to André Rosso, the picture editor in London, who is taping it so he can transcribe it later. Halfway through I break down. My voice cracks as I am talking about how everyone in the mosque is just a civilian – someone's brother, someone's son, someone's grandfather. It's horribly upsetting, remembering events which are still so vivid – yet I don't ever want to forget them either. This is what happens in war. It's hideous and cruel and bloodthirsty. We survived, but so many didn't, and – I keep on remembering – they are going through this torment still in Zawiya. André is terribly upset on my behalf but is wonderfully understanding, brushing aside my embarrassment with a firm 'Please don't worry, Alex.'

We are on the way to Tripoli airport. It feels like we've been inside Libya for weeks, maybe longer. But we arrived on Thursday night and it's only Tuesday now – only really four full days. The office has got us tickets to Tunis. We're all just focusing on getting out now. I don't really think about the airport before we actually arrive. I am busy writing and reading out more of my online script all the way there, confessing, rather guiltily, to the others that I have already had an emotional moment – and it's been taped – while trying to make light of it all at the same time. The others don't say anything, just listen. If I had had time to think, perhaps the scene on arrival wouldn't have been such a surprise, but I don't have a moment.

Our first inkling that the situation is far from normal is when our taxi cannot get near the airport because of the number of people who have set up a huge camp inside the perimeter. The driver drops us off some way out – a mile or two away – and we drag our bags through the crowds and crowds of mainly immigrant workers living in tents. They are desperate to flee Libya, desperate to be part of the exodus, but it looks as though they have been there for a while. There is washing hanging from lines, fires lit and food being cooked. There is rubbish everywhere, but stacked neatly in piles rather than just randomly dumped. No one looks like they are going anywhere fast, certainly not out of Libya.

Perhaps this is a place where they feel a bit safer. There have been lots of reported attacks on immigrant workers by locals who mistake them for Gaddafi's military mercenaries, and they've been beaten, abused, some killed. There's a fair amount of hatred here for those paid soldiers from other countries – and few questions asked to determine the truth. I can't resist taking pictures on my BlackBerry as we walk through this huge sea of misery and desperation. It is an extraordinary sight to me, a story as yet untold, and it seems to encapsulate just how desperate people are becoming here. Martin tells me to stop, but not before a guard has seen me from some distance off. Shit. He beckons me over. I ignore him, hoping he's talking to someone else. I pretend I don't know what he's saying and look blankly at him. He roughly grabs my BlackBerry, rips off the back and pops the memory card out, then hands the phone back to me. Damn, but it could be so much worse. I realize I'm falling into the trap of thinking it's fine now. I need to stay on my guard, be alert, until the plane's wheels leave the runway.

As we check in there are more crowds inside the terminal, all thrusting forward to the check-in desk, some of them just holding wads of cash and piles of passports. Everyone is desperate to leave. There are Gaddafi posters stuck over the monitors which normally would be announcing the flight numbers and destinations. The airport is heaving, full of people, standing room only. We feel incredibly lucky waving our pre-booked, pre-paid tickets which the London office has arranged and we head off to the departure gate.

But we don't feel safe even when we are on the plane. We are in a row of three and I am in the middle. 'The plane's going to fall out of the sky or something, isn't it?' I say. Martin smiles, but agrees. He's anxious too.

We take off and we all fall asleep instantly. It's a really short flight – only a few hours – and we are soon touching down in Tunis. Even here, I can't relax. I don't feel entirely safe. We spend a night in the Tunisian capital and meet up with the Sky team, led by Sam Kiley, which has been covering the exodus of refugees crossing the land border with Libya. I don't want to go out. I don't want to join them. I just want a long bath and to stay in my hotel room on my own. But Tim gently persuades us all, or is it just me he has to persuade? Anyway, he is so right. I feel much better spending a few hours with them talking about things other than Zawiya, pretending to be the tough correspondent who's not affected by anything. It's an act, but it's an easy one. To complete the charade, I drink too much wine and fall into a disturbed sleep, one which isn't restful at all.

When British soldiers return from Afghanistan they are sent to Cyprus to 'decompress'. Here they spend a few days with their colleagues to give them time to come out of the zone they have been in for months on end. It allows them to unwind and to let their adrenalin levels drop, hopefully making them easier to live with when they get back to the 'real' world. Correspondents who have had intense experiences in hostile environments are not that much different. The sudden dip in adrenalin levels brings on incredible tiredness, irritability, fractiousness. The team tends to feel very bonded because of the shared intense experience, and even if there has been tension and arguments and rows among the group, which there often are, each member feels wrenched from the unit – a slightly disturbing emotion – on the first few days home. Everyone, of course, is desperate to get back home, to familiarity, to love, to security, to just being among their own possessions again. But often the first week or so is hard, coping with all the physiological changes as your mind and body adapt. We all know there will be difficulties in varying degrees. We all expect it.

But right now all I can think about is being home. I want to see my children. I want to hug them. I want to smell their gorgeous smells and listen to their school stories and hear about their adventures with their friends. I know Richard has been crazily worried and I want to reassure him, be with him, and just be a family again. Just be a family in a place where there isn't any firing and people trying to kill you. I just want to be safe.

We land in Dubai and I switch on my phone again. It comes alive with messages. Many of them are comments about the report. Several are from news organizations around the world asking me to appear on their programmes to talk about what's going on in Zawiya. The attack on the town is still going on and we're the only journalists who have somehow managed to get inside, film the brutality, and get out in one piece, along with our equipment and the pictorial evidence. Our report is running, trimmed back to twelve minutes but sharpened up and polished by Steph and Armin in London and then reviewed and reviewed again by Sarah

Whitehead and John Ryley. Tim has left us to fly back solo to his family in London while Martin and I are returning to our homes in the United Arab Emirates.

We're still collecting our bags off the airport carousel as I am going through the requests – including from CNN and BBC World Radio, two of Sky's main rivals. This, however, is a story which has already transcended traditional rules of competition and this feeling in the industry looks like continuing. But I am stunned. I hoped for a reaction, a response from the world, and it is coming first from quarters I really did not anticipate. I am still standing looking for our bags when a producer named Alex from CNN's Anderson Cooper programme rings through. She is keen to get me on air as soon as is practicable, tonight if possible.

Sky's foreign desk duty news editor, Karine Mayer, rings me up to tell me a US State Department official has said the White House has seen the pictures and is reviewing its position on Libya. This is exactly why the people in Zawiya wanted us to get the report out. They knew we would have an impact as Western journalists which they could not hope to get from their mobile phone footage uploaded onto YouTube.

I immediately ring to tell Martin, who is heading off to his house in the Arabian Ranches in a separate taxi. 'Well, that makes it all worth it, Crawfie,' he says. I knew he'd think that. I knew he'd feel the same.

My taxi takes me past the guardhouse entrance to the Lakes, where we live on the fringe of the Emirates Golf Club's Faldo course. It's a gated community which might have been a template for Jim Carrey's *The Truman Show*. Everything is perfect. The guards aren't keeping out militants or rebels here. I'm not quite sure who they are keeping out because crime here is virtually non-existent. They don't have guns or any other weapons for that matter. Speeding and parking violations are about their limit.

Litter has no place here between the sparkling white villas, and the verges and hedges have already been manicured and clipped that morning by the green-uniformed tame workforce of Pakistani and Indian immigrants. It is probably a little too perfect and as a polar opposite to ravaged Libya it does a pretty good job.

When I walk through the door of the family home, the first people I see are my in-laws in our sitting room. They are back from their cruise. 'Well done, well done,' my mother-in-law, June, says. 'What a brave girl!' She is meaning it kindly, but I don't feel brave at all just now.

My girls run up to me, fighting for hugs and kisses, the little one, Flo, pushing through and demanding to be lifted and carried like a baby despite being 8 years old. I want to burst into tears – again. My son, Nat, now towering over me at six foot one, walks up, trying not to show his obvious relief, and gives me a hug. 'Glad you're back, Mum,' he says.

Richard is just behind them. He looks shattered, worn down, with worry all over his face. He looks like he might have been in Zawiya himself. I can't imagine what it's like being on the outside looking in at someone you love being shot at and trapped. But his face looks like it is agony. But right now he's just pleased I'm here and in one piece.

Straight away I'm thrown back into the chaos and busy, bustling world of a large family. 'Mum, can we go to see a film?' 'Mum, can I show you my maths test?' 'Mum, I got an A plus for my English.' 'Mum, is it OK if Kelly and Bianca have a sleepover tonight?'

'Mum, Hannah says I can go stay, can I?' There are a million stories of life at school to catch up on, after-school activities, friends' parties, friends' arguments. I have to be updated on who has fallen out with whom and who is best mates with whom now. I'm so weary. My mind is still imprinted with Zawiya images. But I feel enveloped with love here. My children don't care much about my job or what I do beyond knowing it takes me away from them. Now they are the happiest bunnies ever, delighted that I am around the dinner table with them. Richard has a meal prepared and we all sit down, talking so loudly no one can hear each other above the noise. But I can't stop thinking all the time about where we've just come from, what we've just done, how it is still going on.

You don't get to stop just because you're home, and I feel my work covering Zawiya is not yet over. Later or the next day I tell Sarah Whitehead about the interview requests from CNN and BBC World Radio. She doesn't seem surprised and has already provided an edited version of the pictures to a number of news organizations with the proviso they mention these are Sky News pictures. They are now running on Arabic channels too and have been put up on YouTube by several Libyan Opposition supporters outside the country with Internet connections.

However, Sarah is still concerned and mindful about the impact all this might have on the Sky staff who remain in Libya and the backlash they might suffer from the regime. The Sky staff in Tripoli are worried too. There are emails between the Sky Tripoli team and the Sky London office about the wisdom of my doing interviews with other news outlets. They feel they are going to be the ones who may be targeted because of our report detailing Gaddafi's atrocities. They well might be, but right now I can't see their point of view. My first reaction is not an empathetic one, it's not a kind one, it's not one of which I'm proud. I'm incandescent with rage.

I keep seeing flashbacks of the injured people in Zawiya, in particular one man who had his brain blown away but was still alive and muttering. I can't get this man's face out of my head. The sight of him being carried into the mosque by his friends, his skull with a big hole in it, his brain spilling out, keeps popping into my own mind even while I'm awake and talking. It's not a ghostly apparition, just a niggling constant which I keep trying to push away. But it never goes. It's like you're watching a film and keep seeing the same scene over and over again.

I feel this huge duty – this massive responsibility – to tell people. I feel so, so strongly we have to get the word out about Zawiya. I don't want to listen to Sarah telling me to rest. I don't want to listen to Richard telling me to rest and spend time with the children. I don't want to hear about my colleagues' worries from inside the relative luxury of the Rixos Hotel. I don't want any curbs on the coverage of this story – a story we have nearly died for, an ongoing story in which people are still dying and being horribly injured.

I am incensed at the suggestion – however small and probably imagined – that somehow I'm doing this to advance my career, or increase my standing in the field of television news. I'm getting emails and texts from well-meaning friends and colleagues congratulating me. Many make comments like: 'You are going to win the Royal Television Society award for journalism for the fourth time,' and 'More awards, Crawfie, well done.'

Oh my God, they are thinking I did this for an award? That somehow I was driven to do this because I wanted a bit of silverware recognition on my mantelpiece, because it's some sort of competition? That feels offensive and trivial.

I know that, by appearing on other news outlets, the news about what is happening in Zawiya will be taken to a fresh audience. I know I'm being irritable and very aggressive with Sarah and almost everyone I have dealings with. My euphoria about being home has quickly descended into impatient sniping at the children and a raised voice, which I am immediately regretful about but can't seem to stop repeating a few minutes later.

I have an anger I don't recognize in myself. It's raging the first few days, absolutely red-hot. It subsides a little over about a week but it's still there, simmering, waiting to froth up at the slightest excuse for weeks to come. But the more Sarah tells me I'm tired and I need to take some time off, the more I insist I'm fine and I absolutely do not need it. I insist, in a foot-stamping, temper-tantrum sort of way – a little reminiscent of Flo when she was a few years younger – that I am definitely going to talk on CNN and any other outlet which happens to ask me. I go on CNN via Skype from Dubai and, because of the time difference with the United States, it is in the middle of the night, around three o'clock.

I can feel the emotion rising volcanically within me. I'm tired and I'm nervous about speaking well in an articulate way so everyone who is listening understands just how serious the situation is out there. I get through it. Anderson Cooper talks to me live for eighteen minutes, an incredibly long time for any television channel to devote to one story. And Sarah has been watching. She says I did well and that she was worried I was going to be too emotional.

I realize she is right. I *am* too emotional. I know I am. I can't stop crying. I try not to in front of the children. I am not sleeping much or well. They go back to school and I hide away from my in-laws, who are staying with us. I spend my time trying to catch up on shopping and sobbing on the way to the supermarket. I go to the hairdresser and feel guilty that I am spending time on something so frivolous. I try to help with domestic chores like washing and cleaning, but it all feels pointless and my mind and thoughts are elsewhere. I am getting terribly irritated with Richard – who is exhausted and stressed himself – and who is also struggling to handle this highly charged, emotional woman who just snaps at him all the time.

BBC World Radio ring up to cancel their interview request and I feel irrationally angry with them. The producer suggests there has been a discussion about the appropriateness of using a Sky reporter, a journalist from a rival organization. I am dismissive and angry with her explanation. I even suggest she doesn't need to mention I am from Sky. Just use my evidence and quote me as an 'eyewitness', is my unformed strategy, and then I realize how utterly ridiculous that sounds. I am behaving badly all round. This is not about channel rivalry, I am screaming inside. This is not about Sky versus BBC. This is not about Alex Crawford. This is not about anything but people being killed in a small city in Libya which no one has really heard of.

I can't stop watching the news and keep seeing the regime's spokesman, Moussa Ibrahim, appearing on Sky, the BBC, everywhere, telling people there has been no massacre, civilians weren't killed, the Libyan forces do not fire on unarmed people. I am furious that he is even being given airtime and incensed that reporters feel they have to 'balance' their reports by interviewing him. I feel like he is not being challenged enough and journalists don't seem to realize there *is* evidence of atrocities. Why aren't they verbally beating him with it?

I ring up Karine Mayer, the foreign desk duty news editor, who is incredibly supportive and warm. I tell her I need to get in touch with William Hague, Britain's Foreign Secretary. I have never contemplated anything like this, before or since. What? Contact a secretary of state? I want to talk to him personally and tell him to watch the pictures, then use them to persuade other politicians that the international community has to help these people who cannot survive on their own. Karine gives me the number, but I don't use it. It feels incredibly presumptuous, even arrogant. I reason with myself that they will have seen the report in the Foreign Office.

A few days after I'm back I drive out on my own to the coast at Dubai's Jumeirah Beach Resort and park the car. I am aware I am feeling the after-effects of what we've experienced in Zawiya but this doesn't help me feel any better. It's a near out-of-body experience, knowing, understanding why it is happening but being unable to stop it. I just sit for a while on my own. I can't stop crying. I just can't hold it back. I feel pathetic and a bit silly and very out of control. I want to be on my own, yet I don't want to be on my own. I'm just not used to feeling quite so raw. And yet I don't feel I can sob in this completely uncontrollable, venting way at home because it's frightening me, never mind my family. Martin has taken two weeks off work – which is most unusual for him – but he has recognized he needs to shut down and spend time on himself, healing.

I want to talk about it, but I just can't put my family through all the naked details. I talk a bit to Richard, but he is hurting too. I tell him: 'I am sick, Rick. I have to get well.' But it is said in a very snappy, impatient, angry way, totally lacking in sympathy for what he has been through.

When I log onto my laptop there is a string of emails from colleagues in the industry and also from people whom I don't know. Many of them mention they think we will win awards. But all the talk of prizes makes me feel physically queasy. I worry my reputation in the industry is becoming one of a woman utterly committed to winning awards and beating her rivals no matter what, rather than a reporter utterly committed to journalism, finding and telling the truth.

My old boss, the former head of Sky News, John O'Loan, writes: 'Brilliant. Brilliant. Brilliant. Good looking word, eh? Hardly does justice to such a great report! But take really good care – so you can file more. Buy you a drink or two when all of this is over. JOL.' The subtle reference to the risks and dangers hits me, especially when I find an email which must have been painstakingly typed out by little Flo because she can't work a keyboard properly yet. Written on 4 March, it has the title 'Mummy please come home'. It says: 'Mummy I miss you sooooooooooooooooooooooooooooooo much. Please call.' There follows a string of hearts.

Oh, my poor little girl, and I *didn't* ring when she was sending me that message. I never got it at the time of sending. I was travelling and sleeping and just trying to get home. What sort of a mother are you? Why didn't you think of ringing anyway? How could you put your children, your little ones, through this? The children haven't seen the report or heard my phone calls from inside the mosque. Richard tells me he has stopped them from watching the news as soon as he realized I was trapped in Zawiya.

Sarah is trying to reassure mc constantly that the story – the report – is getting the airtime and showing it deserves. She sends me an email: 'An amazing half hour is still underway on air all around your film,' she writes. 'Lisa [Holland] presenting, Hillary Clinton [US Secretary of State] interview with Kay Burley [Sky presenter] about it, Marie Colvin [*Sunday Times* foreign correspondent] live with Lisa in Tripoli, Ming Campbell [Liberal Democrat MP with expertise in foreign affairs] and the chairman of Libya Watch. Amazing. And both of your online pieces are gripping reads and on the site. I'm full. S.'

It does the trick, but only for a little while. I'm getting emails now from Libyans who seem astonished that Western journalists have taken such risks.

Tom Parmenter, one of the Sky News correspondents, passes on an email from a Libyan living in the UK: 'I would like to thank Alex Crawford for her commendable effort in putting together what has been, thus far, the most comprehensive and accurate account of the ongoing plight of the Libyan population. Her and her team's exceptional commitment to the profession has without a doubt revived my faith in responsible journalism. The scenes from Az'zawia resonate the massacres committed by militias loyal to Gaddafi and his sons, in many other cities across Libya, including my hometown Benghazi. Until now, the accurate account of events portrayed in Alex's report was communicated solely through amateur footage finding its way onto the Internet. The downside to this vast amount of material was that in most occasions it couldn't be independently verified. Although the massacres have been mentioned, they have not been shown on mainstream TV here in the UK in such a deserving manner. I hope that you will be able to pass on my gratitude to Alex, Lisa and the rest of the team currently reporting from Libya. Kind regards, Enes.'

And there are others which I grasp at eagerly as evidence that maybe we are making a difference. This, from one of the rebel outfits: 'Hi Alex. Just wanted to commend you on the amazing coverage you broadcast to the world on the plight of the Libyans fighting in Zawiya last week. Real journalism from the front line at its best and the Libyan people will salute you for having the courage to show the world the brutality of what is going on behind closed doors in Libya. Thanks from all the guys at the Libyan Youth Movement.'

And another: 'Dear Alex, on behalf of all the Libyans who continue to fight for their right to a dignified life, I would like to thank you for your accurate and very moving account of the events in al Zawia. You have risked your life to show the world the true extent of Gaddafi's brutality and I cannot express my gratitude in words. May God bless you and protect you, Heba.'

So, perhaps it has been worth it. I forward this last communication to Martin and Tim. In fact, I forward all of them. My name is continually the one being mentioned because I am the 'face', the front person, or, as my former Foreign Editor, Adrian Wells, put it: 'You are the singer in the band.' I loved that description when he first gave it to me. It encapsulated the set-up exactly. I can't do anything without my whole crew and it is all of us who were in that mosque, all of us who struggled to get out, all of us who watched and experienced it all. I want the team to know or to feel it has all been worth it. That it was important to do and that ordinary people are grateful for what we have been able to show.

Sometimes newsrooms wonder whether in between *EastEnders* and *Britain's Next Top Model* there is an appetite among the viewing public for reports from across the world, from countries they will probably never visit, from places people may struggle to pinpoint on a map. The Sky newsroom, the management, the producers, the directors, the presenters have all swung behind our report big time. John Ryley has insisted it is showcased on the channel and it is beginning to be noticed. Guests are being lined up to comment, and graphics and maps are being made to accompany the report. It's presented on the website. In fact, everything is being done to make sure it is out there, in the public domain.

I am conscious at this point, though, that there is a personal gloom which refuses to shift. I just can't drag myself out of this overwhelming feeling of hopelessness and helplessness. My friends and work colleagues talk to me with voices heavy with concern. 'Are you OK?' 'How are you coping?' 'You *sure* you're OK?' I don't know how to respond and am unfairly irritated and angry with them for asking, which doesn't make any sense at all. I say I'm fine, but I know, deep down, that's not entirely true. Something is wrong.

I want to talk to Stuart Ramsay, Sky's chief correspondent, because he has often spoken to me about post-traumatic stress and how he copes with the extremely shocking events he has reported on. I know he won't consider what I'm feeling as a weakness. He is direct and to the point and very practical. We use each other as sounding boards. There's an unwritten code between us that the conversations go no further. I feel he will be able to give me advice with coping, that I won't have to explain anything, just listen. But Stuart is on his way to Japan to cover the tsunami and earthquake and he's out of contact.

I don't want to tell the office about my feelings because I'm worried this may impact on what I do next. I don't want them – or anyone for that matter – to think I'm somehow broken by this. I don't want to stop doing my job. I don't want people to think I'm a head-case and avoid me. And I think they will if I tell them I am hurting in my head and in my heart.

I worry about Richard and what he will think. Will he think I have brought this on myself, that I shouldn't be working this hard anyway, that I should be avoiding war zones when I have a young family and a husband? He's never said anything like this. He's been nothing but supportive and proud, but I know too he just wants me safe and sometimes wonders about my priorities. He's not as ambitious as me, not as driven by his career, not consumed by his work like I am. He loves writing and loves working for newspapers, but he doesn't feel he has to prove anything to anyone. Perhaps that's the difference between us.

Sky's human resources department sends me a reminder that I may wish to contact an expert in these matters, the psychologist Dr Lesley Perman-Kerr. They send a similar letter to the others too. But I know Martin has already turned down the offer and I doubt Tim has taken it up either. Indeed, Tim has returned to work extremely quickly after our return, just a few days later. He gets straight back on the bike. I'm wondering, why is it just me who is so tearful and affected? Why are the others apparently coping and I'm not? It makes me feel very weak.

I know Lesley. I have met her before and found her interesting and approachable and this makes me think about calling her. She came out to us when I was in the Asia bureau based in New Delhi in India. She came to talk to my team about hostage-taking. She spoke to us about research she had done based on working with hostages and the families of hostages for more than a decade. She is one of the principal advisers to the charity Hostage UK headed by Terry Waite. Terry Waite was the former envoy for the Church of England and a hostage negotiator, who was himself held hostage in Beirut between 1987 and 1991. But I hold back from actually ringing her.

Sky's managing editor, Simon Cole, comes out to Dubai on a holiday. He takes the Dubai bureau team out for dinner, but I ask for some time on my own with him. The next day I meet him by the pool of his hotel. I don't want to tell him I am thinking of consulting the office 'shrink' and I skirt round the topic, but he is too much of an old hand not to know what I am meaning without actually saying. Without my mentioning it, he encourages me to ring Lesley, to concentrate on my family and to look after myself. 'You're too thin,' he says by way of suggesting I am not looking after myself. I'm not, but he's letting me know he is worried.

It is a very poignant concern because this is Coley's first holiday without his wife Magda, who has just recently died from cancer. He is not morose. He is not self-pitying. He is, in fact, very good company and has me laughing with his irreverent tales of the newsroom gossip. But he is just gently reminding me of what he has lost and what I still have and telling me to get better and cherish it all.

I send Lesley an email and she rings me back within the hour. I tell her how I am feeling, how angry I am with everyone and everything and how I weepy I am. Within hours she is on a plane to Dubai to see me for a face-to-face talk. I immediately feel guilty and worried, alarmed that she is moving so quickly. Am I that bad? I know I'm not mentally deranged. I know I'm not 'mad', but I also know I'm not myself. Slowly – but too slowly for my liking – it is easing. Maybe that is because I'm gabbling to almost anyone who comes into my path. I go for a coffee with an old mate, Lucy Martin, a former producer at Sky who's now based in Dubai with her family. The poor girl has just suggested a meeting to catch up but I end up blubbing into her arms. She says although she did a psychology A-level she's not quite sure she's really professionally trained enough to deal with my level of 'madness'. It makes me laugh, but, of course, that's why she says it.

At the same time, I'm getting emails and texts from people in Bahrain, some of them from contacts who helped us when we were in the Gulf state covering their protests for change. They feel forgotten and neglected by the international community. No one is listening to their stories of repression. They're entirely overshadowed by what's going on in Libya and Egypt and now there's the Japanese tsunami to take the world media's attention. The emails are direct pleas to me *not* to forget them, to do something about it. They want help from reporters like myself who work for international companies and who may be able to present their plight on a world platform.

They include emails like this one: 'Alex, please help Bahrain. The Saudi Army is killing people now in Sitra. They are using live bullet. They started these actions even before the martial law [emergency law]. They are shooting whoever in the street. Many bodies in the street where we can't go to take them we don't know whether they are alive or not.

'Pls help. They are shooting even the hospital in Sitra with live bullet. They didn't allow the help to come in even the medical crowd have been attacked when they came to Sitra. Dr's are calling for help. People are dying they do not have enough support. Please do something these people do not have any mercy. The international community has to do something.' (I am leaving out any identifying details because the persecution is still going on in Bahrain as I write this.)

I feel terribly guilty, somehow slothful. I feel I'm not doing enough. I can't keep up with all the repression which needs to be reported – which I want to report – and I'm burdened by the feeling that somehow we foreign journalists are in the very privileged position of having a voice which is listened to.

Lesley arrives in Dubai and we meet in a hotel room. Richard knows, and encourages me to meet her. He wants me back to normal. I don't tell my in-laws where I am going. I don't tell my workmates, apart from Martin. I do tell Sarah Whitehead. I decide I need to be upfront with her, and although HR and Lesley assure me of confidentiality I know Lesley's plane tickets have been arranged and booked through the news desk and it won't take much for anyone with access to the office computer to discover that Dr Lesley is travelling to the United Arab Emirates and the place where two Sky staffers who've just returned from a war zone now live.

But I make light of it, joking with Sarah, but at the same time I let her know that I know she knows. I am trying to reason with myself at the same time.

Come on, I wouldn't be normal having seen what we've seen and not be upset, would I? We are humans. We aren't robots. We are 'trained observers' as journalists but not trained observers without hearts. Why are you so twitchy about people knowing you are seeing a head doctor, Alex? I can't answer my own question.

I spend a few hours with Lesley. She is reassuring from the start and doesn't treat me like a sick person, which was what I was afraid – actually terrified – she was going to do. I don't want to be sick. I especially don't want to be sick in the head. I want to get back to work as soon as possible. I want everything to be the way it was before. I don't want to be halted in my reporting career because of this. But she understands me and understands the journalistic culture very well. She says to me: 'Alex, if you picked up bacteria in Afghanistan, if you had a headache, would you just carry on and not take medicine? This is the same. It's just good housekeeping, that's all.'

It makes sense, of course it does. But even as she's understanding and convincing me, I'm thinking, is she really *understanding* or is she just very well trained, very good at her job? Is this paranoia usual too? But she gives me practical reasons why I appear to be feeling pain more acutely than either Tim or Martin. She tells me women can be (but not exclusively) more susceptible to bonding that occurs in traumatic situations as they excrete more of the bonding hormone oxytocin than men and therefore tend to respond to threat through befriending rather than defending. It is the same hormone secreted during sex, she says, which explains why females feel more attached or bonded after sex compared to many men. She says that while trapped in the mosque we would all have secreted this hormone, but me, as a woman, probably the most, which is why I feel so bonded, so responsible, so connected to the people of Zawiya.

At the same time, surges of hormones secreted at times of danger are known to affect brain structures related to emotion, memory and concentration. Ah, so constant weeping, tiredness, my failure to read even basic material, remember simple instructions all seem to make much more sense.

Lesley elaborates, saying that when these structures are affected, then the mechanism inside to switch off from the danger – from the shocking experience – doesn't work so well. You can still feel very much on 'red alert' as if the trauma is still ongoing. And the point is, she says, this response is automatic, not chosen.

Lesley also asks me if I'm having any flashbacks or trouble sleeping. I don't recognize them as flashbacks, but I tell her I do keep seeing some of the disturbing sights we witnessed, one in particular – the man with his head half blown off. It doesn't obscure what I'm looking at when my eyes are open. I mean, I can still see everything around me. I'm not bumping into tables or colliding with doors.

The image is transparent. I can look through it and see Lesley in front of me, sitting there asking me questions and listening, but the image is there when I blink or when I concentrate or when I try to sleep. And I just can't dislodge it. I can't get rid of it. It's difficult to explain and doesn't make any sense, but she seems to understand what I'm talking about. That in itself makes me feel better. I haven't mentioned the image and the problem I'm having with it to anyone apart from Martin, but he is away on holiday now and I'm conscious he must be trying to cope with things too. I don't want to infect him with my problems.

Lesley gets me to do a physical exercise to try to dislodge the image. It involves her patting my thighs while I close my eyes and concentrate on the 'film' in my head. I am cynical about even trying it. I feel silly and a bit embarrassed. I don't go to doctors usually. I don't even take headache tablets. I pride myself on being physically fit and healthy and I often boast about my 'iron' constitution. I'm often the sole one in the team who does not get diarrhoea in an earthquake zone or in some of the other dirty places we have to report from. But now all that seems hopelessly macho, especially for a person of the female gender. So I go through the exercise to appease Lesley. After all, she has come all the way from London to Dubai to talk to me. She's here to help me. Besides, she is sitting right in front of me and it seems impolite and frankly a bit difficult to refuse. I'm astonished when it appears to work.

I'm feeling drained, exhausted. I desperately need more energy. Lesley says try taking some exercise, not too much but a little just to get the endorphins going a bit. The sudden evaporation of adrenalin after it has been surging through me for days is like suddenly coming off a drug. That's why I'm so spent. I ask her if she will talk to Richard. I know he's finding it hard to talk to me about the stress he has been under. I know because when I speak to him about it he says, 'Yes, but it's nothing to being in a mosque surrounded by Gaddafi forces.' But I can tell by his face he is hurting. I also know he feels helpless about how to help me because I'm not talking to him in any great detail about what happened.

I go home and virtually beg Rick to talk to Lesley. He is a bit taken aback by my suggestion. But somehow I persuade him. It makes me feel better, somehow assuages my guilt that I have put him through such pain.

By the time Lesley leaves Dubai a few days have gone by. I'm sleeping a bit better, I am going to the gym and running. I feel a bit more myself. My irrational and illogical anger against everybody is still there but it is starting to dissipate. It's not gone, but I don't want to throw things at the television any more. Well, not all the time. I know now what they mean by time being a healer. It takes time. But, at the same time, I don't want to forget. That would be just as bad as the alternative.

However, I still don't feel too much like socializing when the Dubai World Cup week arrives in the UAE. It's the celebration of the richest day's horseracing in the world and an event which Richard has reported on since it started. He is involved again and has got us tickets to the event's pre-race Arabian Nights Desert Party near the Bab Al Shams desert resort, about an hour out of the city. I want to go and support him, see his old racing chums and former colleagues, but I just don't feel much like chatting and breezing the night away, pretending there are no cares in the world.

We meet our old friends Chris McGrath of the *Independent* and Greg Wood of the *Guardian* and the racing organizers put on a magnificent entertainment of fire performers, acrobats and horse displays. The climax of the evening is a pyrotechnic show and, this being Dubai, it's a little more than a box of sparklers. As the stream of bright bombs explode violently in the desert night for a good half an hour, Richard can feel me shuddering by his side. It feels horribly reminiscent of Zawiya. Suddenly I am back there hearing the noises. I want to crawl under the table and disappear. I don't enjoy it at all.

My co-worker Stuart Ramsay comes back into mobile phone territory around the same period. It's convincing hearing about his own field experiences, hearing it from someone who is doing the same job and also having to cope with the difficulties which go with the territory. He describes a detailed timeline of the different physical and emotional stages I will go through based on his own experience: trauma, anger, rage, guilt, sleeplessness, helplessness, exhaustion, emotional meltdown. 'It'll take a week to ten days,' he says. 'You have to recognize it, try to do normal things, mundane things, like shopping, ironing, chores, then you will feel a bit better. It's normal. It's what we do. Oh,' he adds, 'and don't let this define you.'

I recognize what Stuart says, and the stages. I definitely don't want to let this define me, of that I am certain. I feel like a cliché, but now I have given up fighting not to be a cliché.

The medicine Lesley talked about seems to be having an effect. I remember her words, and those of Stuart, who has been down this track so many times he should have a season ticket. It's time to get back to work.

Chapter Six

RETURN TO LIBYA

We're going back to Libya and Martin and I are nervous. There's no doubt about it. It's a bit like falling off a horse. You have to get back on – and get back on as soon as you can. You can't let your nerves beat you. Not if you want to carry on doing what we do, and Martin and I both want to do just that. We're certain of it. There's no doubt at all in our minds, absolutely no hesitation from either of us. But that doesn't mean there are no butterflies.

This time we are trying to get into Misrata – the latest Libyan city to be besieged by Gaddafi's security forces. We meet my close friend the producer Neville Lazarus in the Egyptian capital, Cairo. We worked together for nearly five years when I was based in India and it's great to see him again. We've covered war zones, earthquakes and volcanic eruptions as well as tales of Indian snake charmers and real-life 'Slumdog Millionaires'. We hug warmly. This is going to be fine. But Martin and I are constantly reassuring each other nonetheless. 'I just want to get on with it,' says Martin. I know what he means. There's a long build-up to actually getting inside Libya.

We've already taken a plane from Dubai to Cairo, where we stay overnight. Then we're all up at 07.00 and back travelling again, this time by road, all day, to the Salloum crossing point on the Libya–Egypt border, an area which has been pretty well secured by the rebels.

Then, once we cross into Libya, we continue overland again in a different car to Tobruk, finally arriving at 19.00. By then it's dark. Waiting for us in the lobby of the hotel is the Sky News editor, Roger Protheroe, foreign affairs editor Tim Marshall and cameraman/editor Ed Bayliss. We're taking over from them. They've done their stint, with Tim anchoring much of the Libyan coverage from Benghazi and reporting on the rebels' haphazard struggle to keep control of the east while also trying to push forward, closer to the capital.

The three of them are pretty tired and desperate to get out and back home. We have a meal together so they can do the handover and update us on the situation as they see it and give us tips about working in Benghazi based on their time here. It's such a fluid situation and keeps on changing. The Libya we visited a few weeks ago is not the same now. Now few crews are operating inside Libya without a security expert with them, and Sky is no exception.

Clive Mills has been working with Tim and company and he's staying on to be with us. No shore leave for him. He says he's former Special Forces and seems pleasant. He's quiet and on an internal reconnaissance mission, just watching and trying to work out what his new team is like. I think I may be coming over as a little aggressive to the outgoing team.

I tell Clive we need to get into Misrata, which is no easy task. It is besieged and unreachable by land, surrounded on three sides by

Gaddafi forces. There is a port which the Opposition fighters have control of for now but which is constantly coming under fire from the regime forces. The only possible way into the city is via the sea. Roger says the National Transitional Council (NTC) – which is the rebels' political body – is sending a few journalists on the few ships which are going into Misrata, primarily to pick up civilians trying to flee the fighting or to pick up the badly injured. But even if you get a lift on a boat, you have the problem of getting out again. It all sounds difficult, but we didn't expect anything else.

We're off and out of the hotel early next morning for the next leg of the overland journey to Benghazi, and arrive in the early afternoon. We go straight to the NTC offices and the set-up seems chaotic and none too friendly or welcoming to journalists. They seem a little worn down by the worldwide interest and the requests of the unceasingly demanding reporters. I think they've lost sight of the big picture. You *need* the journalists to care, I want to tell the NTC official, but he's rather officious and imperious. He's telling me there are too many journalists trying to get to Misrata and they feel responsible for their safety. I'm really astonished at his attitude. I'm thinking of the people of Zawiya and how desperate they were for the attention of journalists and how crucial they felt independent reporting on their plight was and still is. The NTC official says there's a waiting list for reporters to go on the aid ships and we are something like twenty-fifth on the list.

As a rule, reporters are no longer staying in the city. The trend seems to be to go down to the hospital in Misrata and quickly interview casualties and medics before returning to the relative safety of Benghazi on the same ship which brought them in. That way there is a guaranteed passage out. Everyone who goes is fearful

– and their editors are even more fearful – about being unable to extract their staff from the besieged city. ITN's Johnny Irvine and his cameraman, Sean Swann, have just had a narrow escape when the 'safe' place where they were staying in Misrata was shelled. A child playing in the grounds was killed in front of them.

It seems hopeless to try to get into Misrata under the NTC's auspices. We can't wait for its officials to get to us at the very bottom of their list. We head off to the port ourselves, frustrated and impatient. We've met up with our Libyan translator, Hytham, with whom Neville worked when he was last here. He is eccentric, outgoing and chatty, chatty, chatty, and seems to know everyone by virtue of the fact he won't stop talking to all and sundry. Hytham is about 40 but seems a lot older and has wild, curly hair which doesn't look like it's seen a brush in a while. He speaks good English because he's studied engineering in Egypt. Neville says he met him when he was travelling through Benghazi a few weeks earlier. The two got talking, with Hytham ending up by saying he would take Neville to see his sister's house, which had been shelled. He became part of Neville's team day in and day out, even taking them to the front lines. Neville says Hytham insisted he did not want to get paid. He was simply helping those who were helping his country, was how he put it. But he treated it like a job, religiously turning up on time and sticking with them. 'Don't start a conversation with me,' he'd say to Neville, 'or I won't be able to stop.'

We're looking for a ship on which we can hitch a ride. There is one. It's a huge passenger vessel with the words 'Ventouries Ferries' on the side. The gangplank leading from the belly of the ship is down and there are workers in the hull. We walk on board and get taken straight to see the captain, who is Egyptian. He has studied at the same Egyptian university as Hytham. We sit and have tea with him – quite a few cups actually – and chat to him about the Egyptian uprising, the Arab Spring, the changes in his country and others in the region. Then business. Finally we get round to the point. The captain says he has taken his ship into Misrata three times already and come under fire twice. Clearly he's not easily spooked. He feels he's performing a necessary humanitarian mission. He usually takes in doctors and medicine and brings back a cargo of injured. He agrees to take us along. After all, the ferry will be like the *Mary Celeste* on the way in. But he insists that he cannot take Hytham. No Libyans allowed. It's non-negotiable. We talk about how long he will be in the Misrata port. It's only a few hours, just the time it takes to board the injured passengers.

Neville, Martin and I agree there is no point going to Misrata for a day trip. If we're going to find out what is happening we have to be prepared to stay a while. So long as the rebels keep control of the port, we've a fairly good chance of getting back out on an aid vessel. The captain tells us to come back in the morning, first thing. Great. This sounds hopeful. Our best chance yet.

We go back to the hotel in Benghazi and begin planning what we're going to take on the trip. We want to travel light, taking the minimum amount, but that has to include essential supplies such as a medical kit, some food, water, sleeping bags and our body armour. It needs to be carefully thought out. We're just sorting everything when the news desk rings our hotel room, which is doubling up as our office.

It's the duty news editor, Jules Morrison. He tells us they are getting news in London that a British journalist has been killed in

Misrata – the first Western journalist to be killed in the current fighting. Shit. I break off from the phone call mid-conversation to tell the others. They are thunderstruck. Jules says the word is the journalist is Tim Hetherington, but no one is releasing his name until his family have all been contacted. Tim is a big figure in the industry, a bit of a Boy's Own hero. He's not only fantastically experienced in working hostile environments (Liberia, Afghanistan, Darfur, Libya, among others) and exceptionally talented (he's won World Press Photographer four times), but he's achieved what few journalists have. He's seen his documentary *Restrepo* – about the war in Afghanistan – nominated for an Oscar.

Jules then says: 'You might want to think about what you want to do.'

What? At first I don't even understand what he's getting at because this option hasn't crossed my mind. Then I realize what he means. 'Well, you might not want to go to Misrata now,' clarifies Jules. But it's in a voice which suggests he knows what the reaction is going to be.

'No, I don't think it makes any difference,' I say slowly. Then I turn to Martin and Neville. Their reaction is exactly the same as mine. We should carry on. They are stunned and saddened on hearing the news and maybe even nervous just like me, although neither of them says so. But they want to press ahead with our task, our job. None of us knew Tim personally but we recognized he was one of the most respected members of our profession. Of course it brings home the dangers of our journalistic lives much more acutely when a fellow reporter, photographer or cameraman is killed doing the same job. By the grace of God, we're all thinking. If Tim Hetherington can get killed despite all his years of experience, if *he* can die in spite of his years reporting and filming in the worst war zones you can think of, then ... We have plenty of time to think about it as we spend the evening reporting on Tim's death and what happened.

Another journalist has died with Tim. He is Chris Hondros, who was based in New York and worked for Getty Images. He was also extremely experienced and his work has been nominated for a Pulitzer Prize. These guys aren't rookies. A third person, Guy Martin, who is also a Briton, has suffered severe wounds to his pelvis and is critical and having surgery. (He survives.) A fourth photographer, Michael Christopher Brown, has suffered shrapnel wounds to his left shoulder but his life is not in danger.

It seems Tim and the others had been returning from Misrata's Tripoli Street – an area where there had been fierce fighting since the city came under siege seven weeks earlier. They were on the way out, finished for the day probably, when it happened. There was a mortar attack and the three of them ran to take shelter behind a wall which ended up being hit.

Pictures are released of the images they'd taken just a few hours earlier. They're dramatic and powerful and really capture the house-by-house, street-by-street fighting. They're frightening images to look at, not just because they're incredibly vivid, but also because they're the pictures taken by men killed while trying to catalogue the impact of war. In one, the photo-journalists are following rebels up the stairs of an apartment building as they chase Gaddafi snipers. The next series of photos show the rebels entering a room, throwing grenades, and firing. In this city where these journalists lost their lives, an estimated 360 people have already died over the past two months. That's why the men took these risks, that's why they went in when so many thousands of the town's own citizens are trying to flee the place.

The last tweet on Tim's Twitter account reads: 'In besieged Libyan city of Misrata. Indiscriminate shelling by Qaddafi forces. No sign of NATO.'

I find myself reading out tributes to the dead journalists on air from our 'live' position on the balcony of the hotel in Benghazi, counting down the hours until we too are heading into Misrata. Jay Carney, the White House press secretary, issues a statement before the news of Chris Hondros's death is confirmed. It goes: 'We were saddened to learn of the death of film director and photographer Tim Hetherington while working in Misrata and we are deeply concerned about the wellbeing of other journalists who were wounded alongside him. Journalists across the globe risk their lives each day to keep us informed, demand accountability from world leaders and give a voice to those who would not otherwise be heard.

'The Libyan government and all governments across the world must take steps to protect journalists doing this vital work. The United States will work to do everything possible to assist those who were injured in getting the care they need. Our thoughts are with these brave journalists and their loved ones.'

The initial reports suggest that the journalists might have been deliberately targeted, which only increases our concern and worries. The suggestion is that they were working together as a unit so would have presented a bigger target for snipers watching them from the rooftops.

We finish working well after midnight. I can feel the anxiety climbing inside me and I go to sleep worrying if we'll get into the city and then worrying what it will be like if and when we do. At this stage the worry about *not* getting in is far outweighing the worry of getting in. I don't want to fail.

We're up early and down at the port side by 08.00 the next day. We're treated like special guests by the ferry crew and each given a cabin and invited to the canteen for a meal. Later we're joined by a team of doctors who will be caring for the injured on the return leg. Many of them are Libyans who now live in Britain, America, Canada, but who want to do their bit to help their fellow countrymen and women. The whole venture is being funded by the Qatari government.

By night we see another vessel entering Benghazi port. It's the boat returning with hundreds of fleeing citizens of Misrata and also the boat bearing the bodies of Tim Hetherington and Chris Hondros. It's being met by representatives of the British and American embassies. Those poor men. Their poor families. Tim, at 41, was apparently about to start a family with his partner, telling friends how he was ready for a less eventful lifestyle. Now it's too late.

We can't ever forget the huge numbers of Libyans who are being killed and hurt right now but these are two of our own – people just like us – who didn't even need to be in Libya. They could have stayed at home taking pictures of underwear models or actresses on red carpets, but they weren't men who wanted lives like that. They wanted to make a contribution and they worked hard at getting at the truth and telling it – and now they are dead.

It's a very solemn evening. We still can't make any sense of it. How did they get caught out? Were they targeted? How can that be so? Surely the Gaddafi troops aren't that organized or even precise? My instincts tell me they must have just been terribly,

terribly unlucky. That, despite all the years of experience between them, their luck just finally ran out. We hear they weren't wearing any protective armour. The Egyptians have been very difficult at the border with Libya, sometimes refusing to allow journalists to take over body armour, exacerbating an already difficult theatre for journalists to operate in. We've managed to get ours across, hiding it under cases and bags and boxes of equipment. Body armour is a pain to carry – especially if you aren't actually wearing it because it weighs so much – but it could be our life-saver, so none of us is complaining.

We're all asleep by early evening but something wakes me a few hours later. I look at my watch. It's 23.00. I sit up, wondering how much progress we've made across the high seas. But when I look out of the window I can still see the port. What? Have we not set sail yet? There seems to be some sort of argument going on, port side. The NTC is insisting the vessel takes on board Libyans who they say are 'returning' to Misrata. But the ship's crew has strict instructions not to allow any Libyans on board for fear they will be accused of taking in 'fighters' and 'weapons'. The sea is being patrolled by NATO and many vessels have been stopped, boarded and searched and found to be gun-smuggling. There's even a bit of shooting on the port side as tempers flare. Eventually we set off from port after 01.00. We've been on the boat for seventeen hours already. Martin, who is not the world's best sailor, is overwhelmed by nausea caused by the swaying of the ferry. And we're not out of Benghazi harbour yet. Despite all the sea-sickness tablets he's taking, Martin's still looking decidedly green round the gills. He's a man of many talents and enormous bravery and skill – but he's very definitely not going to make it as a sailing cameraman. We chuckle at the absurdity of the situation – even Martin – but wish we were already in Misrata. The adrenalin is there, the tension is there, but we're nowhere near. We're tired and we're still about 265 nautical miles and the breadth of the Gulf of Sirte away from where our job really starts.

Friday, 22 April

When I next wake I'm relieved to see there's no land in sight. We spend all day on the boat, doing a couple of live broadcasts while at sea, talking about the journey and the difficulties of getting into Misrata. It's Libya's third-largest city but it's been cut off by land from the rest of the country by military forces loyal to Gaddafi. They're trying to snuff the life out of the place, hoping to starve it and kill, maim and frighten civilians into submission. It's been the scene of intensive close-quarters fighting for weeks now. But as long as the rebels keep control of the Qasar Ahmad dock they can and are surviving. Fishermen are regularly smuggling tiny boats across, packed full of weapons.

An NTC official tells me, off the record, that the Benghazi rebels had even smuggled over wooden crates full of money, which they had 'liberated' from the central bank in Benghazi. They were transporting medicine and food and they were also taking over men, expertise and knowledge on how to tackle the regime. Misrata is not alone, not at all.

The medics on the boat spend their time preparing the vessel for casualties. They transform it from a holiday ferry into a floating hospital ward. The carpet is covered with plastic sheeting. The chairs and tables are all stacked away and mattresses are laid out on the floor with oxygen tanks and drips placed next to each. Their aspiration is to stabilize the patients as much as possible and keep them that way until the vessel docks again. The plan is to take the injured refugees to Malta. The doctors and nurses are unwrapping their medical equipment, antibiotics, bandages, saline bags. Boxes and boxes of medicine and equipment need to be unwrapped and organized so that when the casualties come aboard it's all immediately ready for action. The medics are cheerful and focused. They're a good bunch. Many have taken time off from their normal jobs to do this. Some are going to stay in Misrata to see if they can help out at the hospital. This is their bit for the war effort.

The sea seems vast. It's cold and unwelcoming. It's not especially choppy, but it feels turbulent to our fragile stomachs unused to sea crossings. Martin has stopped cracking jokes, which only ever happens when he is at sea. Somehow the water seems to dry up his sense of humour. We're also finding it cold compared to the heat of Dubai, despite the clear skies and sun. The winds at sea mean I never venture out without several layers on, and I keep having to go outside to make satellite phone calls to London. I keep checking my watch to monitor the hours going by, ticking them off in my mind. There are no landmarks, nothing but the hours going by to suggest we are getting any closer. I can't wait until we stop, but I am worried I won't feel well enough to be up and running straight away.

We reach the dock in Misrata at the end of the day, just as light is fading. We can hear shelling and everyone dockside is working quickly and nervously. There are still burn marks on the port where grenades have landed recently. No one wants to hang around here for very long. It snaps us out of any lingering seasickness. We're just grateful to be on solid land again.

We film all the injured coming aboard. There's a little boy who has been blinded by a shell. He's clinging to his father, frightened out of his wits by all of this. He won't let go of his dad's hand. His father looks tremendously worried. It's a sad tale but the two of them are now on the way to safety.

The doctors are having to make tough decisions about whom to take on board and whom to turn away. Strictly speaking they're not supposed to take people whose injuries or illnesses are not the direct result of the recent conflict. But among those trying to get on the ship and away from this war-torn city are some who've been paralysed since childhood, as well as those with long-term injuries or illnesses. Under Gaddafi's rule health services are free, but years of UN sanctions have taken their toll on the facilities – and now this siege has squandered what they had before. The country has a life expectancy of more than 70 years – among the highest in the developing world – but, right now, statistics are meaningless. Everyone is just anxious to get out of a city which is under almost constant bombardment. There's shouting and begging and much crying when the doctors refuse entry. The ferry is a lifeline, a route out of the war, the fighting and the random attacks. These would-be passengers have already negotiated the treacherous journey to the port and now they're being turned away.

We leave behind the moral dilemmas and heart-breaking decisions and get a ride in an ambulance which is now empty and returning to the Hekma hospital to pick up more of the injured. Once there, a Dr Mufta tells us there might be a floor we can sleep on in the hospital's physiotherapy section, which is about ten minutes' walk away.

When we get there we are led down to a basement which was once the physio department's gym. There are treadmills all along one wall, medicine balls scattered around the place, as well as piles of weights. There are also people in sleeping bags, most of them gently snoring or just asleep. One or two are reading by head torch. It's difficult to make out just how many people there are here in the dark but it looks like there could be about a dozen. We pick our way through this impromptu dormitory and put down our sleeping bags and food provisions in a row along a bit of vacant wall. We're each handed a pancake-thin mattress, but it is a mattress. Oh joy.

I'm murmuring to Neville that we don't want to be with a crowd of other journalists. We need to find somewhere else to stay. We all hate being corralled. But we're tired and this will have to do for now. It's not actually that bad. It's got power, operated, I think, by a generator, and there are toilets and two showers. It could be worse. We find a small spare room on the floor above and, around half-past midnight, Martin and I begin work on putting together a report for the morning programme, on the injured being evacuated from Misrata.

Neville stays up, hunting for hot coffee and putting together little snacks out of our bags of provisions until we both tell him to get some sleep. He'll be up early and before us in the morning, trying to make contacts and find out how we can connect with the fighters in the city. It doesn't sound as though we'll have much trouble. We can hear the reception of constant, distant shelling and explosions all through the edit and until we finally fall asleep. We're here in Misrata at last.

Chapter Seven

BATTLE FOR MISRATA

Neville is busy. Actually that's not much of a revelatory statement to anyone who knows him. Neville was born busy. But – luckily for us – he was also born with oodles of charm and he makes friends easily. He looks like an incredibly studious, fresh, clean-cut young Indian, with student glasses and a tidy haircut: the sort of dependable young man any mother would love their daughter to bring home. He has a big smile and oozes dependability. He comes over as soft and gentle, terribly conscientious and considerate, unfailingly polite. In fact, he is all of these things. But this passive exterior also disguises an inner core of strength, resilience and courage. People often make the mistake of thinking Neville's a pushover. They only ever make that mistake once. Inside this benign persona lies the Indian tiger. His bite is worse than his bark.

By the time Martin and I are down among the injured, watching the casualties come in, Neville has already met and chummed up with half the hospital, including an ambulance driver called Adam. Well, he's not really an ambulance driver. He's a schoolteacher who has given up the classroom while this war is going on and is now voluntarily driving to the front line, retrieving the injured and bringing them back to the Hekma hospital.

The hospital is so overwhelmed the medics have set up a tent outside, a holding bay where most of the casualties are first taken. The whole city's at war, under siege, and shut off except for the port. This is not a pure field hospital away from the fighting. It's right in the centre of the city, where people are under attack and have nowhere to run.

Adam has a tiny ambulance. There are two seats in the front, one for him – the driver – and one for a passenger. That's where Martin will go. In the back, the entire space seems to be taken up by a stretcher on wheels. There's a little perch next to it for the medic, who will be treating the victim. That's pretty much it. I'll have to ball myself into a foetus, squash alongside the medic, and just try not to get in the way. Adam says two of us can come with him to the front line. He can't take any more. He'll have to bring back a casualty and the medic plus us two. There's no room for anyone else.

Neville reluctantly stays behind at the hospital. He would love to come with us. In fact, he's itching to go. We make arrangements to ring him using our satellite phone at set times. He'll co-ordinate with the London office, monitoring the situation at the hospital and keeping them updated with any developments. But crucially he'll also be the one who raises the alarm and organizes our route out of here should either of us get injured or anything else goes wrong.

It's an essential, critical part of the job and requires 'testicles of steel', as one of my colleagues once put it. It's an arena in which

Neville is expert, having in the past already managed (under the guidance of Stuart Ramsay) to organize the US military to storm a building in Afghanistan to free my crew and me.

While we're driving with Adam through Misrata, Martin films him and I chat through the window separating the front seats from the rear. There's a labyrinth of makeshift checkpoints which the citizens of the city have erected to try to halt the progress of Gaddafi's forces – or at least make it much more difficult. There are piles of sand and chunks of concrete, trees, branches and steel piping strewn across the roads. A working man's blockade. It's a chicane of obstacles which all the vehicles have to go through. Gangs of armed rebels are at each of these checkpoints with rebel flags tied to sticks, pinned on wooden boards, painted on the concrete. They have even put up effigies, tying them to lampposts or hitching them onto sticks in the middle of checkpoints or roads to try to draw the Gaddafi sniper fire.

Misrata is big. In normal times it has a population of around 300,000 and is a city renowned for its business links. It's considered rich, educated, civilized and cultured in comparison to many other cities and towns in Libya. It's home to many of the country's intelligentsia.

Adam tells us how he's lost so many friends and family in this bloody war, how the whole of Misrata is now fighting for survival, and how they cannot afford to give up or give in. He can't help crying while talking to us. But he's not ashamed or particularly embarrassed by the tears. These tough, brave men risking their lives every day, driving through gunfire and shelling to rescue others, well up and sob when they pause, think and remember. They don't have time for that much at the moment and I feel awful that I seem to be the one making Adam feel all this pain. But I also think what an incredibly inspiring, selfless person he is. And how his innumerable daily acts of bravery should be recounted.

There's news that the Gaddafi forces are trying to lay mines around the port area to stop aid ships and reinforcements coming in. The British destroyer HMS *Liverpool* is among the international warships off the coast of Libya. It's patrolling outside the port of Misrata, engaging targets both at sea and on shore and, critically, helping the rebels keep control of the port and gain control of the airport.

However, Misrata has been under siege for two months now and Adam and his like are worn down and emotional. The whole city has become battle-hardened and battle-weary. The rebels are making some inroads, though. On the night of Tim Hetherington's death (Wednesday, 20 April), they manage to gain control of the airport and take over several high points in the city from which the Gaddafi forces had been shelling.

Accurate information is hard to come by because the city is so hard to access and the UN humanitarian chief, Valerie Amos, is telling reporters in Benghazi that they have very little sense of what is going on across Misrata.

We discover that most of the 'journalists' in our underground former gym appear to be freelance bloggers who are in their twenties and have funded their own trips out here. Also among our new housemates is a French TV crew, a team from the *Daily Mail* – writer Andrew Malone and photographer Jamie Wiseman – and *Guardian* reporter Xan Rice. I don't know anyone else. I know *Sunday Times* writer Marie Colvin is somewhere in the city but she's definitely not in the basement. Lucky her.

Hala Jaber, who also works for the *Sunday Times*, has already been over and spent time in this city, becoming the first from a British newspaper to witness the siege of Misrata and write about the terrible hardship being endured by its people. Still information is hard, incredibly hard, to come by, largely because it's just so dangerous to move around. The firing and shelling from the Gaddafi forces across the whole of the city are far too indiscriminate.

Adam drives us down the back streets until we come to the edge of Tripoli Street. It's the main thoroughfare in Misrata and where Tim Hetherington and the others were shelled. As we are making our way through the city I'm thinking, Where are all the fighters? Are there any? I see clusters – individuals and pairs sitting at the many rebel checkpoints – but where are the big fighting units? Are there any at all?

Photographer Jamie Wiseman has told me he has already been out and about with his correspondent, Andrew Malone, down Tripoli Street with the fighters. He plays down the whole incident – as is his way – but the two of them very nearly got killed after themselves becoming the target for snipers. Their translator, who was also their guide, got shot in the stomach. Jamie pinpoints areas where he knows there have been some Gaddafi soldiers holed up and shooting at anything and anyone that moves below. It's vital information for new people in the city like us. It's information which could save our lives and it's gratefully accepted.

It helps that I know Jamie of old. He's worked regularly in the past with my friend David Williams, the chief correspondent of the *Daily Mail*. Dave and I began our careers on the same regional newspaper in England – the *Wokingham Times* – and although we weren't there at the same time he has been incredibly generous with his help and advice to me over the years. He introduced me to Jamie when we were both working in Pakistan several years ago.

Now we're inside the besieged city of Misrata together and Jamie's knowledge of the routes and the roads based on his few days here already is hugely important from a safety point of view. He's bright, alert and very talented, and his advice, born out of years of working in hostile environments, is definitely worth listening to.

Martin and I are aware that to get a sense of just how well the rebels are coping, how well armed they are and how organized they are, we need to get to the 'front'. We have to get to the area where the rebels are taking on the Gaddafi forces. And the 'front' seems to be situated on shifting sands. Adam takes us down a dusty, uneven road, so narrow that the ambulance takes up its entire breadth.

And then we see them.

There are dozens and dozens and dozens of them. Fighters sitting up against the wall of a building looking as though they're on a break. Others are milling around, chatting, and more still are under a roof, sheltering from the sun. There are many of them. This is the fighting unit we suspected might have been a myth. But now they're very real.

They are all armed and there is evidence of weapons and ammunition lying everywhere. At the end of the road, at the corner of the building they are waiting behind, there is an anti-aircraft gun mounted on a pick-up truck. The vehicle has had sheets of metal welded onto the body for reinforcement. Another truck is parked farther down, just waiting to go.

We get out and walk down through the hordes of men. I'm wondering how they will react to two foreigners just turning up and wandering onto their battlefield. Martin has his camera in hand and I'm carrying the microphone and cable so there's no mistaking we're journalists. They seem relaxed, although we can hear the sound of firing and explosions very close by. One or two of them look up and say 'Salaam' (peace) as we walk by. We return the greeting.

There's no aggression here, at least not towards us. We're both wearing our blue armoured jackets and helmets and I feel slightly awkward as none of the fighters are similarly protected. None have flak jackets and very few have helmets. A few have taken to wearing their motorbike crash helmets. Most of them are in their own clothes – jeans and T-shirts, trousers and shirts – yet there is an unusual uniformity about them. Perhaps it's the bandannas, the headscarves, the neckerchiefs which many of them are wearing. There's just something which seems to bind them sartorially. They're a team, a unit, a fighting force.

Martin and I take a peek – one after the other – around the corner they're firing from. In front of us is a scene of devastation. I can see a petrol station across the traffic intersection in front of us. I wonder if there is petrol stored there and flinch at the thought of what will happen if a rocket lands on or near it. It's a two-storey building and I can see fighters on the ground hiding at the back and more on the second floor and rooftop. They're ducking behind the rooftop barrier wall and occasionally bobbing up to shoot.

In front of us is a crossroads. Two articulated trucks have been crudely parked here to form a barrier. They're already burnt out. Still, they're providing some protective cover for teams of men to run, hide behind and fire from. Another vehicle is on fire, and there are clouds of smoke coming out of the building on the other side of the street. There are still more fighters in the middle and waiting elsewhere. Large numbers of them, in fact. This is a full-on battle. Their focus is a building where they believe there are Gaddafi soldiers, and it is slowly being attacked and fired upon from a number of different angles.

I feel the twin emotions of excitement and fear rising in me. I sense straight away the fighters we're with have the upper hand. It may not last. It may just be transitory, but right now the rebels are the ones pushing forward and attacking. I draw a lot of comfort from their obvious confidence, but the fear is still there. Everything here is unpredictable and it takes only one stray bullet – even one fired by mistake – to end it all. We are constantly on edge and have to be.

It is our first glimpse of the Misrata fighters in action, and nearly two months of siege mentality have turned them into a cohesive civilian fighting unit. They seem to be very much on the up. There doesn't seem to be any shortage of fighters or volunteers to go into battle. They are communicating with each other, co-ordinating the fight with walkie-talkies.

It's a very different picture from the one that has been reported so far – the one detailing ramshackle groups of men advancing and retreating along the road from Benghazi to Ajdabiya to Brega without any real sense of direction or plan. And it's very different from our personal experience in Zawiya in March when the civilians just did not possess sufficient firepower and were crushed by a much stronger military force.

This set of combatants has all the appearances of an army – with a major difference. I interview a bunch of them while they're waiting for their turn to move into battle. They keep running into the crossroads and the articulated truck barricade, firing, ducking and diving, letting off more shots, then returning for a brief rest. I address a group of them during one of their breathers. 'What do you do? What training have you had? Where do you normally work?' Not one I talk to has had any training. Well, no warfare training. They are largely a white-collar army of teachers, mechanics, university professors, dentists, doctors, shopkeepers, and lots and lots of students.

The students are taking a break from studying to emulate their fellow fighters, to become doctors, lawyers, engineers. They used to be concerned with going out, meeting girls, clothes, hair gel and computer games – mostly computer games. Now they're risking their lives for freedom. They're young too – mainly between 17 and 20 years old. A number have already been injured, not just once or twice but several times. They've been patched up and are now returning to the front, some still with their hands bound with bandages or their shoulders strapped.

Occasionally we hear the thunder of a Grad rocket being launched from behind the Gaddafi lines. It's a roar which is truly terrifying. The rebels call them 'hounds', but the closer they sound, the safer we probably are because they're so imprecise. We can see the empty casings of cluster bombs lying around, bombs which explode in a hail of ball bearings, bombs which are banned in international law. And we hear mortar bombs come crashing down. But these young lads, some of whom are fighting alongside their lecturers and teachers and many not yet out of their teens, are simply not daunted.

There's a roar from the crowd of fighters farther down our alleyway and shouts of excitement which make everyone stop and look up. At first I can't see anything but the shape of a mob moving towards us. In the centre of this advancing, near-hysterical group is a man in Gaddafi uniform. His face is black with dirt or ash. He looks terrified. He's right to be. He's unarmed now and he's being pushed and bundled along quickly by the mob. Occasionally different arms and hands reach out and lash him, whacking him on the head or thumping him violently on the back. There's a lot of shouting as the rebels issue commands to each other. They angrily spit in the soldier's direction, in his face, at the back of his head, anywhere in his general direction.

As we try to get closer to see him, talk to him, film him, the crowd try to push us back and one or two try to elbow us out of the way. Somehow, Martin holds his own. He is six foot three and strong and he sticks with it. But, after a few minutes, the soldier is pulled away and out of our section of the crowd. He's taken off by a much smaller group, numbering about five. As we follow, they tell us in threatening tones, holding their weapons up, to stop and to take no further video. We drop back and I shout out after them: 'Where are you taking him? Can we talk to him?'

We turn back to the bulk of the crowd. We can hear the sound of fighting still going on farther down the road. This was just a brief distraction, but I feel terribly nervous for the soldier. 'Jesus,' I say to Martin. 'What are they going to do to him?' 'Leave it, Crawfie,' he says. 'They're all fired up. There's nothing we can do.'

The soldier looked frightened and resigned. We've no idea if he will be treated well, if he will be looked after, if he will be allowed to live, or if the rebels will use him to get information about where the Gaddafi forces are based, hiding, or fighting from. His colleagues – the other Gaddafi soldiers in this area – are still trying to shoot and kill those all around – including us. Why on earth do we feel sorry for him? Perhaps because he is one human, one man, on his own, and now defenceless in the hands of his enemy. It's hard not to feel his terror and helplessness, his utter personal defeat and failure. War is repugnant and this is its face. He is now at the mercy of a band of men who are still under attack from his side and fighting for their lives. He has to hope they're going to play by the international rules his own side and his paymaster did not abide by. It's a big ask.

After about fifteen minutes a rebel comes up to us. 'Come,' he says in halting English. 'You see the prisoner.' We follow him. He's telling us to hush, be quiet, don't arouse a lot of attention from the other fighters. He doesn't want any of them following us.

We walk in the opposite direction to the fighting and down dusty back streets until we reach a house. We wait outside for a little while and then a car drives up. Its doors open and we see the soldier being led out towards us. His hands are tied in front of him with rope and he's being guarded by a large man with a gun slung over his shoulder. Everyone gets out of the car apart from the driver. There are four in all, each man armed. One has his hand firmly under the soldier's arm. 'Ask your questions,' one of the rebels tells me.

'Where are you from? What did you do before? What were your orders?' I ask my questions through one of the rebels who is attempting to interpret. I'm trying to get as many in as possible because I can tell the rebels want to leave almost as soon as they have driven up. The replies come back slowly and reluctantly. He's from Sudan, used to work on a farm, came to Libya to earn money. He's one of Gaddafi's mercenaries. He has been ordered not to let anyone live. 'Not to let anyone live?' I ask. I'm not sure I've heard correctly. Yes, the rebel interpreter says. No one was to live. I'm still not sure I've been told precisely what the soldier said. Is the interpretation an honest one? I simply don't know. It seems so, that's my impression, my instinct. The soldier seems less afraid now, more resigned. I've only been able to ask a few questions. I want to ask so many more. But my time is over.

The car which transported the captive has its engine revving. The soldier is told to get inside even while I'm urgently asking the fighters where he is going and what they are going to do with him. They shout back that he is being taken to where the other Gaddafi prisoners are, but no one wants to say exactly where that is. Oh, come on. He will be treated as a prisoner of war. Really? He is considered valuable and may be able to give some information about the Gaddafi forces. But, after these snippets of information are divulged, he is driven off. Someone shows a peace sign to us out of the back window and then they're gone. It's hardly any information at all but I suppose something is better than nothing.

We head back to the fighting zone, just a few minutes' walk away. The rebels are still filing in and out of the crossroads and weaving their way in and out of the barricades they have created. The rebels want us to go farther, to see them finally finishing off the rest of the Gaddafi forces inside the building in the far right-hand corner of the crossroads. Martin and I run forward together into the crossroads and behind one of the articulated trucks. Not for the first time I feel heavy and sluggish carrying all my hardware. Move quicker, move quicker, I'm saying to myself. My legs just won't respond as quickly as I want them to. We crouch down behind the truck on our haunches and wait for a while to see

Left: On board the ferry to Misrata, with Martin Smith who, despite his enormous bravery and skill, will never make it as a sailing cameraman.
© Neville Lazarus

Left: Tripoli Street in Misrata, where fierce fighting took place and journalists Tim Hetherington and Chris Hondros tragically lost their lives.
© Neville Lazarus

Above: Making my way through one of the rebel-made tunnels on Tripoli Street, which were used to go house-to-house and avoid snipers.
© Neville Lazarus

Above: A Gaddafi soldier being treated in a tent outside Hekma hospital in Misrata.
© Neville Lazarus

Above: (from left to right) Martin, me and Clive Mills in the physiotherapy department gym in Hekma hospital, where we spent our first night in Misrata.
© Neville Lazarus

Above: Libyan international footballer turned leader of the Tripoli Street Brigade Ibrahim Shanibah, aka 'Grande', stands to my left. That's Neville Lazarus on my right, with Clive next to him, and Martin on the far right.
© Neville Lazarus

Above: Misrata rebels, whose vehicles could have been lifted from the set of Mad Max.
© Neville Lazarus

Left: A flag is raised by a rebel on the tallest building in Tripoli Street in Misrata.
© Neville Lazarus

Above: The impossibly upbeat and energetic Garwen McLuckie. © Garwen McLuckie

The taking of Martyrs' Square in Zawiya. I take cover while the rebels fire on Gaddafi troops (top), and tanks fire on the Square (above). © Garwen McLuckie

Above: Andy Marsh, with the cable across his face, and Jim Foster filming me on the back of a rebel pickup truck as the rebels enter Green Square in Tripoli. © Garwen McLuckie

Above: Dr Salah Rodwan, who showed such kindness and bravery in the face of terror, gives me a hug when we meet again in Zawiya. © Garwen McLuckie

Below: Green Square is taken by the rebels. © Sky News

EWS HD   TRIPOLI

EAKING NEWS LIBYA CONFLICT
BELS REACH GREEN SQUARE
02 BELS REACHED CENTRE OF TRIPOLI   BREAKING NEWS   GADDAFI'S ELDEST SON MOHAMMED CONFIF

Top: The Bab al Aziziya compound is invaded.
© Garwen McLuckie

Above: Jim Foster and I bump into Stuart Ramsay and his team as we're leaving the Bab al Aziziya compound. © Tom Rayner

Left: Rebels sitting atop Gaddafi's symbol of power – a golden fist crushing an American fighter jet.
© Garwen McLuckie

[Photo strip]:
Mr Hisham Alwindi, proud owner and wearer of Colonel Gaddafi's hat ... and inspiration for the title of this book.
© Sky News

Above: 'Where are you now, Gaddafi?' screams
Irish-Libyan rebel Tareg. © Garwen McLuckie

Above: With the family in Wadi Rum, Jordan, in
between revolutions. Richard and Nat looking
comfortable (left). It took Flo (on my lap),
Frankie (centre) and Maddy (right) forty-five
minutes to summon up the courage to get on
the camels.

where the firing is coming from and how safe it is to advance. Rebels are running up behind us and going past us, firing as they go.

One stops and waits with us, smiling and exchanging pleasantries for a few seconds. Yes, really. We've chatted to him earlier. He's a geography teacher when he's not fighting revolutions and in his mid-fifties, if not older. He has a white-grey beard and matching wispy hair. You can't see much of it, though, because it's wrapped inside a red bandanna tied around his head. Courtesies over, the geography teacher leaps out into the open space, spraying bullets from his machine-gun as he runs forward yelling, 'Allahu Akbar.'

We can see the rebels launching grenades into the building just in front. From behind the truck where we're crouching they're using machine-guns and firing RPGs over and over and over again. They're moving into the building, trying to clear it room by room.

Martin films a little and then we move forward even more. But here we feel too exposed. Martin snatches a few shots and we decide to run back, shadowed by a group of rebels who take us back to our starting point.

Adam the ambulance driver is still there. He reassures us that he will take us back to the hospital in his ambulance – but he cannot and does not want to leave this battlefront on a simple taxi trip. He will leave only if a casualty needs to be taken back to the hospital.

It doesn't take long. The Gaddafi forces might be in retreat, the rebels might be winning the battle of this street, but it's not without risk. An injured fighter is dragged, almost carried forward, as others are shouting for the ambulance. Adam springs into action. The back doors are flung open and the wounded man loaded onto the stretcher inside. Mohammed – another doctor turned fighter – beckons me to get in, and then jumps in behind me.

The man on the stretcher seems to have a number of wounds. He has two on his face – one to his jaw, the other on his forehead. But the doctor is tending to the more serious wound lower down his body, I think on his thigh. Martin is again in the front passenger seat and Adam is racing down these back streets now.

We're being thrown all over the place in the back and the doctor is pulling at boxes with syringes, bandages, plaster. He's already beginning to bind the man's leg. I'm sitting near the man's head and all I can see is blood oozing out of his jaw. He's conscious and holding his jaw, trying to stem the flow. I can see it's not a life-threatening injury. I'm thinking, thank God it's not a terrible skull wound or a bullet to the chest.

The doctor is frantically trying to tear open more bandages while compressing the wound in the man's thigh. But he hasn't got enough hands and he's finding it difficult because he's wearing plastic gloves. He can't do this on his own.

I take the sticky plaster, which he wants to use to hold the bandage in place, and tear some strips using my teeth and hand it back to him. He seems surprised at first but is then immediately grateful I've stopped being just an observer, a passenger in both senses of the word. I'm feeling bad enough frankly taking up space in this tiny ambulance and here in front of me – inches away from me – is a man who is hurt and bleeding. I've been trained in first aid like many journalists (certainly those from Sky News) who may find themselves working in war zones. And whoever this man is – rebel or regime supporter – I can't just sit and watch him bleed when I could assist and there's no one else here to do the helping.

I ask the doctor for the swab he already has in his hand and put it on the man's jaw, placing his own hand over it to hold it in place. I tear off more strips to stick the swab down on the man's face. It's an amateur attempt but it seems to stop the bleeding. The doctor meanwhile is trying to insert a needle into the man's hand so he can rig up a drip. He's got his own specific jobs to do and he's left me with the less serious of the injuries.

Adam is driving so fast we're having trouble stopping ourselves falling on the patient. How on earth can the doctor insert a needle and drip into the man's wrist? But he does, and by the time we draw up outside the Hekma the man has all his wounds bound and a drip inserted in a vein in his hand.

The ambulance doors open and he is pulled out by the welcoming medics and whisked away to the emergency room. I glance up and notice Martin has filmed it all from the window separating the front seats from the rear. Hmmm, I don't think that is going to be used in any report I do. I know it won't go down well among certain people. It will probably be seen as self-glorification by those in the industry and partisan by others. What? You bandaged a rebel? How can you be impartial? How can you claim to be independent? I don't talk about it to anyone at the time save Martin and we both agree it should stay out of any report we send back to London. I'm just not sure what people will make of it but something tells me they won't view it in a positive light. But I'm satisfied I did the right thing. I helped the doctor when help was needed. He shakes my hand afterwards. He doesn't say anything, just shakes my hand, and I congratulate him on managing to fix up a drip in such difficult circumstances. He smiles. I guess he's had a lot worse days.

Chapter Eight

CITIZEN ARMY

Sunday, 24 April

We're being taken to see a child soldier. It's all very clandestine because these juvenile fighters are among Gaddafi's troops and therefore now targets. They're among the injured who have been taken to a secret hospital in Misrata and are being cared for and rehabilitated by the medical staff. We arrive and are hurried inside. The doctors are still very twitchy about being seen with any foreigners and they certainly don't want to draw attention from those in Misrata who might be bent on revenge.

A young boy is brought out to us in a wheelchair. He looks very young, but he says he's 16. He has a blanket over his legs so at first I don't notice he has only one foot. When I ask, the doctor pulls back the blanket and I see his left leg has been amputated below the knee. The doctor doesn't want to be identified. In fact, none of the medics want to show their faces on television. They still fear they will be hunted down by Gaddafi's administration. But they are ready to supply us with information.

ALEX CRAWFORD

The young boy soldier was brought to them with a terrible wound on his leg after being injured during the fighting in Misrata. He says he was one of a number of young men forced to go into the army and fight for Gaddafi. He tells us he was told to go to the front of the attack. 'We were less important,' he says. 'It didn't matter to them if we got killed or injured. If we didn't go, we were beaten. I was very afraid of the men in charge of us.'

The poor boy still seems afraid. He doesn't really know what to say and seems terrified of saying the wrong thing. He's surrounded by doctors, all of whom have cared for him and brought him back to health, but he's nervous nevertheless. We leave him and return to the Hekma.

There are a number of tents outside now, an encampment. I wander around just having a look at what's going on and go inside the rear tent, right at the bottom end of the hospital car park. There are three injured men lying on beds inside. But the tent is devoid of medical staff. The casualties have already been seen to and appear to have a variety of wounds. A medic comes in.

'Who are they?' I ask, suspecting the answer already.

'Gaddafi men,' he says without the courtesy of looking at them. One of them is clutching a wad of banknotes spattered with blood. 'That was the money found on him,' the medic says. 'That was the money Gaddafi paid him to kill us.' Blood money.

The men say they are from Sudan and Algeria. By now there are photographers and other journalists inside the tent and the soldiers are staring wide-eyed and silently from their hospital beds at the interest in them.

There's a cry outside which draws some of us away. It's a hubbub. Another couple of injured Gaddafi men are being brought

141

in. The crowd of civilians waiting outside the hospital to hear about their injured relatives is incensed. The two soldiers are on the back of a pick-up. They have obvious injuries, they're bleeding, but they're conscious and now also scared. There's a lot of shouting and lashing out. One man is trying to hit them with his shoe. One of the many armed rebel fighters guarding the hospital from attack fires his gun in the air to scatter the crowd and the fighters who have captured the soldiers drive hastily away.

This is what it's like on the battlefield. The rebels of Misrata, with the help of NATO, are slowly turning the screw on the Gaddafi forces inside the city and there's not much sympathy for the aggressors turned prisoners.

As well as the injured, there are the dead. A truck-load of corpses is driven through the hospital car park, arms and legs poking out of Gaddafi uniforms, twisted in a messy, ugly pile. There's little sympathy for them here, little time for respect. I get the sense the drive-past is deliberate, to show the Misratans mourning their losses that the people of their city have fought, are still fighting, and, bit by bit, they're repelling the security forces.

It's taken a while, though, and the city is hurting. Food and water and gas are running out as Gaddafi troops keep hitting the city's key infrastructure points like power stations, water and food storage plants. Most of the city is without a mobile phone network or Internet. The city is nearing breaking point and has sent an official request to the NTC in Benghazi to let foreign troops in to help them. They're reaching desperation point. NATO has upped the pressure and the bombings. Events are on the turn slightly – at least for now.

We're taken to the rebel 'HQ' in Misrata. We've made contact with an excellently connected Misratan called Abdullah. He's shrewd and smart and of sufficient years to be taken seriously by the armed fighters and to be treated with respect by them. This is his city. He knows it well and he knows many of the influential people. His brother Mohammed has already found himself an unelected position on the city's rebel council and is running what they're calling the Media Centre.

The man in charge of the Tripoli Street Brigade is Ibrahim Shanibah, who is nicknamed 'Grande' because he's so tall. He used to be centre forward for the Libyan national football team and played for his country at the 1997 Mediterranean Games in Italy. Now he's juggling walkie-talkies (an impressive array of them all stacked on a table) and commanding his men to make a final sweep down Tripoli Street to check for any lingering Gaddafi snipers.

After weeks of violent battle in and around the city's main thoroughfare, they believe they've pushed Gaddafi's forces out of the city centre – for the time being at least. They say they have control of 90 per cent of the city. The Gaddafi men are still there – on the outskirts – and now the regime forces are intensifying their long-range bombings – using Grad rockets – but the rebels at least seem to have forced them to the fringes of Misrata.

We accompany the rebels as they move down Tripoli Street. We climb one of the high buildings that the two sides have been fighting over for weeks now. It's eight storeys high, a huge trophy. Some of the tallest buildings in Misrata are along the Tripoli Street strip and whoever controls these rooftops has a massive advantage over the battlefield. Hence the fierce fighting. The insurance building and therefore Tripoli Street are in the rebels' hands for the moment and they hoist an Opposition tricolour. There's no premature sense of victory, though. Yes, they have temporary control, but it's been a long, drawn out and remorseless process, with many, many deaths and injuries. And the city is still being attacked and bombarded with rockets and shells.

The rooftop has discarded Gaddafi military paraphernalia everywhere. Mattresses and blankets beneath holes in the rooftop wall where soldiers have been positioned day and night, raining firepower on those below. There are left-over pots, pans and mugs where they have eaten and drunk, and thousands of empty bullet cartridges and shell casings scattered all around. There's also graffiti saying they will never forgive the people of Misrata and they will return and punish them. I'm scared and I'm not even from Misrata. The rebels we are with pay the warnings scant attention but they have been noted.

From this vantage point we can see the length and breadth of Tripoli Street and gasp at the scale of the destruction. Nothing is untouched. Shops and buildings leading off the main road have been punched through with rockets and bullets and grenades. It's staggering.

We make our way to the vegetable market, picking our way through unexploded bombs and other military debris. We hear from the London news desk that Misrata's port is once again coming under fierce attack. The regime is fighting back. It knows it has to wrest control of the port if it is to gain overall control of the city again. The people of Misrata might have won this particular battle, but the regime is going to hit them again, and hard. The port is crowded with immigrants and refugees desperately trying to get out. One of them describes nine rockets landing in and around the port, with dozens killed.

In the stalls around the centre of the marketplace there are, left behind, the uniforms, boots and helmets of Gaddafi troops. They look as though they have been camping here for weeks. There's a stench of death and we see the bodies of Gaddafi soldiers all along the small routes leading to and from the market.

When we turn the corner, again a gasp. The vegetable market – which is open-sided – has two tanks right in its centre and they're still burning. There has clearly been a NATO airstrike – and not so long ago either. There's a huge hole in the market roof. The Russian tank has been hit with such force that its turret has been blown off and catapulted some distance away. Several other tanks are parked down the side streets leading to the marketplace.

At this point, Gaddafi and his regime are still insisting it does not target civilians. No one believes him, but this is the evidence if evidence was needed. It is a jaw-dropping sight. And chilling too. These huge tanks – like monsters – hidden among the shops and stalls and businesses of Misrata, terrorizing a whole city and holding it to ransom. Just a day ago – a few hours ago maybe – they might have been operational. But the whole of Misrata has united to fight this beast within. We've been with the fighters the day before, seeing them weave through the mazes they've created by smashing holes through the walls of their homes. This was how they could make their way around the city without being shot at by Gaddafi snipers.

We go to one of the hidden weapons factories. I cause a bit of a stir when we first arrive because I've forgotten to put on my head-scarf. One of the older men is shouting and has clearly taken exception. Neville comes up and whispers: 'Please put your scarf on, Alex. They're all staring.' I'm angry with myself. I carry a scarf everywhere with me, just for this sort of occasion, but I've left it in the car. Damn and damn again. I don't want to be the reason, the excuse, for not letting us film here. It takes some time to pacify the objectors and a lot of coaxing by Abdullah and Neville. The locals are nervous of a television crew anyway, so the initially missing scarf has not helped matters. But, finally, headscarf on, they let us film.

While we are negotiating, a European man appears in a rebel truck. He's clearly not a journalist and is with a group of fighters. He's surprised to see us here, maybe even alarmed. These work-shops are meant to be a city secret. Neville and I assume he is one of the NATO 'advisers' helping the rebels mount the fightback.

When they first began this revolt, Misrata had virtually no weapons at all. Now, by capturing Gaddafi soldiers and their guns, through maritime smuggling and through sheer ingenuity, they have built up an arsenal. It's not nearly big enough, but it's better than the alternative. This is one of a number of secret depots, open all hours, every day, where they're assembling, designing and repairing weapons. There is also a firing range where they are test-ing the rebuilt weapons and teaching residents how to use them.

Four-door civilian pick-ups and cars are being converted into fighting machines. Guns are being welded onto the back of pick-ups, metal sheeting is being welded to the sides of the cars, the fronts, the bottoms. They're being painted black to decrease the risk of being seen by snipers. These reconstituted vehicles look hard and frightening, even if they might be only marginally more substantial than their street cousins. The rebels are receiving donations from all over the world, largely from Libyans now living abroad, but the NTC has also plundered the banks in Benghazi and sent crate-loads of cash over by sea – along with weapons and know-how in the form of personnel.

There are men at tables converting land mines and tank shells into other lethal arms. Other men are creating four-sided metal spikes which they will scatter on roads to puncture the tyres of the Gaddafi military vehicles. Another group are scraping out the combustible material from unexploded bombs which they will use in their own home-made RPG launchers. It's a bizarre munitions factory.

These are all men who say they had no experience of weapons or arms before this war. They are dedicated and relentless in their work. They have to be. Their city is under attack. Gaddafi's men may have been forced out but each man here knows they'll be back. That's the Gaddafi way.

Monday, 25 April

There's a lot of bombing around our physio building and it also seems to be getting much nearer to the hospital. We can see the explosions late at night from our rooftop and hear the Grad rockets landing close by. When we wake in the morning, Abdullah tells us a Grad has landed near his father's home overnight. His father – who is in his seventies – rushed out to try to get to safety. A second rocket landed on his car. He was killed instantly. Abdullah seems stunned, not quite believing his father has gone. He seems in shock, but he wants to show us where it all happened.

'This was considered a safe area of Misrata,' he tells us. But now nowhere is safe. His father's house is right in the middle of a residential area. The side of the house where the kitchen once stood has been blasted out, bringing down an exterior wall, the kitchen wall and half the ceiling. The second Grad hit the garage where the car his father tried to leave in still stands. Abdullah is matter-of-fact about it all. He wants to talk about his father. The old man is now a *shaheed* (martyr) and to talk about him – especially to an international television crew like us – is to ensure his father's death is properly marked. We're all astonished by Abdullah's bravery and fortitude. 'This is what is happening to us Libyans every day,' he says. 'This is why we have to get rid of Muammar Gaddafi.'

Tuesday, 26 April

The citizens of Tripoli Street are slowly coming out to survey the damage to the city centre. They can't quite believe what they see. Grande is busy trying to tell everyone to stay away. There are too many unexploded bombs and grenades around here. He shouts at the young lads who are scavenging. But this is one battle he's definitely losing – the battle of the curious. Soon there are dozens, and then dozens of dozens, picking through the debris of their shops and businesses.

Near the rebel offices, we meet a mother of five-month-old twins. Salah Sadawi tells us how Gaddafi soldiers burst into her house about a month earlier and took her husband away. 'Forget him, they told me. You'll never see him again,' she says. Salah and the other women and children were herded into one of the main office blocks around Tripoli Street, she said. They were kept under armed guard and their menfolk were coerced into taking part in pro-Gaddafi demonstrations in the streets below in the centre of

Misrata. If they didn't obey, they were told, their women would be raped and killed.

This is one of the ways the Gaddafi regime is managing to fool the world into thinking he has support. Salah is just a young woman, her head covered with a black *hijab*. She looks demure, but she is furious and full of resentment. Salah still hasn't found her husband but she hasn't quite given up hope. She's praying he's still alive somewhere. However, this is the first time in weeks she's been back in her own home and she hasn't even been able to begin the search for him yet. I leave wondering what other atrocities she has suffered and not been able to tell us about.

There are countless tales from the rebels about their women and girls being raped by Gaddafi soldiers. But rape is such a taboo in Libya – in the whole of Islam really – that I've been unable to persuade any women to talk publicly about it. I feel we've been incredibly fortunate meeting and interviewing a woman prepared to speak about being taken prisoner by the regime. But somehow it doesn't feel good enough. It's only part of the story, only part of how they're suffering.

We return to the former gym in the basement. To our surprise, the *Mail*'s Andrew Malone and Jamie Wiseman are still there. We'd said goodbye to them earlier that day. We had watched slightly enviously as they packed up their sleeping bags and equipment and headed out to the port and home. That had been the plan. They're not long back and are still catching their breath.

They had set out to the port, along with six French journalists, to hitch a ride on a ship coming in from Benghazi. The vessel was due to transport thousands of fleeing residents and immigrants, as well as those injured in the fighting. But, as the ship tried to dock, the port was hit by a volley of rockets and mortar bombs. The driver of the journalists' van did a quick U-turn away from the port and back down the road into the city.

This road is a long, empty stretch and very vulnerable to attack. They were targeted again and this time the bombs fell close enough to rock their van, even lift it in the air. Jamie shows us astonishing pictures he has fired off instinctively as the journalists are throwing themselves on the floor of the van for cover. Another frame shows the rocket landing very close to them. His photograph details the puff of smoke and grit as it hits the ground next to them.

They tell how their driver Ahmed rammed two burnt-out vehicles which blocked their exit so they could escape to safety – or relative safety – back inside the city. It's another incredibly narrow escape. They tell us the ship which couldn't dock today is returning in the morning and they intend to be on it. There's no word of any more after that one. Perhaps now is the time to leave. Perhaps we should take our chances and try to get out of here ourselves.

We hear a French blogger – one of our gym colleagues – has been hit by a sniper or a ricocheting bullet on the way back from the Hekma, a walk we have done many times. He had been over to use the hospital's showers. (The two showers in the physio department are taking a colossal hammering owing to use from all the people bedding down in the building, some of them journalists, most of them those involved in the rebel organization.) The bullet has somehow nicked his spine, and he's paralysed. None of us even knows his name or whom he was working for.

The bloggers with him, who were unhurt, don't want to release his name. Maybe they're too shocked or afraid. He'll be on the boat back with us if we manage to get on it, if it manages to dock. If, if, if. If only he hadn't decided to shower, if only he hadn't walked just then, if only he'd stepped two inches to his right or his left. What if we'd been on that same short journey? It just doesn't bear thinking about. The poor lad – and he's only a lad – in his early twenties, I'm told, cannot move anything now but his eyelids. This is the end of the war for him, the end of reporting, the end of his life as he knows it. What sort of a future will he have?

We fall asleep listening to Gaddafi's bombs getting ever closer. It's hard to relax, even harder to sleep, but, somehow, we all manage it.

Wednesday, 27 April

We're up early, around 06.00, to make our date with the ship. Everyone is a little edgy given what's happened the day before, but the journey to the port is uneventful this time. We sit on the dock for hours and hours – until early afternoon – constantly hearing the sound of shelling not too far away but not actually on the port. It's a little comfort.

Then the trucks turn up. Trucks and trucks and trucks of immigrant workers, piled high on the back of them. They look like they could have come straight out of a Second World War scene. They're young, they're all men and they have an air of desperation about them. They've been trying to get out of Misrata and this siege for weeks now. Many have been living in pretty miserable conditions in refugee camps near to the port, refugee camps which Gaddafi's troops have been attacking consistently.

The port-side crew are desperate too. Desperate to get them and us loaded onto the Red Star One ship as quickly as possible to avoid a repeat of what happened yesterday. The ship pulls into dock and, as soon as it does, it's all action. Everyone wants to get on this ship.

The man from the International Organization for Migration (IOM), which is overseeing this evacuation, pinpoints the problem. There are too many 'journalists'. There is quite a selection of us – around twenty-five or so – as well as Martin, Neville and me. He asks us to decide which ten of us can board. The charge is led by a man from Spanish TV, who just bolts for the ship's hull. So, no orderly discussion, weighing up the pros and cons of who goes on, then? No drawing of lots. If we don't take part in this unseemly rush, then we sure as hell are going to be left port-side. The IOM official gives up.

Disembarking from the boat is a team from Channel Four News, led by Alex Thomson, and another from ITN News, headed by Martin Geissler. I don't see Alex. He is away before we can exchange hellos. But I spot Martin, who is waiting for his car ride into Misrata. I wave to him and go over to brief him quickly about the situation in the city centre. I know he'll head off to Tripoli Street and I want to tell him about the litter of unexploded bombs all over the place. It's good to see him. He is a friendly face and bursting with energy right now despite the long sail over. He'll use the few hours while the ship is being loaded to scout the area and get as much material as possible in Misrata before jumping back on the vessel for the return journey.

And it does take quite a few hours. There are nearly 1,000 people to board – among them more than 800 Nigerians and small groups of Sudanese, Egyptians and Tunisians, as well as thirty Libyan medical cases and fifty accompanying family members, plus the critically injured French blogger. The ship is heaving, with people everywhere. They're sitting and lying all over the outside decks, along the corridors, filling the ferry's lounge areas, and even sleeping under tables. We find a couple of seats in the lounge and collapse into them. Martin Geissler is trying to arrange for us to use the Channel Four cabins. That team is staying on in Misrata. We will have to wait for Geissler to return.

The IOM has a specialized medical team of eleven on board to take care of the wounded. There are four patients, including the French blogger, who require intensive care. One of the French TV crew goes down to the hull to try to make contact with the blogger and returns telling us he's in a miserable condition. It's tragic.

As we set sail again for the long journey back to Benghazi, the IOM official tells us there are an estimated 1,500 immigrants still in urgent need of evacuation and still trapped in Misrata. They will try to return to pick them up. The immigrants on board are cheery, despite how uncomfortable they must be during this long journey. They have no homes, no money, no prospects. Most of them are separated from their families and all they've ever known. Even in Benghazi they'll still be stuck in a war-torn country not their own. But they're out of the immediate line of fire, and, I think, that must be an enormous relief.

Somehow we manage to snag a couple of cabins. I'm sharing with a Spanish photographer, but she's partying down the corridor with the other Spaniards who have been blogging from inside Misrata. I have the cabin to myself for most of the night. We all hear the shouting and giggling and roars of laughter from the travelling band of bloggers and photographers. It's all a bit distasteful while the refugees are crowded outside peering in through the portholes at the Europeans clinking glasses of whisky and beer.

But, of course, we say nothing and do nothing. I guess this is their release, their way of coping.

I am exhausted, as is the rest of the team. I grab a quick bite in the ship's canteen and then crash and don't wake until we arrive in Benghazi at 11.00 the next morning. We have a fantastically long journey back home – car from Benghazi to Tobruk, across the Egyptian border, car journey from the border to Cairo, then a flight to Dubai. It will be another two days before we are back home and in our own beds, but we too are out of the firing line. I was right. It feels very good.

I had worried about this trip, worried because it was the first one back into battle after our experiences in Zawiya. We have done it and we haven't fallen to pieces. There's a trembly-lip moment when Geissler asks me about Zawiya while making small talk in the ship's dining area, but that's all. I'm one big story away from Zawiya now and it's been a fairly substantial full-on one. Although the scar is still there and still red raw – and probably will always be there – it's getting further and further away with every fresh story I do.

Chapter Nine

ZAWIYA HITS BACK

We've been relocated by Sky to Johannesburg. My family and I have spent the summer packing up our belongings in Dubai, shipping them all to South Africa, and obtaining visas, which nowadays seem to be just as elusive as finding the yellow metal in the City of Gold. But now we are here. It feels fantastic. Garwen McLuckie is my new cameraman and partner. He is impossibly upbeat and energetic – always – and bounds up to us, Tigger-style, at the Oliver Tambo International Airport with an enthusiastic 'Howzit?' He and his family are very welcoming, inviting us over to their home the first night we're in Jozi and laying on a *braai* (barbecue) for us.

Garwen is an incredibly youthful 41-year-old South African, brought up in Pietermaritzburg in the province of KwaZulu-Natal, the home of the Zulu nation. His mother is British, from Nottingham, but his heart and soul are very definitely African. He's old enough to have done his conscription service, but young and lively enough to be utterly fanatical about running. And I mean fanatical. Lordy, who does a marathon on the treadmill in the Rixos Hotel's gym, as Garwen did? He's fluent in Afrikaans and he disarms everyone with his command of Zulu, a language he learnt as the sole white constable in the police unit he was conscripted to. He has spent three years as a teenager patrolling the black townships of mid-Illovo at the height of the apartheid violence. Before his twenty-first birthday he'd witnessed shoot-outs, wielded a pump-action shotgun, carried a semi-automatic sidearm and handled an R1 automatic rifle. He's had to investigate countless murders, robberies and rapes. On one Boxing Day he was woken up to investigate the killing of sixteen members of one family who'd all been brutally murdered by having their heads hacked off. With this history, he could be a troubled character.

However, my children are captivated by this amazingly positive, lively personality. Underneath, though, they are definitely tense. Going into every new school, every new classroom, is an ordeal no matter how many times you do it. They might be considered old hands at this moving lark. They've done it three times now. But that doesn't mean it's easy. It isn't. They're going to an international school, which should make the transition smoother. It's filled with children from all over the world (fifty-six nationalities) who live similarly nomadic lifestyles (moving on every two or three years). Everyone there knows the importance of making friends and making them quickly.

The new location causes a bit of a family debate. Maddy has seen online reports about Africa's witch children – those tribal youngsters who are treated as outcasts because they're thought to have the spirits of witches inside them. Maddy led the fund-raising to gather money for the witch children at her last school. Her most recent impressions of Africa have been coloured by coverage of the

2010 football World Cup, most specifically the *Waka Waka* song by Shakira. So it's not all bad.

All three of our girls not only know the words but the dance movements too and are constantly singing it. It feels like our family anthem. But the children do take some convincing. 'Just exactly why did you bring us to the murder capital of the world?' asks Frankie (remember, aged only 14). 'It's not,' I say rather weakly. 'Caracas is the murder capital and the second is Cape Town, not Johannesburg. And, anyway, those statistics are out of date.'

Frankie gives me a very withering look. She's good at those. By the time she reaches her twenties she'll be able to halt conversations and make people dissolve into tears with just a flicker of her eyelashes. Or will it just be her mother?

Maddy is much more focused on making friends. 'You don't remember what it's like at school,' she says. Is that a dig at my age? 'You *have* to be popular.' If Flo is nervous, she doesn't show it. She's more concerned that her teacher is nice. Miss Gina is, and fits the requirements of Flo's perfect teacher, i.e. she's young, pretty, got long hair, is maternal and the sort who does not believe in much homework for Fourth Graders.

Nat is much more sanguine about the move. Given he didn't like his last learning establishment, this cannot be worse, he reasons. It isn't. All four of them come home having made friends on day one and prepared to go back for a second. Phew. That's a relief.

Just as more than 100 boxes of possessions are being unloaded off the back of huge trucks and into the front garden of our new home in Johannesburg, I get a phone call. It's Sarah Whitehead, the Foreign Editor. She wants me to go to Libya. Ian Woods, a fellow Sky correspondent, has been granted a visa by the Tripoli regime. He's just filed a report saying that the government-chaperoned trip from the Tunisian border into Tripoli has been abandoned because of protests en route in Zawiya. The uprising the regime thought it had crushed in Zawiya has flickered back into life. Wow. I had wondered whether they'd rise up again. I can't wait to see if it's true and how it's handled by both sides. Yes, yes, yes, I'm screaming inside. But, hang on. What about the Everest of boxes containing all our worldly goods on our front lawn? I can't, can't, can't leave it all to Richard, even if he is the most long-suffering person in the world. And what will the children say? I've managed to see them into their new school – just – but this is so early in their new lives in South Africa.

'Not tonight,' I say to Sarah, 'not tonight. But what about tomorrow?'

Tuesday, 16 August

By the time we get to Tunisia and Djerba, our new team-mates are ready and waiting: Sky producer Andy Marsh and cameraman Jim Foster, who will also act as our security. They've been here a few days already, preparing for us to go into Zawiya. They've bought up a whole pile of essentials, including twenty cans of fuel, a stash of dried nuts, dried pasta and canned tuna, plus 200 litres of water, tea bags, coffee grains and soft drinks. Oh yes, and twenty-four toilet rolls. Yes, twenty-four!

They have also bought a gas canister, a stove and a generator. Andy and Jim have thought of everything, even tea towels. We can survive just about anywhere with these provisions – and, I'm thinking, with this team. Jim has spent around twenty-seven years in the British Army and is ex-SAS, specializing in counter-terrorism and covert operations across the world. He has managed, planned and carried out undercover assignments in every dirty, despotic country you can think of. In his former life he's trained 'covert agencies' for operations. He speaks fluent French and colloquial Arabic. He's spent his childhood in Libya and Tunisia. I couldn't feel safer with anyone else. Jim is immensely skilled and, for the past decade, has retrained and been operating as a cameraman, director and editor on documentaries and films for television. He doesn't suffer fools under any circumstances. You have to up your game with him and stay there, but, if you can prove you're not a total idiot he might just tolerate you.

Andy too is an interesting and unconventional character. He is meticulous about planning and, well, life in general. He is immensely resourceful: the sort of guy who sets the timer and builds his own motorbike before the Sunday lunch he has planned right down to the colour-coordinated napkins he's pre-ordered. Andy is from Ilkley in West Yorkshire but has spent most of his adult life travelling the world, trekking the length of the Amazon, winding his way through Brazil, Bolivia and Peru on just a handful of Spanish phrases and a very active thumb which even managed a hitch on a tractor. He's launched a bar in Hong Kong, worked in a seafood restaurant in Australia, and attended the University of Nantes on the banks of the Loire, where he honed his French. You imagine his family is run like a military operation. Jim would fit in quite well. He could be a favourite uncle.

We need two cars to carry it all plus our cameras, broadcast equipment, our body armour and our personal kit. We're travelling light, but it doesn't feel like it. We spend the night in Djerba. It is a popular tourist destination so we are mingling with holiday-makers as we're preparing to go into a war. It's decidedly weird but it's probably going to be our last night for a while with clean sheets on a comfortable bed. So we savour it.

Gaddafi has made his first audio address for some time, calling on his people to 'liberate' Libya from NATO oppression. The rebels have captured the key town of Subratha on the road to Tunisia, severing Tripoli and the regime's supply route. Is this the beginning of the end for Gaddafi? It's been talked about so much before and he has always surprised everyone. The world seems to continually underestimate him. But the race is on to see if it is the start of his demise, and journalists from around the globe want to bear witness. The rebels appear to be in their strongest position yet since the uprising began in February. They now control the coast both east and west of Tripoli. The Libyan Interior Minister, Nassr al-Mabrouk Abdullah, has arrived in Egypt with nine members of his family. It looks like another high-level defection.

So we're all raring to go. We wake early, throw down some breakfast and head off for the Libyan border crossing at Dahiba. The road journey takes hours and we're held up for at least three hours at the border. It's not the Tunisian officials or the Libyan rebels who are keeping us waiting. It's our drivers.

They have – unbeknown to us – also done a deal with our competitors, the crews from Channel Four and ITN. We're having to wait for them to catch up so they can share the transport across the border. Right now I'm finding it hard to contain my anger. Our drivers have been greedy and taken two customers. That's the bottom line. There are plenty of drivers, but because ours could not resist turning down a second fare our time advantage has been squandered.

We are tempted – very tempted in my case – to ditch the ITN and Channel Four crews and march on regardless. But that would leave them stranded at the border, so we find whatever mercy we have in our bodies and hang on. In my case, it's not done with much grace. So much for getting up early, so much for getting ahead of the pack. We're back at square one. I'm fuming at the thought that if it had been the other way round I wonder whether the same competitors would have waited for any Sky crew. I'm thinking not. But I'm tired and tetchy and maybe I'm wrong. Anyway, we're all terribly impatient to get going and we cross only in the late afternoon. By this time we're all hugely frustrated.

Once in Libya, we sort out another set of drivers, in Nalut. It looks very relaxed to us here. Not so long ago there would have been fighting. Not now. There are women and children milling about the streets, going about their shopping and playing. There are markets and shops open. It's normality. The rebels appear to be very much in control.

As we sweep east towards Zintan, we notice village after village, community after community, is under Opposition control. Occasionally we see abandoned Gaddafi military vehicles, sometimes tanks camouflaged in the desert landscape, but there's not a green flag in sight. This is very much rebel territory.

It's dark by the time we arrive in Zintan and the Opposition here is utterly unprepared for yet another army, the sudden influx of international journalists. We're directed to the post office, which is being turned over to house the travelling journalists. Andy heads down there to secure some sleeping space. The remaining three of us work on doing some live reports into the 21.00 and 22.00 evening programmes. We're pretty tired by this time but all of us know we have to get to Zawiya as soon as we can. It seems impossible tonight. Our drivers have all left, job done. We have a great mound of jerry cans, food and equipment, and I'm thinking, why didn't we travel with less? We can't get anywhere very easily with this mountain of baggage.

I want to get to the army commanders here in Zintan. They should be able to give us an accurate idea of how the battle is progressing, if it is progressing, and how quickly. We start chatting to one of the men who is hanging round watching us broadcast. He claims to be one of the rebel media team. A media team? Apparently they have one already up and running in Zintan. Well, when you're up against a man like Gaddafi, who is monopolizing the country's state television and radio, then you have to think about your own media. He insists he knows the commander of this area. I'm thinking this guy is bullshitting us, but let's take a chance. So, while Andy is sitting on our post office beds (securing ownership at least for the night), as well as unloading all our equipment and cases and cans of tuna on his own, we set off to try to meet the commander.

We find out about Mr Rebel TV. It transpires he's telling the truth. He takes us to a building which is spilling over with Opposition fighters and Libyan army defectors, many in uniform. We're taken to an anteroom, where there are a few men already waiting. They're young by my standards – in their early thirties, I guess – and at first I don't realize they speak English. They do, very well. They aren't wearing uniform and, although they play down any connection with the army or any part of the Libyan military, my first instinct is that they are military men or working closely with them. They're cautious at first. They don't know who we are or where we're from. They've been educated abroad, speak English fluently, and seem very knowledgeable about just about everything Libyan, particularly the current battles. One is bald although still young and seems to be the most talkative. He's very interested to learn we're reporters from an international television channel. His pal is much quieter and appears to be deferring a lot, but is friendly all the same.

The colonel in charge of the Western Region comes out of his very long meeting. Mr Rebel TV puts in a word for us and Garwen and I jump out of our seats to grab a few words with him. His name is Colonel Juma Ebrahim and he tells us he was one of the first defectors and that his new set of soldiers are making excellent progress. Many men have come down from the Nefusa mountains into Zintan and are now going to press ahead towards the capital. Ebrahim expects to be in Tripoli and to have taken the capital by Ramadan. 'By Ramadan?' I splutter. 'That's only two weeks away.' 'Yes, that's right. Gaddafi will be gone by Ramadan, *inshallah*,' and off he hurries. He has a war to get on with.

I am staggered by his confidence. He didn't seem like the sort to brag. This is a military man, not any old over-optimistic rebel. The two men we have been chatting with earlier have been watching. We still have the problem of transport and they're the only two people who might be able to help. The main man hands us a card bearing his name: Ahmida Anjina. He says he will try, really try, but he can't guarantee anything. We tell them we're staying at the post office and, as they leave, I say: 'We're never going to see you again, are we?' 'No, no, Alex, we will be back,' Ahmida insists, while his friend adds: 'We'll do our best. We'll try.'

We set off for the post office, where Andy has just finished lugging all our belongings into our room. He has secured us four beds and seems pretty pleased with this accomplishment. Garwen and Jim are looking longingly at the soft, flat surfaces. Is this an opportunity for some down-time? But, before our bottoms have made an imprint on the mattresses, the two men I never thought we'd see again are in our room. Not only have they returned and tracked us down, they tell us they bring good news.

'We cannot find two vehicles or two people who we trust to drive you,' Ahmida says. Hang on, that doesn't sound like very good news to me. 'So we will take you ourselves,' he adds.

'When do you want to go?' I look at my watch. It's after midnight. 'Now?' I say somewhat tentatively. But he seems to be expecting this. 'We can't guarantee anything, but we will try.' It turns out to be a Libyan catchphrase.

The others have all perked up suddenly. Andy launches in with the practicalities. 'Can you help us find somewhere to stay when we get there?' he asks. 'Yes, yes, we have friends who will help,' comes the reply. 'Any chance of a local SIM card?' he adds. (The rebels have restored a partial local mobile service.) 'Well, that's more difficult, they are like gold dust, but I will find one.' Nothing is a problem.

They help us load all our provisions and fuel into the back of their two 4x4 vehicles. They don't want payment, but Andy is insisting and, when their eyes focus on the jerry cans, he says: 'How about fuel then? Can we give you fuel instead?' Fuel is hard to come by, more precious than cash. Without fuel there's no movement. They take up this offer eagerly.

The journey is a little tense. It's night-time and there are numerous checkpoints. At one stage all the vehicles heading in the direction of Zawiya are halted by fighting and firing. Once it dies down we continue. At another checkpoint the rebels refuse to let us pass. No explanation, just no go. 'Get out your interview with Colonel Ebrahim and show them,' we're instructed by our new friends. It does the trick. We're allowed to continue.

We arrive in Zawiya in the early hours. We're finally here. It feels like a huge achievement and we haven't even really begun. We are driven to a house which is set in farmland. It's very quiet and very dark. There's no power, so everything is being conducted by torchlight. There are three men already there. Two of them appear to be brothers. They are huge and round and look like Tweedledum and Tweedledee, but much harder. The other man is the owner and doesn't say much at all. I'm not sure it was his own idea to hand over his house to a bunch of strangers, but he's doing so as the two brothers and Ahmida and his friend look on and smile.

We unpack everything and unload it into the bungalow. There are no beds but there are mattresses and two sofas. The bungalow also has a kitchen and two bathrooms. Great. We've really cleaned up here.

We're rushing so we can snatch a few hours' sleep. The boys set up the generator. Power. What a life-saver. We can now charge all our camera batteries and even create a bit of light so we're not bumping into each other quite so much. Suddenly the huge mountain of provisions and essentials Jim and Andy insisted on bringing seems to make perfect sense.

I get a room to myself. Andy calls it my 'suite'. It's bare, with no furniture at all, and the sole decoration of a mattress, but I get to have it all to myself. No skulking behind towels trying to protect my modesty. No wriggling into my sleeping bag and changing clothes in a space that I can't turn round in. No slapping make-up on inside my sleeping bag without the aid of a mirror. No. This way I can emerge every morning wearing eye shadow, mascara and blusher as if I was born that way. Oh yes, totally natural. It's in the genes.

Jim takes possession of one sofa in a small room just off the kitchen. Garwen camps down on the other in a separate room but it's so huge he'll be sharing it with Andy. No one is complaining, well, not yet anyway. We're just desperate for a few hours of sleep.

Thursday, 18 August

In what seems no time at all, Jim is knocking on my door with a cup of milky, sugary tea. 'Morning,' he says, far too brightly. Anyone would think this is the army. But this is our first full day in Zawiya and the tiredness is all forgotten. We have to get up and out and unearth what's going on. Come on. Come on, team. They don't need much geeing up. Everyone is here to do a job and we're all keen to find out what's out there and do the job well.

We hear there's been fighting near the oil refinery and the rebels are claiming they have wrested control. This is why Zawiya is so important to the Gaddafi regime. The oil from the town's refinery is what has kept the Gaddafi forces moving over the past five months. Losing the refinery will mean they lose their oil supplies. Losing control of the town means they lose their supply route – and therefore the replenishing of food and essentials from Tunisia through Zawiya and into the capital. It's a devastating domino effect.

Most of the population is already suffering from the international economic sanctions. The supplies which have been getting through are pretty much reserved for the regime's lords and whoever the regime deems fit to hand them to. We're hearing that NATO war planes intervened by bombing the Gaddafi military vehicles and the fleeing forces from the refinery. We want to go and check it out, but the sprawling refinery is out of town. Let's see what's happening in the town centre itself first.

Our new driver – one of the Tweedle brothers – is Mr Abdul Alsaq Benkora. It seems he was also in the Libyan military before defecting. He doesn't speak English but a little French so somehow we manage to communicate. He laughs a lot, especially at me and my accent. He's charming. He also turns out to be exceedingly brave and daunted by little.

This is my first look at Zawiya since March, when the town's citizens were brutally attacked and their uprising horribly and violently crushed. I'm desperate to see how it's changed. Will I recognize anything? Will anyone we met then still be here? Mr Benkora takes us to the flyover near the East Gate, from where the road leads to Tripoli. It's the same flyover where Martin filmed the tanks opening fire on the thousands of Zawiyans who were marching for regime change. Now there are dozens of Opposition fighters underneath, some cleaning their weapons, others just stopping and checking cars as they enter the roundabout underneath. Wow. This is a very different Zawiya. This is a Zawiya with teeth, one which is not prepared to be pushed around any more. This is a Zawiya which is now armed.

We make contact with a group of fighters – about fifteen or so – who are heading off to the 'front', where they're trying to rout Gaddafi snipers. The front today is near Martyrs' Square, the site of the mosque where Martin, Tim and I were trapped and where we sheltered. None of these fighters appears to be actually from

Zawiya. There are a lot of new fighters in town – from Zintan, from Nalut, from the Nefusa mountains. They say they have come to help the brothers in battle. Zawiya is famous among Libyans. The whole country has seen them aggressively crushed once. They don't want it to happen again.

We haven't been in Zawiya for twelve hours yet but we're soon finding out just how dangerous life still is for those living and fighting here. Gaddafi gunmen are hiding near Martyrs' Square and no lane, no alleyway, no road is entirely safe while they're lurking. We run down one road which the fighters have cleared only to find bullets coming our way on the same stretch just twenty minutes later. It's like the Wild East out here. As usual, the fighters we're with are all young lads. They seem to have little co-ordination and little sense of what they're doing but they're united by one aim: to kill Gaddafi soldiers. It's a hairy few hours running with them between roads and buildings and hearing the bullets whistling by. I think that if this is all they've got they don't stand a chance against the Gaddafi men.

We head back at the end of the day to our safe house on the outskirts of Zawiya. Away from the bullets and rocket shelling, this seems almost tranquil, a haven. However, the sound of the garden cockerel crowing is all too often interrupted by the noise of rockets being fired on the town centre.

Andy is really settling into his new home, busying himself conjuring up a veritable feast out of his dried pasta and tins of tuna. He's the Gordon Ramsay of Zawiya, in more ways than one. Garwen and I are working on our report for the evening programme and Jim seems to have become Andy's cooking assistant. I doubt Jim has ever really been anyone's assistant, but he realizes to mess with Andy's kitchen system is to mess with an unexploded mine. One nudge and you know it will blow up in your face. You would just rather avoid it.

Everyone's happy and pretty relaxed. We're all getting on with each other. We know each other fairly well and we've all been in war zones far too many times before. They're not pleasant but they're a whole lot better when you're with friends and people you trust and can count on. We have a report. We've had a fairly good first day. We have a string of extremely well connected and helpful contacts. We have a roof over our heads and we have food. It's a pretty good start.

Our new best friends visit to check we are OK. They bring with them a Began, which is a highly unusual and expensive bit of kit for any non-professional, any civilian, to have. Ahmida is asking Jim to show him how to use it. Jim has already let it be known he is former British Special Forces and there is a burgeoning understanding and implicit trust between them.

Friday, 19 August

I am hesitant to go to the oil refinery because it's a little way out of town, but I know we have to. We need to see it for ourselves. When we get there rebel fighters are standing guard outside. There's an anti-aircraft weapon at the entrance which has been destroyed. The rebels say it was NATO bombs that did it. The men here tell us when the Gaddafi soldiers heard the NATO planes they fled, terrified. This is one major asset Gaddafi cannot afford to lose and he's just seen it surrendered to the rebel enemy.

We leave hastily because I'm anxious to get back to the town centre again. I don't want to miss what's going on there. None of us does. I feel nervous about being so far out of the centre. I jump into Mr Benkora's car so hurriedly that I leave behind my tiny bag, which contains everything precious to me. In it are my passport, my money, my children's photos, everything. Only I don't discover this crucial fact until we're just about back in the town centre again, some forty-five minutes later.

Mr Benkora is incredulous. He's thinking I'm the Mad Hatter. Is this what I am dealing with? What sort of a halfwit is she? A halfwit who clearly does not deserve to have a tiny bag to look after. Good thing she doesn't have anything like children to care for or anything important like that. OK, he doesn't actually say that, but I sense that's just what he's thinking. In reality, he just laughs and he and Andy head on back down the road to the refinery. Mr Benkora is slightly more cheerful than Andy, who is wondering how he ended up in a war zone with me. He hasn't even done anything wrong to upset Sarah Whitehead that he knows of. They find my bag still sitting next to the carcass of the anti-aircraft weapon where we had been filming a few hours earlier. Andy only agrees to this selfless act, I have to say, after giving me instructions to 'find the fighting this time'.

While Andy and Mr Benkora are in the car making awkward small talk in poor French (well, in Mr Benkora's case anyway; he's fluent in Arabic, though), Garwen, Jim and I have gone back to the fighters we met the day before under the flyover. They direct us to a lane off Martyrs' Square, where they say most of the battle is now focused.

We go there expecting more of the same ramshackle, enthusiastic but directionless fighting we've already seen. Instead we find an old-fashioned 'front'. There are weapons laid out on the ground and fighters sitting around as we approach. As we head on down a small set of steps, there's much more of a concentration of fighters, more weapons, more ammunition, and definitely much more action. The second tier of fighters is hanging back – as though they are resting – waiting to take up the rear or supplement the others when they tire. As we enter this area we're greeted by a young man who says: 'Alex? From Sky News? I saw your report on Zawiya. Thank you, thank you. Tell me if there's anything I can do to help your team.' He's not the only one to make this sort of offer. Remarkably in a place with no Internet, people may not have seen our report but they've heard about it and they're desperate to help us. We're not short of friends here.

We move to the front tier, which is almost merging with the flank of those hanging back. These are the men actively engaged in the firing and fighting. They're crossing a road – back and forth – firing as they track Gaddafi snipers whom they can't see but can certainly hear. Across the way, on the opposite wall, someone has painted the words 'We fight or we die'. This is how these people feel. They have to fight or they will be crushed just like before. There's simply no choice.

Events are really picking up pace now. Some of these men clearly know what they're doing. One man in particular on the corner of the building is taking the lead. He can handle a weapon, is directing the young charges around him, and is the man with all the ideas. Other fighters are more callow, positively dangerous in charge of military vehicles. An anti-aircraft vehicle is pointed along the road to the corner, crashing into the flower-bed verge which separates the roads. The man driving seems to be trying to work out how to turn the turret when it suddenly fires without warning into a nearby building in which many rebel fighters are sheltering. It takes a chunk out of the wall. Everyone does a sort of collective tut-tut and moves out of the line of sight of the anti-aircraft vehicle. They just carry on with their own firing. There's so much combat and noise going on, it barely registers.

Jim is hugging the wall next to the military man who has claimed control of the corner. I'm just behind him watching what's going on. Garwen is a little to our left and slightly behind us, filming the stream of men running across the mouth of the road, blasting down it with heavy machine-guns. One of the men – who is standing next to Garwen but tellingly beyond the corner shelter – suddenly screams and falls to the ground. He's just in front of Garwen. There's no one between them in fact. He's been hit. He rolls over towards us, desperately trying to get out of sight of the sniper who has detected him. Wow, that was close. We watch aghast as other fighters drag him to one side. Garwen follows him with his camera as his friends take him to the waiting ambulance. The bullet has entered his shoulder. You can see a very clear hole through his T-shirt and into his body. He's still walking, he's shocked, and his face is wincing with the pain, but he'll be all right.

The soldier on the corner is now using mirrors to try to see round the edge without actually presenting himself as a target. His colleagues have found some tyres and they're filling them with grass, rubbish and petrol. They set the tyres alight and send them rolling down the road with huge clouds of smoke pluming out of them. They use the smoke as cover to run farther down the road and take up positions nearer the Square and the snipers they're hunting.

We reconnect with Mr Benkora and Andy and we're taken to the main rebel 'office' in Zawiya. We're stunned at the array of weapons and ammunition they have with them. Much of it is still in unopened crates and boxes. Even while we are there, trucks are coming in transporting yet more supplies. They have a tank parked outside and men are preparing it. This is the day. This is the day they take back Zawiya.

We bump into a doctor who remembers me from March when we were filming in the hospital. He tells me that after he and his colleagues gave us an interview then, the Gaddafi forces rounded up thousands of people and he was one of them. They had seen his face on our television report. 'They jailed me for two months for talking to Sky News,' he says. I don't know what to say. I don't know how he has the courage to talk to me again, why he doesn't hate me, how he doesn't resent me and blame me for what happened to him. But he doesn't, he doesn't at all. What material are these people made of? Something special, that's for sure.

We jump in the back of a pick-up with a team which has mortars in the back, ready to fire. They're driving around the centre, not staying in one place for any length of time. A spotter with binoculars is taking a crow's nest position in the surrounding flats. A second man is setting up the mortar tube on a plate. He's feeding the bomb into the tube. I press my fingers into my ears. Whoosh! Bang! They wait a few minutes. The spotter is checking out where the mortar has landed. He's now redirecting his team, telling them how to reset the angle to better hit the target. And the target is always Martyrs' Square.

We move on down the road, uneasy at the idea of mortars landing out of nowhere, anywhere. There's a crowd of people ahead and then we can hear the thunder of a tank making its way along the road towards them and us. Its tracks are tearing up the tarmac. This is people on the rampage. They have some Gaddafi tanks now and from somewhere they have found the aggression used against them months earlier. The tank pulls up alongside us. It turns its gun and blasts off a round. It's loud. It's deafening. Then there's another. My ears are numb. It does this five or six times, then pulls off and retreats to the sound of people cheering.

We go back to the edge of Martyrs' Square again and the corner. Only this time it's empty. The men have moved forward. Rebels are urging us to follow them. Jim has already moved in as our forward lookout. More and more people are edging into the Square. We can hear firing and shooting and much bombing ahead, but everyone is moving in the same direction. Fighters guide us into the shattered reception of what looks like a hotel lobby. Oh my God, it's the hotel where Martin and I stood and watched as the people of Zawiya first prepared to defend themselves in March. It's almost unrecognizable. In fact, at first I don't recognize it at all. There's so much debris around. Everything appears shattered. We hear our boots crushing and cracking through a carpet of broken glass, window fragments, pieces of ceiling, shards of metal. On the other side we can see vehicles heading out of the Square. Still more are sounding their horns and screeching across it.

I'm looking out over the Square and watching the panorama incredulously. There are smoke clouds dotted everywhere, the noise of guns being fired, the sound of wheels skidding and engines revving. People are shouting. The last time I was standing on this spot, Zawiya was being surrounded by the same tanks they have just driven out. The last time we were here they were scared, panicking, but fighting with whatever they had. The last time I was here I didn't think they stood a chance. I thought they were finished – would be finished – crushed by a far superior military force. But, among all this rubble and ash and debris and fire, I feel like I'm watching the phoenix of Libyan hope rising.

They have done it. They have reclaimed the Square against massive odds. It is a hugely symbolic victory. This is the heart of the city. Zawiya is the city Gaddafi cannot afford to lose control of, a city he has been prepared to smother and smash in order to stay in power. Jim is suddenly in front of us. 'They've driven them out,' he says. Jim's talking about the Gaddafi forces. 'The last lot have just scarpered.' We move out in front of the hotel and I see discarded Gaddafi uniforms everywhere. They look new – not at all grubby – hardly worn, actually. I can see cars driven by rebels joy-riding around the Square. They're doing handbrake turns and hanging out of the windows waving rebel flags. It's unbelievable. What a turnaround.

We set up the Began and do a live broadcast as the rebels are celebrating behind us. They're firing their guns into the air in celebration. There is smoke billowing where bombs have recently exploded. Andrew Wilson is the presenter back in London and lets the pictures and audio 'breathe' so we can all just drink in the sight of the rebel victory in Zawiya.

Andrew asks me – live on air – how I feel being back there and in such different circumstances. I get quite emotional thinking about it and recounting this to him. This was a town which was broken when I was last here. A town where we saw so many die and where we filmed and reported on so many being injured. This very place was where we thought we ourselves would die. How do I

answer that question coolly? Being trapped in Zawiya was probably the most traumatic time of my life.

There's a big empty space where the mosque once stood. The
mosque, the sanctuary where we sheltered as Gaddafi tanks fired
all around us, is no more. The Gaddafi regime bulldozed it after
crushing the uprising. All that remains is a barren piece of land
which looks like a car park. But the people of Zawiya have come
back from that terrible crushing. They've licked their wounds and
now they've roared again.

As we walk round the Square we see bodies of Gaddafi soldiers.
Some seem to have been lying there for some time. They're bloated
with the heat and badly decomposed. In one corner there's a
soldier who is still alive. He's screaming in pain and fear. A couple
of rebels are trying to staunch the blood flowing from his thigh and
he's carried away, I hope to get some medical help. There's still a
lot of chaos in the centre, people driving heedlessly around, shooting and shouting. They're tearing down the green flags which have
been tied up all around the Square and burning them in bundles.
But what now? What happens now? And will the Gaddafi forces be
back?

Saturday, 20 August

The euphoria is still evident the next morning. This is the first day
in nearly six months that Zawiya has been free of Gaddafi forces
inside the city.

We go to see what's happening around Martyrs' Square and
notice small groups of the city's people just venturing out to check
out the news, to see for themselves if it's true. They're wandering
about stunned. When they see us, their faces light up for Garwen's

camera and, unprompted, they happily stamp all over broken Gaddafi portraits which are lying on the ground. No one would have dared do this a few weeks ago, maybe not even a few days ago. But the people of Zawiya have beaten back the army of a dictator and they're feeling very brave today.

An ambulance comes racing round the corner with a number of its occupants leaning out from the sliding side door. They are all dressed in their white medical gowns and are screaming like students on an end-of-year night out. They stop next to us and get out, not apparently to view anything in particular, simply to just savour freedom in the Square. They want to smell the air and walk around knowing they can do so without fearing Gaddafi soldiers might unleash a volley of bullets in their direction.

There's not a building left untouched. Every window is smashed, with many hanging on their hinges. There's broken masonry all over the place, as well as burnt, mangled bits of metal and the detritus of war everywhere: shells, bullet cartridges, boxes which once housed bombs. There is the pock-mark evidence of bullets on every building, and substantially larger holes in most of them.

The centre of Zawiya is utterly trashed, but rarely has it been more beautiful for its emerging citizens than right now. They're babbling with excitement. They have huge smiles on their faces. They're laughing and joking, jostling and pushing each other. They're just happiness personified.

They say they are on their way to visit the hospital. They are particularly keen to see it, check it out, find out if it's empty of Gaddafi forces. They tell us that for weeks now it's been occupied by Gaddafi soldiers using it as a base. For weeks before that the soldiers were terrorizing the medics still working there. The doctors speak of dozens of their fellow professionals being arrested and detained. I keep asking about Dr M, trying to find anyone who knows him. I want to hear he is OK, still alive. Some of the doctors are still missing, presumed either dead or in jail. I keep hoping Dr M has escaped this fate, but I know it's extremely unlikely. He was so vocal, so strongly critical and so visible.

The army replaced the hospital director with one of its own. They discharged any injured and ill civilian patients when there was an influx of wounded soldiers. They put snipers on the hospital roof and armed guards outside the emergency operating room. The doctors say they were forced to perform surgery after surgery. They stored their weapons next to the delivery suite. It has clearly been a desperate time for them. Now they hear the Gaddafi soldiers have fled and they want their hospital back.

They invite us into the ambulance with them: 'Ah, Sky News! Sky News! Come in, come in. We love Sky News!' A Spanish journalist already inside the ambulance takes exception to Garwen and me crowding his space and apparently 'hijacking' his intended interviewees. Actually I hadn't noticed him sitting in the back until we climbed in. 'Listen, I got here first. Can you find another?' he says.

The head doctor hears this exchange and stares at the Spaniard. For an instant, the smile is gone. 'Hey, I'm in charge of this ambulance, sir,' he says. 'I'll decide who comes with us or who does not. Sky News is coming.' I'm a little embarrassed at this piffling rivalry within our industry compared to what these doctors have been through, but, at the same time, I understand why the Spanish journalist might not want other media like us clouding his pictures. I'm also pretty surprised and privately delighted at the doctor's robust reaction.

We bump along with them all as the vehicle hurtles far too speedily towards the hospital, but I've been in more perilous ambulances than this. The last time I was in one in Zawiya we were racing for our lives and being shot at by Gaddafi security forces. I remember swearing and trying to grab onto anything to stop myself being thrown against the sides. There wasn't much talking then, aside from my Tourette's-like response to the military shooting. This time the vehicle is filled with a more agreeable noise, with the laughter and giggles of doctors and medics heady with joy.

When we pull up outside the hospital entrance, the medics bundle out of the ambulance and stand together outside the front door much like a football team, singing and chanting, their arms draped round each other. They take photographs of each other celebrating their return, before turning and going inside. We follow as they rush to find the main office. The senior medic sits behind his old desk, beaming. His arms are outstretched and stroking the woodwork. It's not a fancy desk by any means. It's not a fancy office. But it's his again. His junior throws himself on top of the desk and hugs it. 'I've missed you. I've missed you,' he jokes.

As they're checking the supplies, opening the cupboards and going through the cabinets to see what's been left and what's been taken, I hear someone call my name. 'Alex? Alex? Is that you?' I turn round. It's Dr Salah, the doctor who had been so instrumental in planning our escape from Zawiya in March. He was the young man who'd suffered leukaemia, who'd persuaded his friend to drive us out, who'd helped us when we most needed it.

'Oh my God,' he gasps with a huge smile, 'I never thought I would see you alive again. I wondered so much what had happened to you. Where is Martin? Where is Tim? Are they all right? We were so worried about you guys.' His eyes are filled with tears. 'My heart's pumping,' he says. My eyes are filled too. I feel his heart. He's right. It's beating wildly. So is mine. We have so many questions for each other, they're tumbling out, the words colliding. We're both stuttering. I feel like I'm meeting a long-lost friend, a brother. Perhaps I am. We hug each other awkwardly. There's genuine affection on both sides. I feel terribly indebted to this young man. I can't explain it. He showed us such kindness, such bravery in the face of such terror. And here he is, months on, worrying about *me*, this person who has lived in safety and comfort in the interim.

I learn his full name for the first time. It's Dr Salah Rodwan. It seems strange to discover this so late in our friendship when I feel we have such a strong bond. 'We saw your report,' he says, 'but we never knew if you got out of Libya. Really, I never thought I would see you again.' He tells me he hid for months afterwards, too afraid to go out. 'The security forces came round and were arresting everyone.'

The soldiers entered the hospital days after we left, he explains. He was sleeping in the operating room and was woken by a friend raising the alarm. He immediately destroyed his mobile phone to protect those rebels he'd been communicating with and any other information the regime would consider 'treacherous'. He managed to escape out of the back of the hospital with two other medics. He said the soldiers rounded up a lot of doctors and threw them into jail. 'It's hard to believe,' he says, 'that many people working in that hospital were spies with their camera phones, especially the nurses.' The pictures on their mobiles were handed over to the military and used to persecute those medics viewed as 'disloyal'.

He reminds me about showing us a patient with a head injury. 'I explained to you the CT films on the X-ray box,' he prompts me. 'His name was Ahmed Gosbi and he was killed in the hospital by a gunshot in his chest a few days after the soldiers got inside the building.' I had worried these doctors would be targeted. It is worse than I thought.

But this is the vile past. Dr Salah wants to enjoy and delight in the present because the present is glorious right now. They have their hospital back. The Gaddafi soldiers are no long here and life is beginning to seem hopeful for these people for the first time in a long, long while.

I press him eagerly for news of the other doctors. 'What about Dr M, the older doctor? And what about your friend Dr Mohammed who drove us out?' I tell him I had rung Dr Mohammed afterwards when I was back in Dubai. I had used my UAE number so as not to arouse too much suspicion, or so I thought. The phone had been picked up by his brother, who handed it to him. I just managed to say: 'We got the report out, Mohammed. Don't worry, we got the report out.' Mohammed, clearly terrified, had replied: 'OK, OK, please don't say any more.' Then he ended the call.

After that I had worried even more. How could I be so stupid? I had only wanted to let him know it had been worth it, that we had achieved what they wanted. We had managed to get the report out about what they'd gone through in Zawiya. But here I was jeopardizing his safety once again. Stupid, stupid.

They are cleaning up the hospital now, trying to sweep and wipe away the turmoil of the past few months. But it's not yet ready for habitation or use. 'Come with us to the field hospital,' says Dr Salah. They've been running a medical outpost about six miles south of the town while the hospital has been under siege. We follow him there. The journey seems to take a little while. It's not exactly convenient for the wounded and damaged of Zawiya, I'm thinking.

While we're away from the centre, we can hear the thud of mortars landing. The sound of bombs exploding is horribly familiar and is coming from the area we've just left. There are more than half a dozen of them. Boom, boom, boom, one after the other with sickening regularity. What? Are the Gaddafi men back?

Soon the casualties start arriving at the field hospital. Stretchers carrying yet more bloodied men with hideous injuries puncture the party atmosphere instantly. It's like the reclaiming of Zawiya never happened. It's like those soldiers never went away at all. The doctors are back to work. The war is not yet over. Even the field hospital is not safe despite its location out of town. It too has been shelled, several times.

Gaddafi's men are mounting a fightback. As long as the rebels keep control of Zawiya, it cuts off the regime's main route to the outside world. His men will be under orders to mount a counter-offensive and seize it back – and this is the beginning.

We pull out of the field hospital and make our way back to our safe house. We're tired and today my news radar is definitely not as sharp as it could be. I've seen the euphoria in the Square. I've seen the happiness of the doctors. I've seen their joy as they re-entered the hospital and I've also witnessed the fresh casualties at the field hospital and heard the bombings. Somehow I'm not unduly worried. It doesn't feel like March when the Gaddafi forces hit back so hard it knocked the city off its feet. And then they just kept hitting and hitting and hitting. No, this time it just seems very different somehow. Not nearly as threatening, not nearly as frightening, not nearly as menacing. It's not over, sure, not by a long way. But it's definitely not the same military lion which roared in March.

We're hearing reports of unrest in some of the Tripoli suburbs. Residents in Tajura are reported to be fighting after Saturday prayers. But no one really knows for sure because the journalists in Tripoli are confined to the Rixos and are virtually under hotel arrest.

We go about editing our report based on what's been happening around us in Zawiya. We feel tremendously lucky. We're in relatively comfortable surroundings. We're safe and away from the now sporadic bombings. We've comfy chairs to sit on and running water for showers. We've got into a routine now whereby Andy does most of the kitchen work and we do most of the eating. It's working quite well really and everyone seems pleased with the arrangements. Our generator is proving to be an absolute saviour, providing us with the means for cooking food and charging our equipment, as well as powering the Began so we can send the reports back to London. It could all be so much harder, so much worse. We count our blessings.

Chapter Ten

RIDING THE REBEL CONVOY

Sunday, 21 August

'Go! Fucking hell, go!' Jim is shouting, and when Jim is shouting you usually do what he tells you. It means things are bad. Rasan, our new driver, doesn't argue. It's taking all his concentration and nerve to slam the car into reverse. A rocket lands close by – close enough for us to feel the vibration of its impact in the car. The Gaddafi snipers have located us. Jim's right, again. It is time to go.

I am in the back, jammed between Andy and Jim. We all have our flak jackets and helmets on, so it's very, very tight. It's a small, four-seater vehicle and we are all sweating anyway from exertion and anxiety in the forty-something-degree heat. The air inside the car is stuffy as our combined sweat glands go into overdrive. Garwen is in the front filming the dust and panic and chaos through the windscreen.

The rebels are in urgent retreat – and it's a total and complete exodus. No one wants to be last and I count ourselves very much among those thinking that. The panic is contagious. The rockets keep landing just behind us as we race out of there, all of us willing the vehicle to go faster, faster, please go faster. I keep thinking one is going to land on us, we're all going to burn. Come on, come on, get us out of here. The noise of the thudding behind us contrasts with the quiet fear inside the vehicle.

It's only a few minutes before we are out of the range of the rockets, but those minutes seem to stretch for ever. God, it's going to be a long day. I can't see the rebels making much progress. Well, I was right about the first part of that analysis.

We got up that morning thinking this was going to be a quiet Sunday. After all, the town had been reclaimed, the snipers driven out, its citizens were now celebrating freedom from Gaddafi forces for the first time since March. We were actually worrying about what we were going to put in our report that day. I am always worrying, always wondering about what's next, whether we're missing something, if there's something going on that we don't know about. We were actually scrabbling around to find something we could get together for the Monday morning news programme. I had woken suddenly, sweating. How is it the sound of quiet can wake you after days of bombing, shelling and machine-gun fire?

There's no power in much of the town – so no air conditioning in the bungalow we've been loaned. It's early – about seven o'clock local time – but it's already boiling hot. We are due to do some live broadcasts into London, giving them an update of the situation in Zawiya.

We use our Began. It's the size of a laptop, so easily portable, and connects with a satellite to beam data from the camera back to London. It's our lifeline, our way of transmitting our reports back to London and the wider world.

We rattle through the 'lives'. 'Yes, Zawiya is very quiet this morning,' I say. 'Yes, there is still a mood of celebration after the Opposition recaptured the town.' I don't like it. It doesn't feel like good reporting. It just feels like a weather report. I hate it when I have to do broadcasts like these. I want to be out reporting what is actually going on, not reviewing what has already happened.

We've given ourselves the maximum sleep possible short of my appearing on air with a toothbrush still in my mouth. You learn never to waste sleep time when you're out in the field. Sleep is precious and to be snatched at every opportunity. But it feels too quiet this morning and too cut off in this farmhouse. I'm anxious. I'm always anxious. We need to get out and see what's going on.

I want to check out the East Gate. Here, access to the Tripoli road has been blocked for the past five months by Gaddafi tanks and artillery. The capital is only thirty or so miles down the road but it might as well be 130. Zawiya's been cut off since the uprising in March – an uprising which was comprehensively crushed by pro-Gaddafi forces.

Rasan turns up at the house. Our previous driver, Abdul al-Zaq, has given himself a lie-in after days of ferrying us in and out of sniper fire. If only the snipers took days off.

It's in the middle of Ramadan so every Muslim – even the fighters – is very reluctant to get up too early, having spent most of the night feasting. Rasan is very definitely not a fighter and views himself more as our personal Libyan tourist guide. 'I can take you to see the library. It is a very good library,' he says to his bemused passengers, one of whom is getting increasingly irritated (that's me). It's probably not the time to be curling up with a good book.

'We need to go to the East Gate, please, Rasan,' I say.

'But this is dangerous,' he says. He can't quite believe we want to do this.

'Could we just go and have a look … please?' (Barely suppressed impatience here from me.) The guys are used to this and shuffle around in their seats slightly, hoping I am not going to be too snappy with him.

I have no idea what to expect but I pack a small bag with spare pants, clean T-shirt, some make-up and other essential female toiletries. I think we may be on the run a lot of today and I am rather impressed with my own forward planning seeing as I am usually hopelessly disorganized.

When we get to the East Gate, the tanks are gone, the artillery has gone, the soldiers have disappeared. This is a result. It's clear and open. A trickle of Opposition vehicles is heading down the road. They are on the move. The tension and excitement rise in our car. The team knows this must be the start of the push on Tripoli.

But there are half a dozen villages, towns and communities between Zawiya and Tripoli which the rebels have got to recapture before making an assault on the capital. The rebels have an idea that most of them are anti-Gaddafi but they're not sure about what resistance they will get in each of them.

And there is one very significant obstacle. The headquarters of the 32nd Brigade – the Khamis Brigade – is sitting between Zawiya and the capital. The most feared brigade in the whole of Libya, it is headed by Khamis, Gaddafi's seventh and youngest son. It is lavishly funded and its main purpose appears to be protecting the Gaddafi family. The brigade is in charge of controlling the interior

– in charge of internal dissent, in charge of repression. Just in charge, basically.

We follow the movement of rebel vehicles slightly timidly. None of us is saying much. We don't know what to expect. We don't know what we'll see but we're desperate to find out. Within a very short time we find ourselves on the edge of Judaim, the neighbouring town to Zawiya. There's a large collection of Opposition fighters here and we seem to have arrived just after some sort of firefight. There are a couple of vehicles alight on one side of the road. Groups of rebels are resting on the other side. It's a four-way intersection and everyone seems to be buzzing around. Now *this* looks like an advancing force. They have plenty of weaponry, plenty of arms and plenty of people. There are dozens of vehicles – some of them civilian cars, some of them vehicles which have been adapted for war, with anti-aircraft guns mounted on the back of pick-ups or trucks piled high with ammunition and RPG launchers. They are all parked haphazardly, no pattern or order. The red, black and green flag of the rebels is everywhere.

And there are a lot of people without any vehicles, who are on foot, just milling around. The rebels are very buoyant. The lack of Gaddafi forces blocking the exit from Zawiya is a sign that the government soldiers are on the back foot or at least adopting different tactics. A car drives by with two rebel soldiers in the front, one of whom is hooded. They might be confident but there are some who still don't want to be recognized. Call it insurance should the battle *not* go their way. They stop when they see us, Garwen with camera in hand. 'We are beating them,' the masked man tells us. 'We have them on the run. Gaddafi called us rats. Now he and his soldiers are running like rats.'

And the plan? 'We go on to Tripoli.' When? 'I think, maybe tomorrow ...' – he hesitates – 'maybe ... we have something big planned. You will be surprised.'

They take everyone by surprise.

We're excited now. This looks like they mean business. I can feel the adrenalin rising inside me. Suddenly the team has a collective fresh burst of energy. Sunday might not be so quiet after all.

We set up the Began and start broadcasting live into Sky's head office in London, telling them the Opposition fighters are on the move. There are packs of men armed with all sorts of weapons behind us and they are manoeuvring different military vehicles, all getting ready to move forward. There's lots of revving of engines and shouting of orders. They have set alight green flags which they have found still hanging up in Judaim. There doesn't seem to be anyone else around but the fighters – no civilians, no families, no onlookers. Some of the young men are chanting and dancing round the burning material. They are raising their weapons in the air and singing in Arabic. They're a bit rowdy but don't seem threatening. Garwen weaves in and out of them, filming with his camera, and I hover behind him, just minding his back and trying not to get in his way. The mood feels very confident.

A lot of them want to talk to us. They keep coming up and telling us how well they are doing, how they are going to take Tripoli, how they are beating Gaddafi finally. 'He is finished,' they say over and over again. Fine, thank you, I keep saying, but does anyone speak good enough English for me to interview live? Not many here, it seems. I thrust one of the fighters in front of the camera and we have a stilted conversation in English about battle plans (there appear to be few he is aware of) and mood (oh, he's very confident and they're going all the way to the capital) and an update on progress (very good).

The BBC team turns up and parks next to us and starts making telephone calls to their office. We nod a hello to our acquaintances. 'We've got to go,' I tell the team. 'The Beeb are here.' None of us wants to be falling over our television opposition while covering this.

The first tranche of rebel fighters is moving forward. They will push on but leave a group behind. The first wave will check out what the resistance is like ahead and then call the others to follow. It appears ramshackle and chaotic but there is a core of communication and co-ordination.

We set off on foot, running with the fighters down the road to Tripoli. Each of our flak jackets weighs about twenty pounds. It is sweltering and it's awkward. My vest clunks against me, my helmet feels like it is wobbling from side to side. But as we're running we aren't in the open ground between buildings for too long. I'm thinking, I'm going to be the big, slow one lagging behind, whom the snipers see and take aim at. I'm desperately working hard to keep up with the others. Garwen regularly runs double marathons and Jim, well, Jim is ex-SAS and therefore has to be fit. I'm struggling but somehow fear and excitement keep me going. We are all soaking already. Our shirts under our vests are wet through. Perspiration is dripping down our faces. Our hair is wet under our helmets and now sweat is seeping through our trousers. It's so hot. I'm thirsty. I'm tired. I'm panting. I can hear my breath. I'm heaving and gulping, trying to fill my lungs with air, trying to find energy from somewhere. The gunfire keeps me moving.

Every few hundred yards the fighters stop, halted by the sound of firing from snipers ahead. The snipers are positioned in some of the tall buildings and from that vantage point they are firing on the advancing rebels. We are constantly diving behind trees and buildings as we hear bullets whistling past. There are so many fighters running all over the place, we will be extremely unlucky to be hit among all of this lot. That's how I reason with my inner fears, but even as I do it doesn't sound too convincing. Instinctively everyone ducks behind vehicles, buildings, trees, each other, as the bullets frequently fly overhead. We keep trying to set up the Began to do updates whenever we think it's a bit calmer, or the noise dies down, but we're constantly interrupted as the battle lines keep moving – backwards, then big leaps forward, then back again. If we don't move quickly we'll get caught out here, I fear.

So Rasan is cautiously following us in the car some distance behind with Andy and all the heavy equipment while Jim, Garwen and I run on with the fighters. By now he realizes we'll probably have to leave the library for another day.

At one point we take shelter down an alley between two large government buildings. This is the way with battles. There are often periods of waiting, waiting to see if the fighters are going to advance, waiting to see what lies ahead, waiting to see if there's any return fire, waiting to check if there are booby traps. There can be a lot of waiting. I remember it's Garwen's birthday and take the camera from him, telling him to say something I can record for his three children. I thought it would be nice for Reece, Kiara and Amber (and of course his wife Kerrin) to know what Dad had been doing on his birthday.

Garwen immediately springs into action. 'Well, it's so nice of so many people to come out to share my birthday,' he says with a big smile on his face. (The place is crawling with combat-clothed Opposition fighters with weapons draped over them, some sitting, some scouring the area to try to find out where the shooting is coming from.) Not a cake in sight, though. (Andy tells us he *did* buy some ingredients, though Lord knows where he found them. He'd planned to make Garwen a surprise sweet offering.)

While I am filming, Jim and Andy enter the camera frame and start hugging Garwen. In the background you can hear the boom, boom of rockets landing close by. Incredibly, none of the guys flinches and it's only much later when I watch the recording that I realize that Garwen's poor family would not be much comforted at all by the video.

Seconds later, the rockets land close enough for the rebels to decide it's time to pull out or at least pull well back. People start running everywhere, but ultimately always back the way we have just come. I jump into Rasan's car, which happens to also be very close to where we are cowering. A man follows in behind me. 'No, no,' I shout, 'this seat is taken.' I feel awful pushing him out, this man desperately trying to get to safety, out of this war zone. These are split-second gut reactions, not always laudable. Jim and Andy arrive at that point and the man realizes he's no match for the two of them and runs away to try to catch a lift elsewhere. 'Go,' Jim yells to Rasan. 'Go!'

It's during one of these stop-start-stop moments that we decide we'd better head back to Zawiya to try to file something for the evening news from the safety of our house. We have a lot of material already in the bag, with much Opposition firing, Gaddafi sniper attacks, chanting and buoyant war songs from the rebels. We have more than enough to show the advance of the rebel group and their apparent confidence. And besides, the rebels seem to be stuck at this point, unable to clear the Gaddafi snipers.

We head back. We're all starving and incredibly thirsty, dehydrated and needing some energy from somewhere. We've been out for most of the day without food or drink or access to a toilet – although the serious heat seems to alleviate that need. But I've got a throbbing headache from the relentless seeping of moisture out of me. I bet the guys are the same. I cobble together some scrambled eggs, which is most unusual. And not just for the taste. Normally it's Andy or Jim doing the cooking while I'm working, but I'm the only one unoccupied at this moment as the guys are busy with the technicalities of downloading the pictures and setting up the edit and feeding (transmitting) equipment. So I do my share of the feeding.

We all gulp the food down and Garwen and I set about putting together the report in double-quick time. We're all anxious to get back out again because we sense it's not over yet. We don't want to miss a thing.

Once it's edited, Andy will 'feed' the report back to London using the second Began unit we have with us. This can be a slow process and is prone to cutting out. When that happens, and it happens often, it involves someone restarting the feed and sending the remainder of the report. It can take hours. It's always frustrating.

It's decided Andy will stay behind to monitor the feed while the three of us (Jim, Garwen and I) head out down the road to Tripoli to see what progress the rebels are making.

But, before we go, we are going to do a live broadcast from Zawiya to update on what's been happening. As we set out from the house we see a convoy of about a dozen vehicles – each packed with rebel fighters. They look impressively tough. We follow them round the corner, where they are massing on a patch of farmland. They are from Misrata. Their mission: to take Tripoli. Mission improbable, it seems. We do a broadcast with the fighters in the background announcing this ambition to the Sky viewers. The Misrata brigade are very different from those we have seen in Zawiya or even those who we have just been with on the road to Tripoli. They appear and *are* much tougher, much better armed. They seem to work better as a homogenous unit. They have adapted ordinary cars and welded large sheets of metal onto all sides as reinforcements, cutting holes into sections through which they can point their guns. Their vehicles look like they have been lifted from the set of the film *Mad Max*, like they are survivors from some sort of post-apocalyptic world. I'm not using the analogy lightly. They actually *do* look like the *Mad Max* characters. They're hard, tough, their clothes adapted for war, their vehicles turned into fighting machines. They have evolved through months and months of fighting the Gaddafi military inside their besieged city. They not only survived that, they beat Gaddafi's soldiers back. They feel invincible.

(We noticed their resilience when I was in Misrata in April 2011 with cameraman Martin Smith and producer Neville Lazarus. Misrata had been shelled and bombed by Gaddafi troops for months. The city was cut off bar the port, which the Opposition still held. The port was key. This way they were able to get medicines, fuel, money, and obviously ammunition and weapons shipped in from their comrades in Benghazi. But often the ships came under fire themselves and the port was frequently shelled. This was not a trip for the faint-hearted. Misrata had closed in on itself and was working as one, defending itself against the constant Gaddafi attacks. Everyone in the city was pretty much involved in defending it. They had set up a political council, organized gun and ammunition runs from Benghazi, had ammunition factories working 24/7, and were operating as an impressive army. Many talked about getting help from 'foreign' forces. Britain and France were among the countries which said they would give 'logistical support' and many of the fighters gave us anecdotal evidence of being 'trained' by them.)

Here the same Misrata fighters were in Zawiya. They were battle-hardened and had the look and feel of desperadoes about them. Fresh from their own success, they were raring to go into battle again.

There's no holding them back now. One of the fighters says they have been told to wait for an order but they don't want to, can't wait any longer. They set off. I try protesting with them. Wait, just wait a bit longer, I say. I'm mindful our report is still chugging its way back to London. They don't listen, don't want to hang around any longer. We automatically decide to go with them. We say a quick goodbye to Andy. He hesitates. Just as we're moving off in Rasan's car again, Andy decides he won't stay behind with the Began after all. If the report cuts out, well, it cuts out. It's a gamble and we definitely won't be very popular with the office if they end up never getting the report they've been waiting for all day. We decide to take the chance. It's a roll of the dice. We have to do it all the time, make these instant decisions. Andy jumps in with us. It turns out to be the best gamble of the whole trip. We've just rolled a double six.

Chapter Eleven

GREEN SQUARE

Everything picks up speed suddenly. We pass the four-way junction near Judaim, where there are still fighters congregating, but the bulk of them are no longer there. We see yet more discarded army uniforms, a green jumble of them strewn across the road. They have been ditched by the Gaddafi men, who are probably now trying to pass themselves off as frightened civilians.

We pass the next village, Maia, now recaptured. From the road it's difficult for us outsiders to imagine this is a community. It is so small, but the civilians standing by watching the crews of rebel fighters tell us this is an enclave. The rebels have little heavy weaponry but they do possess one enormous advantage. They have Western air power on their side and we are seeing the evidence of their activities as we go along. There are the jagged holes of NATO's bombs through buildings and restaurants and offices all along the route.

A few civilians are on the street watching the hordes of rebel fighters streaming down the road. They look astonished. Village after village has fallen. 'Is that ... no, is that the Khamis headquarters?' I ask the guys. 'Yes,' says Garwen, jumping out of the front seat, 'it's the 32nd Brigade headquarters.' Rasan is gaping. None of us can believe it. This is, after all, one of the four 'gates' that Gaddafi has built to form a fortress, a defence for the capital. Opposition soldiers and fighters are streaming in and out of the main entrance. There seems to be a fair amount of pillaging going on. Men are ransacking the offices and everything else inside the grounds. Men are walking out of the building where people were once tortured and interrogated, carrying whatever they could get their hands on. They are just pushing past us, some firing their weapons into the air.

It feels like we don't have much time. I want Garwen to film everything that is happening right in front of us but somehow it feels like this is just the rear group, just the opportunistic ones, not the fighting force we saw a few hours earlier down the road. It doesn't feel like we're in the right place. While we were editing and scoffing scrambled eggs, the fighters were pushing, pushing, pushing and making what appears to be tremendous progress. I'm cursing myself inside. We shouldn't have stopped. We shouldn't have eaten. Now we're behind, now we have to play catch-up again. We set up our Began for another live broadcast just outside the entrance of the HQ and next to a pick-up truck. The truck has been piled high with office chairs, tables and a television, all tied down with rope.

Next to the truck, three men are poring over files they have got from inside. They are files of men who were signed up for the Khamis Brigade. There are pictures of each of the recruits plus their nationalities and a brief description of their previous jobs – they are Algerian farmers, Sudanese labourers and unemployed young men from Chad. They are mercenaries, paid a fee to fight against the Libyan people. I hold the file up to the camera as evidence while the fighters fire rockets and guns into the air in delight at having taken this very symbolic building. The brigade's HQ is now under the control of the Opposition and it is a huge psychological boost to all the rebel Libyan fighters involved. I am aware even as I'm broadcasting that this will be a clarion call to Libyan civilians who may be watching. The Khamis Brigade HQ is empty, they'll be thinking. He's gone, his troops have gone. If anyone is wondering which side to support they surely will be swayed by this turn of events, I think.

The sun is going down at this point – on the Khamis Brigade and on the horizon – but the rebels show no sign of stopping. While hundreds are still running and walking through the spookily empty building, whooping and firing and pillaging, again the bulk seem to be getting themselves together to move on. But there's a problem.

Rasan decides at this point that he hasn't signed up for a battle into Tripoli. He might have imagined an afternoon browsing between the reference and non-fiction aisles. Becoming a character in a real-life drama is not part of the deal. 'I can't go any farther,' he says. Abdul al-Zaq has also turned up to witness this spectacle at the Khamis Brigade's headquarters, but he too says the demarcation lines of territory mean he can't (or won't, or both) go further. The brigade's HQ may be one of the capital's four defensive 'gates', but it's also known as Gate 27 because it's twenty-seven kilometres from the heart of Tripoli. However, the Opposition is already through that gate and heading on – and there's no way we are going to let a reluctant driver hold us back. I'm feeling worried and frustrated now – worried we're going to be left behind, frustrated we have two cars here and neither of them is going to budge. Who can we get to help us? Abdul al-Zaq is busy making his own enquiries on our behalf. He feels responsible for us and has a word with an older man with a white beard and who is wearing army uniform. He has the air of someone in charge. He agrees to take us, but he's not moving quickly enough for me. He's occupied organizing his men. I'm looking round frantically for another ride while we grab all our equipment out of Rasan's car and load it into the rucksacks on our backs. We think we have everything, but my handy little bag full of essentials is left behind. I will regret that many times over during the next week.

I spot two young guys next to a pick-up which is empty apart from boxes of rotting tomatoes in the back. They are just about to set off. 'Can we come with you?' I say, using very expressive hand language to compensate for my lack of Arabic. 'Yes, yes,' one says, trying to lift some of the boxes out. They are so rotten that half of the bottom of the boxes falls away. The fruit smells and squelches over our boots as we climb on board. Why didn't I wait? The older guy would have been a much better bet. The young lads set off after the other cars.

Only about ten minutes down the road we draw to a halt as the rebel vehicles are all congregating in one big mass. OK, we have a second chance at getting it right. By now it's dark. We jump out the back of the pick-up. These guys are obviously just a couple of young opportunistic lads swept along with the excitement of these advancing troops. They appear to be just tagging along. They don't know the fighters and they aren't part of the fighting group, not part of the rebel army. They are a convenient ride for us but we need to be with men who know what they are doing and are preferably part of any decision-making process. The boys seem more like farmhands carried along by the momentum. They are obviously delighted to be helping some foreign journalists, or *sihafis*, as they call us. But this is our chance to find a better lift.

We spot the older commander again, and I rush up to him. There's another older man with him, a commander from Zawiya whom we have met, spoken to and interviewed before. They recognize us and smile. They in turn talk to other drivers and Opposition fighters, and it doesn't take long before we find someone who is not only willing to take us but who speaks good English too.

He is Mosab. He's spent some time at Bournemouth University and, more importantly, he has a Toyota pick-up with room enough for all of us. Mosab is quite a find. For a start he knows Sky News and is keen to help. He doesn't look much like a Bournemouth University student at this point, with his army combat trousers, his AK-47 and bandanna – but we do have lots to talk about. 'Bournemouth is so lovely,' he tells me. 'I love England. I like the weather.' 'Yes, yes, I say, but what about the revolution?' They don't have revolutions in Dorset, Mosab may have thought. But what about Tripoli? I ask to make sure we were by now on the same page. Will you get there tonight? And then what?

The convoy is now quite huge – with cars, trucks and adapted military vehicles all inching along, because there are so many. We're filling the whole road. It's actually giving the team time to rest a bit. We are no longer running, no longer heaving the equipment around. We travel light, but nothing seems light when you have a flak jacket on your back plus full rucksacks, filled with the laptop and the Began, with satellite phones stuffed in our pockets. We have plenty of time to get to know Mosab. He seems ever so young and has a lovely open face and a great smile. I keep asking him if we are actually *in* Tripoli yet. As soon as we are, I want to telephone London and tell them the Opposition fighters have entered the capital. I am impatient, but not as impatient as the fighters, who are a mixture of excited, nervous and edgy all at the same time. It is an intoxicating brew.

We're moving so slowly, Garwen and I are able to get off the pick-up and film a piece-to-camera walking through the vehicles, talking about the traffic jam of Opposition cars heading towards Tripoli. Garwen is worried about light as it is pitch-dark and he is just using the Paglight attached to the top of his camera. It's limited but will be enough to light up my face during my report. I have to do the piece-to-camera several times as I keep fluffing my lines and am getting increasingly irritated with myself. We get one 'clean' one and climb back on the pick-up, which hasn't made much progress down the road. There are two other fighters on the back with us, perched on either corner while Mosab is at the front on the left. They don't say much at all and don't seem to know much English but are constantly watching, looking around, guns ready. They seem to know what they are doing. I feel safe with them. Mosab seems very much like a Bournemouth University student who has been given a gun, but they seem like professional soldiers, probably defectors from the Gaddafi army.

There are no street lights – probably because the power has been cut – and this huge convoy of several hundred is travelling very slowly with no lights on at all. We are almost feeling our way blindly into Tripoli.

Mosab is getting nervous. As Jim lights up a cigarette, Mosab tells him not to smoke. 'The snipers will see,' he says. Jim snorts and carries on. He is not impressed and he does not think smoking is going to be the death of him. Not today anyway.

I notice the streets are not so empty any more. There are small groups of people – and the groups are getting bigger. They are standing by watching virtually open-mouthed at this huge caval-cade of vehicles with the rebel tricolour flying from many of them, defining their allegiance.

The fighters we are with just sit on the back of their pick-ups, saying nothing, watching impassively, looking grim and daring a response. Then one man comes up to our vehicle and hugs Mosab. The man is beaming. He slaps Mosab on the back and then goes along the pick-up, slapping all our backs. I'm nearly knocked off at first and think he is hitting me – but when I turn round he is running alongside the other vehicles, slapping anyone he can reach, yelping with what appears to be joy. Within minutes more join him. The fighters are noticeably relieved. This is a welcoming committee – and they're being joined by many, many more.

Soon there are crowds of men, young and old, surrounding the convoy. Their faces are shiny with sweat. Some are crying. Others are delirious with excitement. Even more are smiling. They are shouting and yelling: 'Gaddafi go!' and 'Free Libya' and plenty more in Arabic. Some yell 'Freedom' in English. They don't know much English but they know that word. And then, for the first time, I see there are women out on the street, dressed all in black and trilling with their tongues – the noise they save for celebra-tions such as weddings or births.

As more and more people come out of their homes, the drivers begin sounding their horns. Someone fires his gun in the air, and that sets off the entire crowd. Soon there's constant gunfire – all in celebration. Andy has rigged up the satellite phone so I can telephone London and tell them we are in Tripoli. The Opposition fighters are not only meeting with no resistance, the population of Tripoli is welcoming them with huge relief.

The presenter on the other end of the line is Steve Dixon, a lovely man with boy-band good looks who is a solid journalist. Tonight he can't believe what he is about to see or hear. He keeps asking me who the people on the streets are. 'Where are all the Gaddafi supporters? Just to be clear, Alex, there is no resistance whatsoever?' There is understandable doubt in his voice and I find myself saying to him: 'Steve, to be absolutely clear, these people are coming out of their homes and they're welcoming the rebels.' I'm immediately a bit embarrassed that I have allowed myself to be so transparently tetchy with him on air. 'Steve, we'll try to get some pictures back to you so you can see for yourself. It's a bit difficult because we are moving in a convoy, but we will try.'

Andy has heard the whole conversation, and agrees. We need to put the doubts to rest. If Steve has doubts, then probably people watching my broadcasts are doubting us too. But in order to send pictures back live we are probably going to have to get off the pick-up and set up the Began on the pavement next to the road. I have no doubt they will be good pictures. There are plenty of people on the streets and plenty of action, but we're going to end up being stranded and lose our transport. 'You know we're going so slowly the Began might just work if we try from the pick-up,' Andy says. I think he's as wildly deluded as the Opposition fighters. But it's worth a try. Roll that dice again.

Now, Begans are notoriously temperamental. I provoke tut-tuts all round when I describe them as menstrual but I am a woman and I know every month there's a time when I get moody, impatient, tired, tetchy, and sometimes, some might say, not very co-operative. It's called hormones. Well, the Began is like that. Every television journalist working today will tell you how tricky a Began can be. You can be in a totally secure environment on solid ground in the back streets of, say, France or Italy or comfortable Sardinia (substitute any well-known location where you would have good infrastructure) and the Began won't work, for no discernible reason. It's just having an off day.

A Began also drains power. It has its own battery but doing a live broadcast immediately uses up large amounts of its battery power. But Andy has a cunning plan. He plugs it into the pick-up truck's cigarette charger. Problem number one solved. But the Began needs line of sight with the satellite. It needs to 'lock on' to the satellite and stay locked on to transmit. Even then, the pictures are often fuzzy and become fuzzier if the subject in front of the camera moves.

Whenever we are out in the field transmitting by Began, we try to avoid swaying trees, flags waving, anything which might move and therefore cause the picture to fuzz or freeze. Here, as we're travelling through Tripoli, making our way to the centre, we are not only moving ourselves, but everyone in the background is jumping, walking, shooting, shouting, hugging and screaming. Asking them all to stand still probably won't work. Surely the Began won't either. Andy sets it up on the bonnet of the pick-up alongside the laptop – which is connected to the camera. The camera at this stage is in Jim's possession. Garwen is hanging off the back of the truck filming the ecstatic scenes and trying to capture the emotion. Men are holding up toddlers to the convoy as we're passing. Some are weeping. The atmosphere is incredible.

The team is desperate to capture some of this on air and we're all scrambling to untangle the cables and plug them into all the right places in the dark. Andy gets a signal – a high-pitched noise is emitted from the Began, showing he has locked onto the satellite. Bingo! Now he has to keep it locked on. As we're moving he slowly turns the Began – as if he's handling gelignite – so it remains in sight of the satellite. Problem number two solved. Almost instantly I can hear the studio in London through my earpiece. 'Alex, we can see you, coming to you in ten seconds ... nine, eight, seven, six, five ... And now we can cross live to Tripoli, where our correspondent is with the rebel convoy heading into the town, Alex ...' Steve says but still scarcely believes.

We'd done it. I start babbling about the scene, telling him these people are welcoming the Opposition fighters, there is no resistance, and the gunfire they can hear is celebratory gunfire – men firing their weapons into the air but not at each other, not at anyone intentionally. There are bullets flying everywhere, though, and showering the back of the pick-up. It's dangerous in its own right. Several land on Jim's arms as he is trying to hold the camera steady. He holds fast and they singe his skin. Afterwards he's left with a lot of red weals on his forearm. I feel one land next to me and stupidly I pick it up and drop it instantly – it's burning hot.

I'm trying to reassure the viewers, who I know in the past have been horrified at the sound of gunfire behind me and do worry about my crew and our safety. I am also bearing in mind that my boss, John Ryley – who is Sky's Head of News – is monitoring these pictures as they are coming in and he will want to know that everything is under control and I am not jeopardizing any of my team's safety. He wants to count us all back.

'I am wearing this flak jacket and helmet not because I am afraid or fear for our safety,' I say on air, 'but because there are so many bullets flying around due to the celebratory gunfire.'

The pictures and audio we are sending from the back of the pick-up go through a 'gallery' in London which acts as mission control. The gallery is full of the essential behind-the-scenes staff who actually make sure our reports and broadcasts get on air. 'We're staying with you, Crawfie,' says the producer in London, Adam Jay. 'The pictures are great.' That's all I needed to hear.

It's not yet eight o'clock, London time, on a Sunday evening – perhaps the quietest hour of the week. But it's becoming one of the most exciting days of my working life. I don't feel nervous. I don't sense the rest of the team is either. Everyone is fired up and motivated, anxious to do well, anxious to do a good job, to record what immediately feels like a very significant moment in Libyan history. We don't want to mess it up. The fear of failure is far stronger than the fear of anything else. There's a lot of guns being fired, so much so it's difficult to talk to each other without shouting and even then we can't hear what each other is saying most of the time. We've gone into automatic. This is what we've been working for, what we've been waiting for on this trip. But still I feel like I can do better. I'm grasping around for adjectives, trying to fill the air with descriptions just in case the pictures aren't too clear. I'm trying to give whoever is watching a taste of the atmosphere, but no amount of superlatives quite cover it.

'It's amazing, just amazing,' I hear myself saying once too many times. Think of other things to say. I'm cross with myself. But events are moving so quickly, we're just reacting. Jim is reacting to where I am moving on the truck, trying to follow me with his camera as I move around, frequently losing my balance and falling over. Garwen is reacting to what the young lads are doing, jumping up and down in front of him alongside the pick-up. Andy is reacting to the truck's movement, trying to keep the satellite in line constantly. We're all just concentrating intently. But we have each got our own radars, honed after days of being in the middle of the fighting, after years of reporting, after decades of living – and right now this doesn't feel frightening. It feels utterly exhilarating.

Soon the pictures are being beamed around the world. And within minutes I hear Steve Dixon, the presenter in London, reading out comments from the United Nations, the White House, Downing Street – and we are not yet in Green Square. I realize we must be the only ones showing these pictures, the only ones here – even better.

Sky management quickly realizes the significance of the moment and rallies extra staff into the headquarters in Osterley, West London. Another army is on the move. An executive producer, Ronan Hughes, is called in and takes over the direction in the gallery. There is a change of tempo. Around the pick-up there is a cacophony of horns honking and gunfire. I can barely hear myself yelling down the microphone, but as the pictures are arriving in London I think I can still hear the sound of jaws dropping.

We are effectively marooned from the rest of the world, with no Internet, no mobile phone network, no television, and no radio. But I know now we are the only ones broadcasting this live. We have to keep going, otherwise I have no doubt the Gaddafi regime will deny it happened.

We are approaching Green Square and I can see fireworks going off just ahead inside the Square. We have about twelve, maybe more, vehicles in front of us. By now there are hundreds of people out on the street, many of them showering the trucks going by with water and hugs and more slaps. We are still moving very slowly.

Garwen is off the pick-up filming the road scenes when suddenly something spooks those at the head of the convoy. In an instant the atmosphere changes. Whatever it is that starts it, the alarm spreads quickly and uncontrollably. No one asks any questions. They just run. Vehicles screech into reverse, including our own, and are crashing into each other and knocking down pedestrians (of whom there are many) in their desperation to get the hell out of there.

Garwen jumps back onto our truck as we're all thrown backwards by the force of it suddenly accelerating. People are firing their guns wildly now and I see men running away from the Square. Bullets are being sprayed everywhere. The fighters – so confident a minute ago – are terrified. Perhaps the most terrified of all appears to be our driver. 'Calm down,' shouts Jim.

I lean forward into the driver's cab as we are being thrown all over the back of the truck, and pat the driver on his shoulder. 'It's OK, it's OK, *shway, shway* ["slowly, slowly" in Arabic].' But he doesn't acknowledge my pat or my words and just keeps careering down the road, dodging other vehicles. We don't stop until we are out of the city centre and at a huge roundabout where many of the other Opposition fighters have gathered. My heart is pumping at the sudden mood change. And yet, although I can't be sure, it just didn't feel like an attack. It felt very much like someone had just freaked and the fear had spread. The team thinks the same.

In the rush we have broken transmission, but Andy quickly connects again. Everyone in London will be very worried at the sudden movement and sudden shutdown. Andy is on the phone again, reassuring them even while we are still muttering among ourselves about what has happened. We get back on air. 'There was something which frightened them,' I say to Steve, 'but I think it's just a sign of their nerves. I don't have any reason to think they were being attacked. There were fireworks going off. I think they were just nervous.' Within a few minutes the convoy which had broken away has rallied itself and we are heading back in. The collective nerve has returned.

As we turn the corner into Green Square there are two cars alight. An Opposition pick-up has driven past ours with a young fighter on the back with his gun around his shoulders, dressed in a dirty white sleeveless T-shirt. He's looking at the burning cars like us, astonished, like us. His face is grimy with dirt and sweat. He turns round and sees us and puts up two fingers in the peace sign and smiles. I think, God, it looks just like a scene from *Apocalypse Now*. We are actually living through a real-life movie. It feels surreal somehow.

The noise had been tremendous until now but when we drive into the Square it goes up several more notches. Green Square seems to have just been 'taken' by the rebels and it's just filling up with people. There are hundreds of people pouring in. They are all men. They are carrying machetes, guns, penknives, kitchen knives – it seems to me some have just grabbed whatever they could from their homes and followed the crowds. They look ready for a fight, but there isn't one. Their faces all have that sheen of sweat caused by fear and excitement and adrenalin. They are shouting and firing their weapons. There are some anti-aircraft weapons mounted on the back of pick-ups and one is being pointed at a huge Gaddafi poster which is draped down one of the buildings. The firing is taking huge chunks out of the building as it tears into the Gaddafi façade. They're going mad. They just can't believe it. We're pretty incredulous too. A lot of the time I feel like I am struggling to say anything because we're still broadcasting and I am myself astonished at the scenes in front of us.

There is a digger which has a group of Opposition fighters standing in the claw's mouth. The claw is being raised so the fighters can tear down the green flags still festooned around the Square. Everyone I see clamouring around our truck is smiling, dancing, swaying, holding each other. I find myself smiling back at them. They are shaking hands with our driver, hugging him, thanking us too, as if we have somehow been responsible for this. We drive around and around and around – all the time broadcasting live. It is dizzying for many reasons.

Some men are praying. Others are dancing on the walls of the fort which is on one side of the Square. Someone has set fire to more flags so there are fires now at two ends of the Square. They cannot believe it. Neither can we.

After months of stalemate and fighting, in just a day they have careered down the road from Zawiya and ended up not just in Tripoli but right inside Green Square. Here Gaddafi himself had given speeches and demonstrated how much loyalty he had among the population by gathering crowds of his supporters. I had reported from here in March and seen busloads of Gaddafi supporters arriving to shout their allegiance to their leader. Garwen had also been here as a 'guest' of the regime, reporting from the Rixos Hotel with Sky's chief correspondent Stuart Ramsay, and filming the apparently pro-Gaddafi crowds. Where are they now?

The mood this night is a victorious one. It's difficult not to be infected by the rebels' enthusiasm and the feeling that they have somehow conquered something, even if only their fears of the dictator and his regime. 'Gaddafi is gone,' they shout. 'He is over! It is the end of Gaddafi and the beginning of something new!' They make cutting motions at their throats as they say his name and others are tearing with knives at posters of him. They are jubilant and delirious with excitement and victory. No one – least of all me – thought we would be in Tripoli's Green Square within a day. How we underestimated them.

When we come off air, Garwen throws his arms round Andy and gives him a big kiss. 'How the hell did you do that, *boet* [a term of endearment in Afrikaans]? Bloody well done.' We are all delighted and exhilarated too. We have been tremendously lucky – in the right place, at the right time, with the right people – and everything has played in our favour. The dice had been loaded. We feel like we are witnessing an amazing page in Libyan history.

The rebels appear to have made astonishing progress. Mosab tells us he has information that they have captured two of Gaddafi's sons, Saif al-Islam and Saadi. I listen, slightly unbelieving. Surely not, but then no one expected anything like this tonight. I pass it on to the office and hear that the prosecutor of the International Criminal Court has confirmed this news. But even Mosab does not seem overly excited. Perhaps he doesn't believe it either. The support for Gaddafi seems to have just melted away. His forces seem to have been utterly beaten back. I can't imagine they have totally disappeared, but, for now, they seem to have been cowed at least. Barack Obama is calling on Gaddafi to recognize his rule is at an end and to immediately resign to save Libya from further bloodshed.

'The momentum against the Gaddafi regime has reached a tipping point,' the US president says in a statement. 'Tripoli is slipping from the grasp of a tyrant. The Gaddafi regime is showing signs of collapsing. The people of Libya are showing that the universal pursuit of dignity and freedom is far stronger than the iron fist of a dictator.'

It's in the early hours. We're not really aware of the time but we decide to call it a day and try to find somewhere to stay the night. 'What about the Rixos Hotel?' I suggest. 'Maybe we should check it out.' Two of our colleagues, Jude Burrows and Darren Skidmore, have been trapped there by the regime for weeks now – and Sky's satellite dish is there. The hotel has power and beds. It seems like a good option. The others aren't so convinced but I ask the driver to take us there anyway. He isn't too keen either and, besides, he doesn't seem to know where it is. As we pull out of the Square, we spot another television crew arriving. 'I think it's Al Jazeera,' Garwen says. I see someone who I think is Zeina Khodr getting out of a white van. They are hours behind us. We leave them to it.

En route to the Rixos the driver goes by one of the hospitals. We spot an ambulance arriving and Garwen jumps out, instinctively keen to film what is going on. He and Andy disappear inside the hospital while Jim and I opt to stay with the truck for fear it will leave and we will be without transport again. Possession, at this point, is even more than nine-tenths of the law.

Within minutes there is firing outside the hospital's entrance. Several fighters are running down the road which we have just come from and which leads to the Square. One of the men is hit in front of us and falls on the hospital's ramp. Jim and I duck behind the pick-up, which is alongside the ramp, and we edge our way to the hospital doors and slip inside. It isn't all over yet by any means. I am thinking of Zeina in Green Square. The shooting is coming from that direction. Is she OK? We left just in time, but did she?

Just after midnight Gaddafi has gone on state television again via audiolink. He's not giving up just yet. Christ, I think, he is one stubborn man, but history tells us that dictators who've been in power for far too long fail, in the end, to see the writing on the wall. They fail to see what is blindingly obvious to all those around. It is what, ultimately, does for them.

Gaddafi tells the Libyan people: 'There are criminals, they are coming to destroy Tripoli. They are coming to steal our oil. Now it [Tripoli] is in ruins. They are coming. They are destroying it. Come out of your houses and fight these betrayers. Hurry up, hurry up, families and tribes, go to Tripoli. Call the tribes to go to Tripoli.' It is his second address to the nation this Sunday.

But the rhetoric from the Western leaders on seeing the scenes of celebration in Green Square is just as firm and uncompromising. From Number Ten comes this: 'It is clear from the scenes we are witnessing in Tripoli that the end is near for Gaddafi. He has committed appalling crimes against the people of Libya and he must go now to avoid any further suffering for his own people.'

The NATO Secretary General, Anders Fogh Rasmussen, says: 'The Gaddafi regime is clearly crumbling.' He, too, urges him to go.

I'm thinking, could Gaddafi really still be in Tripoli? As he's vowing again to fight to the end, to the very last 'drop of blood', it seems he is definitely trying to give that impression. The Misrata military council is saying units of Misrata rebels have made a beach landing near Tripoli, delivering weapons and ammunition to the rebels and arriving in force. NATO has been bombing the Gaddafi compound, with jets hitting targets inside the complex early on Sunday. We hear that one of the largest military bases in the capital has been overrun, with thousands of people who were imprisoned there now freed and caches of weapons seized and distributed. There is battling going on around the airport and the disused airfield amid fears the dictator will try anything to leave. But, despite all these gains, all this momentum in the rebels' favour, the word among the Opposition fighters is that the Gaddafi forces are heading their way. The last remnants of the regime are fighting back.

We find out later we're transmitting these astonishing pictures which show the tide has really turned for Colonel Gaddafi at the same time as *Celebrity Big Brother*, but people are tweeting to turn over. Watch Sky News, they say, they're in Green Square. Soon the pictures are being spotted by our competitors, Al-Arabiya, CNN, the BBC. By 21.30 UK time, CNN has lifted our pictures on a 'fair-dealing basis' and is running them with the strap 'Sky News World Exclusive' across the bottom. The American network CBS takes huge chunks of our coverage and puts it out on their evening news that night, as does the American Fox Network. The decision is taken that these are pictures of such importance that Sky *will* share them with other broadcasters so long as our competitors give us an on-air credit acknowledging the pictures come from Sky News. Daniele Pinto, Sky's foreign desk duty editor that night, says: 'When the pictures started coming in the whole newsroom was amazed. We couldn't believe it. And the quality was so good. You don't get that quality of picture from a static Began, never mind one which is on the back of a moving truck. We were just amazed.' He went on: 'The whole evening's broadcast assumed a life of its own. We were just babysitting this connection and just rolling with it live – three hours of rolling coverage.'

Steve Dixon says later: 'There was this stunned silence in the gallery as we saw the pictures. Up until then we had been told Gaddafi had tremendous support in Tripoli, and yet here they were just driving into the capital with no resistance whatsoever.'

Soon the news is being picked up on Twitter and being tweeted round the globe until, remarkably, 'Alex Crawford' began trending worldwide. Now I am not an expert on Twitter by any means, having got most of my Twitter knowledge from my 12-year-old daughter Maddy, who was the first in our family to set up her own account. But 'trending' means Alex Crawford (and obviously the Sky News team) was among the most mentioned names on the planet for a few hours. Luckily all of us were completely unaware of this at the time and for days to come.

Chapter Twelve

THE ONLY WORKING HOSPITAL IN TRIPOLI

Monday, 22 August

The first person I see as we run inside the hospital is a doctor from Zawiya. The entrance is a mêlée of doctors and nurses and people who are crying. It's chaos. A group is still taking in the latest casualty, rushing his bloodied body through on a stretcher to the emergency ward. I'm trying to get out of the way of those who are working when I hear my name being called. 'Alex, Alex, oh my God, you are alive.' I look up and cannot believe who is in front of me. It's Zacharia, Dr Mohammed, the young doctor who drove Martin, Tim and me out of the town in March when Zawiya was surrounded by Gaddafi troops.

We hug, both equally surprised the other has survived. I'm stuttering thanks and hellos and bombarding him with questions all at the same time. He looks exhausted. He has red eyes as though he's been crying. And the smile I saw a minute ago has quickly been replaced by worry and frowning.

'How are you, how are you? How is it? You must be pleased about Green Square,' I say. 'What do you think, Alex?' he replies.

'How do you think I feel? Look at these people. There are too many deaths, too many people hurt. It's still going on.'

I feel immediately chastened, embarrassed by my own lack of thought. Embarrassed at feeling jubilant. I'm still on a high from Green Square, but the mood here in the hospital is utterly different. Here people are dying and suffering. The party atmosphere we have just left seems in a different country. In this land, they appear desperate. 'I'm so sorry,' I say, 'I didn't mean ...' I feel like I have let him down somehow. He turns away as if he can't hold back the emotion any more and walks off. I realize he's still very scared: scared maybe Gaddafi will return – or hasn't actually left – scared about talking to me, scared about being seen with me, being associated with a Western reporter. We never see him again.

Garwen and Andy reappear from the direction of the emergency ward. We have a brief conversation. A doctor is among the injured they have seen, shot through the head as he was unloading a patient at the entrance. The two of them have also suddenly sobered up considerably from the great excitement of the Square.

That settles it. We aren't moving out of the hospital. It seems far too insecure outside suddenly, and we're far too tired. We're going to have to stay here for the night. I look around for anyone in a white coat who speaks English and the first person I talk is a man who says he is Dr Muhammad (not to be confused with the Dr Mohammed we met earlier). He takes us to a small office used by the medical staff. 'Stay here,' he says. 'You can be safe here. Don't worry.' I virtually beg him to let us stay the night and then go one step further, cheekily asking if there are any spare beds. He looks at me. He's shattered too. 'I'll see what I can do,' he mutters.

We wait half an hour – maybe longer – for him to come back. It's a chance to take off the flak jackets and helmets at last. Andy and Jim are buzzing around trying to find out if there's any water or coffee or anything else to drink. Garwen is worrying about charging his camera and downloading pictures. I don't feel like I am doing anything very useful at all. My energy levels seem to have plummeted.

Yet we still have to edit a report for the morning. I'm trying to think of the first line, the first pictures to use in any report. 'Jesus, we never expected this!' As an intro this might stun the morning producer a little, but that's all I am thinking. I sit there for what seems like an eternity, just holding my pen and looking at a blank bit of paper in my notebook. Did we just survive all of that? Has it all just happened in one day?

Dr Muhammad finally returns and leads us up some flights of stairs. He unlocks several doors to let us in and we are taken into a ward which is unused. It looks new, like the Waldorf Astoria of Tripoli. 'This was kept as the Gaddafi show ward,' he explains. 'It was not allowed to be used by the ordinary Libyans.'

The doctor says the hospital was under the command of the government and the Libyan soldiers up until two days ago, and we would never have been allowed in. Nor would anyone have been allowed – or been brave enough – to talk to us. 'You can sleep here,' he says. The regime is crumbling so quickly we are now staying in the showpiece hospital ward of the dictator. And his people don't give a damn.

We grab at this offer, immediately claiming beds. There are six altogether. Garwen chooses the window bed, where he is already setting up the Began, trying to balance it on the window ledge to get a signal. (The Began has to have line of sight with the satellite, as I said, so doesn't work indoors or where there are many high-rise buildings. If Garwen can get a signal from here, then we can feed our report back without having to camp for hours outside in the hospital grounds.)

Jim strides in and dumps his flak jacket at the foot of the bed right next to the bathroom. God, Jim, are you sure? I'm thinking. It's never a good idea to be so close to the ablutions. Andy leaves a discreet spare bed between himself and Jim and takes up residence next to the door. I choose the one next to Garwen. I don't want to be too far away from anyone and even one bed away feels too far right now.

Each bed has its own white sterilized medical cover and a little blanket folded on it. Seeing the small bathroom in the corner makes us realize none of us has actually been to the toilet all day. The heat, the dehydration and constant perspiration have somehow done away with that requirement. The bathroom has a toilet with a small hose for washing it down, a hand basin and some running water. While the rest of the hospital looks worn and threadbare, this showpiece of a ward which no ordinary Libyan ever saw is clean and freshly decorated. The Brother Leader had no qualms about saving the best for himself during a quest to impose uniformity among his nation.

Andy has typically already sorted out all his gear, laying out the parts of his sat phone and iPhone with all their matching cables and extensions neatly in rows next to his bed. The two of them collapse onto their hospital beds. They have nothing fresh to change into but strip down to their underwear and hang their shirts and trousers over the safety rails around the bed to dry out.

All our clothes are soaking wet with sweat. I am very envious of them. I would love to take off my sopping top and trousers but don't feel I can in front of the men.

Jim and Andy will do the early start in the morning. They know Garwen and I have hours of work ahead. Garwen and I start going through the footage the two cameramen have recorded in Green Square and we begin the process of editing a report for the breakfast programme, which, scarily, is on in just a few hours' time.

Dr Muhammad comes back into the ward. 'My cousin is on the phone from London,' he says. 'He wants to talk to you.' I take the mobile phone from him and hear a very English-sounding voice down the line. 'Hello, is that Alex Crawford?' he asks. 'Oh my God, I cannot believe I am actually talking to you. I have to tell you, you are a hero with the Libyan people. I've been watching your reports all evening. I cannot believe it ...'

The supposed hero is stunned. I did not expect this. I cut him short, embarrassed. I mean, what can you say to such a statement? 'Thank you, thank you,' is all I can think of. 'Can I put you on to my cameraman, Garwen, who is the person who filmed all the pictures you saw?'

I look up and see the doctor's quizzical face. Like us, he has been cut off from everything, so he has seen no television, maybe not even heard radio reports, and there's definitely no Internet. He doesn't know who this rag-tag group is. They certainly don't look like heroes to him. But his cousin in England has clearly told him about our broadcast. Maybe this explains the Gaddafi show ward, the best room in town.

Garwen edits the report really quickly but there's still hours left for it to chug its way to London via the satellite. I nip into the bathroom and realize at this stage I have left my handy little ruck-sack with all my essentials behind. Damn. There is no soap but there is a pile of those white medical sheets and I use one to dry myself off.

Two of the nurses come in to check we are OK and ask if they can get us a drink. We immediately ask for whatever they've got. They take ages to come back with half a pot of very thick, black coffee and lots of sugar. We gulp it down.

Jim and Andy are already asleep and Andy is making some deeply impressive farmyard noises, with the help of his nose. Garwen and I chuckle at the regular explosions coming from the far side of the ward, all the while feeling quite jealous of them. 'You go to sleep,' Garwen tells me. 'This is going to take hours to get to London and I'll set my alarm to wake myself up.'

I think about saying no. No, Garwen, you can't do that on your own. I'll stay up and talk to you and keep you company. But I can hardly keep my eyes open now. I feel guilty but I can't fight it any longer. Within seconds I am asleep. Two hours later I hear Andy's voice telling me to wake up.

Getting ready doesn't take very long as I have no way of brush-ing my hair and have no change of clothing. None of us has. Andy gives me a toothbrush which he has saved from his plane flight over from the UK. Great. I feel so much better after a quick brush of my teeth. I think, not for the first time, I am going to look really rough and instantly think how superficial I am too at having that thought when so many people are injured and dying.

Jim, Andy and I leave Garwen sleeping and descend the stairs into the hospital's quadrangle, three floors below. It connects the building where we are staying with the emergency ward and main entrance on the opposite side. The guys have already set up the Began in the centre of the open space but we notice some medical staff scuttling down the sides of the walls of the building, running to get inside. One shouts: 'Not there. Lots of firing. Not safe.' Even as he shouts to us, there is the sound of shelling close by. We pick up the Began and cables between us and set up, this time tucked in near a corner, behind a parked car. As we are waiting to connect to London, a woman runs round the corner. She is panting and nervous. She passes us to get into the hospital and tells us that two other medical staff were shot while they were in this quadrangle. Christ. I put on my helmet and flak jacket.

We do the first broadcast into the early morning programme at 06.00 London time. The 'sunrise' producer, Neil Dunwoodie, has selected a series of clips from our previous night's coverage in Green Square. He gives me instructions via my earpiece, telling me they will run some of the clips, then they will 'cross' to our Began as well as to my fellow Sky reporter Ian Woods, who is in Garayan with the rebels there. Eamonn Holmes, the presenter, will ask both of us to give a 'sit-rep', a situation report, of what is going on in our area. 'Great stuff so far, Crawfie,' Neil says. 'Tell the team they have done a great job.'

I pass it on and the boys nod appreciatively but we are far more concerned with coping with the sound of fighting going on around us just outside the hospital's walls. And then we are on air. I can hear this babble of noise in my earpiece and the sound of a woman shrieking above it and then realize through my tiredness it is me from a few hours earlier in Green Square. Then Eamonn is asking me about any celebrations in Tripoli this morning. Even as the director in London cuts to us, there is the sound of firing and shelling near to us. 'There doesn't seem to be much celebrating here, Eamonn. Rather there is still the sound of firing outside the hospital where we are,' I say. 'The medical staff here are frightened and worried.' I then relay the news about the injuries among the medical staff. Where Ian is, it seems, it is quite a different picture. He talks about the joy of rebels there at the news that Green Square has been 'taken'.

But far from any calm descending on the capital, the situation seems to be getting considerably worse, at least where we are. By this time Garwen is up and downstairs helping us as we edge farther and farther into the corner for our breakfast broadcasts, which are every half-hour. At one stage a rocket hits the side of the hospital building above us, showering us with dust and bits of masonry. After the breakfast programme we power down the 'lives' by disconnecting all the cables from both laptop and Began and pack everything away in our rucksacks. Garwen and I need to go and have a look round the hospital and record what's happening.

We run across the quadrangle and go first to the emergency ward where Garwen had filmed the night before. It is packed. There are crowds of relatives around the entrance to A&E, some crying quietly, others howling and pacing. Their grief hits us like a wave but we go past them and enter the ward. Every bed lined up against the wall is filled with an injured person. Others are lying on stretchers which are stacked up against each other. There's a riot of noise as we first enter, with the sound of the monitors constantly going in the background. But as we go farther inside the ward, it becomes much quieter. The medics we see are all moving quickly and they're concentrating furiously, but it all seems like it is spiralling out of their control. They can't do enough, quickly enough.

Some of them are huddled around two or three beds, trying to plug a bullet wound in one case, trying to blow air into the lungs of another man, working to resuscitate a third bloodied man, pummelling his body, which is not responding. His stomach is moving rapidly up and down, his legs are twitching. One of the doctors is trying to force a plastic hose down his throat to open his airwaves. His eyes are shut and another medic is pressing on his head, trying to staunch blood we can see pouring out of his head and dripping onto the floor. We know instantly he is dying, in front of us. The medics know too but they press on. And this has all happened within the first few minutes of us entering A&E. The medics barely register we're there as they're rushing around, grabbing swabs, mopping up, filling needles, bandaging.

Garwen and I are both shocked, overwhelmed, stunned. Our senses are in overload. We can barely take it all in. After everything we have seen and been through the night before, we thought, hoped it would all be over. No wonder Dr Zacharia was so upset with me. No wonder the doctors seem so fraught, so tired. It's havoc and there is a really strong smell of blood, of death. In fact the dead are just put to one side, round the corner from those being treated. There's no time for anything at the moment. No time to deal with those who cannot be helped. As we turn the corner we see them, left on their mobile stretchers, some covered, most not. Those who loved them are young men, probably brothers or sons or maybe just friends. Whoever they are, they are distraught. One is clutching the wall, just howling. He sounds like an animal. It is an uncontrollable, wild sort of sound, oozing pain. Awful to listen to.

Another has dropped to his knees, his head in his hands, crying. His friend is the man we have just seen being tended to, with the severe head wound. The doctors haven't given up on him yet but it can't be long now. The uninjured friend gets up and implores another doctor, begs him not to give up. Please save my friend, he seems to be saying. Please don't let him die. His hurt is so raw, so awful and so deep, it is terribly difficult for Garwen and me to remain composed. I am struggling not to cry myself. I don't know any of these people but their pain is so obvious, so strong, it's incredibly hard to watch and listen to. I hear Garwen singing under his breath. He is struggling too. He tells me it's the only way he can keep going. He is singing 'Amazing Grace'.

The ward is in a shockingly dirty state. There is rubbish piled up in all the corners and along the walls. One of the doctors is trying to mop the floor in one area, dragging the pools of blood with a plastic wiper along to one side. It keeps swilling back. There's just too much of it. Several times men just come up to Garwen and scream into the camera in Arabic. We don't need a translator to work out their grief and anger at what is happening to them. Occasionally they shout words we recognize. 'Gaddafi! Gaddafi!' they say, clutching at their shirts, which are covered in blood. 'Gaddafi did this!' they sob and point to their wounds.

A woman is standing silently holding the hand of a young girl. One of the doctors tells me she is 11 years old, the same age as one of my daughters. Her head has a massive bandage around it which has blood already seeping through. She isn't moving but is on her side as if she is sleeping. Is she unconscious? Is she already dead? Is she going to survive? Her mother is clutching her hand and crying quietly. She has a headscarf on but the material which is covering her neck and chest is soaked red with her daughter's blood. The blood is all over her shirt too. I take one look at her and realize she has picked up her child who has been shot through the head, I'm told, by a Gaddafi sniper. She has cradled her baby to her, her daughter's blood going everywhere as she rushes her to hospital. Christ, it's awful, awful. We are, all of us in the Sky team, parents. We have eleven children between us. It is impossible to see this suffering without thinking of our own children, our own families, seemingly millions of miles away in a different country. I realize in all that's happened I haven't spoken to them for what feels like ages. I desperately want to see them, talk to them, hear their voices. I want reassurance they are alive and well and well away from all this. But that will have to wait.

We see Dr Muhammad, who tells us the hospital has no power. They are running off a generator, so, aside from the emergency ward, the hospital has no lights. There is a shortage of everything and the fighting outside the hospital means many of the staff just haven't come into work. We interview him. It's the least we can do. 'Please, anyone who can help, please come in,' he says in a terribly tired voice. His English is being tested to the limit. 'We need orthopaedic surgeons, we need anaesthetists, we need nurses, we need anyone who can help, please.' It is a startling, desperate plea. And even as he completes that short sentence you can make out the sound of shelling in the background.

Around the corner in the corridor there is another child, about 3 years old. Her eyes are half open but she isn't conscious. She has a bullet wound to her stomach. The doctors say she was watching the Green Square celebrations and a bullet fired up into the air in victory somehow ricocheted into her stomach. Her father, who was holding her on the balcony of their flat at the time, is sitting bending over her still body, wiping his eyes with his T-shirt. It is a desperate scene. A short time after Garwen films them, we're told, the little girl dies.

We leave the ward and start to go upstairs. We have to edit this and get out another report. But before we get there a man comes up to us. He tells us he is the father of a boy who has been injured. 'Please, please, help me. He is going to lose his leg. Please help. We have to get help. We have to get him out of Libya to another country.' We go to the ward where his son is. He looks about 15. His leg is bandaged and as we get close we can smell the wound. It is rotten and obviously giving him pain. He has been waiting for surgery but the lack of doctors and the lack of oxygen in the hospital has meant his wound has gone gangrenous. He will probably end up having his leg amputated. 'There is no food here, no water, no doctors,' his father tells us. 'The people are afraid, everyone is afraid because of the shooting outside.' There are still Gaddafi posters on display in the hospital ward, a nod to the very recent past here.

Outside we see doctors lying on the waiting-room chairs, asleep, exhausted. We leave to edit, but no matter how quickly we are working and editing, we can't seem to keep pace with what's happening here. The fighting outside is so frequent and so fierce we abandon our live broadcasts in the quadrangle altogether at one point during the day and do a number of them from inside the ward where we are sleeping. Dr Muhammad manages to persuade one of his superiors to appear on television to talk to us. He is Dr Fathy Abossnina. His voice is trembling as he talks to us, shaking with emotion, tiredness and a little fear. He describes in graphic detail the scenes we have just witnessed, urging the international community to help, to bring help and bring it soon. I hear the sound of more rocket fire outside and wonder whether the noise is being picked up by my microphone. Will they hear that back in London? I hope so.

It's only been a day but it feels much, much longer. We are all feeling trapped, hemmed in by the constant fighting outside and strung out ourselves because of lack of sleep and strong emotions. Our report goes back to London but even as I am watching it I think it doesn't quite convey just how terrible it is. You can't smell the fear and desperation in a television report. You can't pick up the odour of fresh blood everywhere. The powerful, rotten smell of death doesn't fill your nose and lungs. God, I'm thinking, this is Zawiya all over again. We're going to end up being trapped here. These people are all going to die. I am going to die. I am never going to go home. But I recognize I am panicking. It's panic. Stop it, Alex. Get a grip. If I lose it now, I'll never get it back. I wrestle hard with my thoughts and push them away.

While the report is being 'fed' to London, I try to get the satellite phone to work so I can ring home. I have to go outside to the quadrangle. I get through to Richard, who sounds calm and relaxed and glad to hear from me. I immediately feel better. It seems mad where we are, trapped in this world of non-stop firing and suffering. His is the voice of the 'normal' world. He tells me none of them saw what we did the night before in Green Square. I am disappointed at first but then pleased the children didn't see it. It might have been frightening for them. 'Well, they had school,' he reminds me. Oh yes, school, their new school. Thank God for that. They are all making friends, all seem happy, all settling in, he tells me. God, I think, I should be there. I should be with them. I hope he can't hear the firing, which is starting up again. It's a fairly short conversation. It's always torturous on a sat phone. It's hard to hear or be heard sometimes. We all realize we haven't drunk anything or eaten since our scrambled eggs in Zawiya. Andy and Jim go on a hunt for food and water. There's no point begging the few staff here for anything. None of us can take food away from the injured, who can barely move, never mind go searching themselves. 'Don't go anywhere without telling me,' Jim says to Garwen and me. We nod assent. Well, you don't do anything else with Jim.

'We're just going up to see what's going on outside,' we say. Our intention is to go to the first rebel checkpoint, which has been set up just a short distance from the front entrance of the hospital. We can see the rebels standing about half a mile down the road from where we are at the hospital door. We can also see a plume of smoke beyond them at the end of the road where a bomb has landed. We're told Green Square is about two kilometres north of where we are; the Rixos Hotel, which is said to be still in the hands of the Gaddafi forces, is about two kilometres south; and the Gaddafi compound, Bab al-Aziziya, is about two kilometres east. The only working hospital in Tripoli at this point is slap bang in the middle of this volatile triangle.

As we walk towards the checkpoint, the rebels see us and call out. They seem tired too. They don't look like fighters either. They are dressed like civilians, in T-shirts and jeans, except of course that they have guns. 'We have prisoners,' they say. 'Come and see.' We hesitate, remembering Jim's warning. 'How far away are they?' I say. 'Close, close,' says one, who is in charge of a van. 'Jump in.' We do. Minutes later they are driving us down the back streets, down alleyways where only a single car can fit, until we enter a courtyard. There we see a table with food laid out on it. They are waiting to break the Ramadan fast as soon as the sun goes down, which is soon. They seem raucous and high, but in a tired sort of way. A huge guy with dreadlocks tied up at the back and carrying two rockets swaggers up to us. He kisses the tip of one rocket. 'This is for Gaddafi,' he says. Another man wearing glasses starts talking very earnestly to us. He says he is a lawyer called Mohammed and invites us to have *iftar* with them, an evening meal breaking fasting during Ramadan. We're very tempted because we are very hungry. We take the plates offered to us with unrecognizable squares of something which is very edible. 'Where are the prisoners?' I ask. 'Can we see them?'

The men are brought out of a building adjacent to the court-yard one by one. Their hands are tied together and they crouch down on their haunches up against the wall. They all seem well dressed and clean: in fact a lot better dressed and a lot less dirty and sweaty than those who are holding them captive. I get the impression they haven't been fighting. 'This one is the sniper,' Mohammed the lawyer points. 'And he is the man who recruited everyone,' he says, gesturing at a bookish-looking, white-haired man of about 50. The man looks down at the ground as we stare at him. He is the only one who appears to understand English and who seems to be listening to our conversation. About ten prisoners are lined up. The rebels say they have about twenty more inside. Their plastic hand ties are cut and each of them is given food so they too can break the fast. I ask to talk to one of them and he tells me he is well looked after. Well, his captors are standing over him with guns. What will happen to them? I ask. They tell me they will be taken and handed over to the NTC. We're getting anxious now. It's getting dark. We've already taken far longer than we antici-pated. We have to get back to the hospital. Besides, Jim will be going off his head with worry. One of the group offers to take us back and within ten minutes we are outside the hospital again.

Jim and Andy are already upstairs in our ward. They have managed to find a shop across the street which has opened its shutters for ten minutes. They have a cardboard box full of biscuits, processed slices of cheese, water, some fizzy drinks and cans of tuna. Jim is a little put out we didn't take him with us on our short excursion to see the Gaddafi prisoners – not because he believes we broke any safety rules (he knows us better than that) but because he just hates missing out on anything. He listens intently while we describe the prisoners and their state. Andy is much more upset when we let on we shared *iftar* with the rebels. 'What? You what?' he exclaims in *faux* indignation. 'You went out for a meal while me and Jim have been eating biscuits and cheese you could mend tyres with?'

Andy has somehow managed to wash himself using the hose which is above the loo. It's a test of dexterity in itself. When I check out the option later I conclude the only way of getting the hose high enough for water to drip on you is to actually stand in the toilet bowl. Andy is in his undies, having hung his shirt and trousers up to dry. His chargers are all lined up as if ready for inspection, or has he already done that? Jim seems to have attempted washing as well because he is bare-chested too. Suddenly I am envious. I don't feel I can strip down to my undies but I would really, really like to take these damp clothes off and have a break from them. The constant talk now is who among us has managed to go to the toilet and pass anything. We are all suffering from constipation because of being so dehydrated and having few liquids. 'It's been three days now,' says Garwen. These things matter!

COLONEL GADDAFI'S HAT

There's still the sound of gunfire not too far away from the hospital. We fall asleep to the thud of rockets. Tripoli is still far from secure and the rebels are a long way from being able to claim they have 'taken' the capital.

Chapter Thirteen

INSIDE GADDAFI'S LAIR

Tuesday, 23 August

There's a crackle of gunfire – and the man next to Jim collapses. He's already dead before he hits the ground, shot through the head. His brains and blood are all over Jim's neck and shoulder. There's so much, at first I think Jim's been hit. The brain matter has also sprayed all over Garwen's camera lens.

The three of us are outside one of the security walls of the Bab al-Aziziya compound – Colonel Gaddafi's home – the huge complex which is the heart of his empire, where he and his family have lived and have hosted heads of state.

Jesus. Seconds earlier I'd been talking to Garwen, telling him not to go round that corner. One of the rebels has been beckoning us forward. 'Come, come, it's fine,' he implores. But I want Garwen to film the anti-aircraft gun to the side of us, the one which looks as though it is about to be fired. 'Wait, Garwen, wait,' I nag. But if I hadn't been so bossy, if Garwen hadn't stopped to listen to me, if he hadn't hesitated, he would have been shoulder to shoulder next to

Jim. Garwen would have taken the bullet instead of this stranger. The guys are stunned. We all are.

'Fucking hell,' gasps Jim. 'Look, look at my shoulder.' His shoulder is smeared with blood and stuff I really don't want to look at too closely. 'Fuck, it's over my lens,' Garwen says, pointing. I'm thinking, oh Christ, please don't let any of it be over me. I wipe Garwen's lens with some tissue I have in my pocket. I'm trying not to let it get on my fingers, my skin. I don't know why. As if that makes it any better. And then I turn to Jim. The brain matter is sticky and thickish. The smell reminds me of the hospital, of the mosque in Zawiya. I feel vomit rising in my throat. I think I am going to be sick. Jim catches the look on my face and sees me retch. He takes us both to one side farther along the wall. 'OK, let's just stop a minute.'

But Garwen is furious, which is highly unusual. He just doesn't do furious. I've known the guy for about fifteen years and I've never seen him even talk that sharply to anyone. He is Mr Nice Guy, the person who everyone loves, who gets on with anyone and everyone. He has a wonderfully positive, sunny personality. But he's mad angry now.

'That was so fucking unnecessary.' He spits the words out. Wow, he's angry. He's seen everything that's happened. One of the Opposition fighters has just let loose with his machine-gun, carelessly spraying bullets down the alleyway, out of control. The stranger has been shot by one of his fellow fighters.

The three of us stand there quietly, close to each other and a little apart from the group of fighters, who are still firing regardless. All I can do is try to breathe slowly, try to avoid hyperventilation. A few of the rebels try to drag the dead stranger away.

Garwen automatically starts filming. 'Garwen, don't,' I say. 'Don't put yourself through that.' It's an image which neither of us can get out of our heads for a long time.

Hours earlier we had woken up in our hospital ward, sweating again. There's still no power. The newsroom in London tells Andy that Saif al-Islam, far from being captured and under arrest by the rebels, has turned up at the Rixos Hotel. The 39-year-old son of Gaddafi has spoken to the journalists inside, including our colleagues, who are held there as unwilling guests of the regime. He's insisted his father is still in Tripoli and the capital is still under the control of loyalist forces. He's not only spoken to the reporters, he's taken some of them back to the Bab al-Aziziya compound and addressed crowds of supporters there. It's unbelievable. Members of the Gaddafi family are still in the capital after all. And they're either so confident or so brazen, they've even ventured out to try to rally support.

'The situation in Libya is excellent, thank God,' says Saif. 'We are going to win. The people are with us.' He is clearly deluded or attempting to delude, but he has managed to stage quite a performance and, to do that, he had to have some security back-up. The rebel council has been made to look foolish at the very least – conniving and manipulative at worst – by claiming they had arrested him and his brother. If the claims were true in the first place, they have blundered by not holding onto them. At this stage no one has time to question exactly what happened and where the claims came from in the first place. Events are moving very rapidly and it's taking all of our skills to keep up with them.

We're in the quadrangle again and I am plugged into the Began, listening through my earpiece to a report put together by one of my colleagues at the Sky headquarters in Osterley. She is talking over pictures which seem to show Gaddafi supporters lining the streets and waving green flags. But how? That cannot be true, I gasp to the others. That means the Gaddafi supporters would have had to be out on the streets just near to this hospital, streets we could not safely get around a few hours earlier. How on earth did he manage it, never mind rustle up a whole load of supporters? He must have used a tunnel, surely? Those supporters cannot have been on the streets round here. There's no one on the streets but fighters and men defending their homes with guns. The 'crowd' must be the staff and family members staying with Gaddafi in the family compound. But the world seems to buy the lie. The rebels don't. The news seems to galvanize them.

Power is becoming a bit of an issue with us too. We have none for the cameras. We had set out on what was meant to be a day trip nearly three days ago and we haven't got any chargers for the cameras. We had carried numerous batteries but now most are flat and we're running dangerously low on juice.

Andy is going to have to somehow get back to Zawiya along an insecure route, get to our house and raid our supplies there. He can recharge the batteries using the generator, pick up the chargers, and, at the same time, get some fresh clothing for us. Great. Now all he needs to find is a vehicle and a driver willing to take him. He manages to get a lift with an ambulance which is ferrying injured back to the more secure hospital in Zawiya. We're reluctant to split up the team but there seems no choice. He heads off with a long list of all our personal items to pick up too – toothbrush, pants, T-shirt, socks, soap, Tampax. (That last request was from me. The pile of medical sheets is running low. Bye, Andy, please take care. Please don't get hurt. Please come back and please, please, please bring the Tampax. Don't worry about odour-eaters)

Opposition fighters are gathering at the intersection just near to the hospital. Soon there are hundreds of them on foot as well as with vehicles. They are just waiting, sitting beneath the underpass, prepping their weapons, chatting, resting. We sit with them. After more than an hour they set off. They're going to Bab al-Aziziya. They're going to confront Colonel Gaddafi himself.

Playing tag-along has already worked for us once, so we stick to the trusted system. We follow the hordes and find ourselves down a lane fifty metres away from the compound's exterior wall and the West Gate. The fighters have fanned out and are attacking the compound from all sides, but there is still a large number of them here. They are firing their weapons at the wall, trying to punch holes through it and break it down bit by bit. Occasionally a group drives an anti-aircraft weapon up within sight of it and unleashes a volley, hastily retreats to avoid return fire, and relocates around a different corner. They're throwing grenades and using machine-guns and weaving in and out of lanes and houses, taking pot shots at the wall. The Gaddafi soldiers behind the wall are furiously firing back but this seems to inflame the rebels even more.

It's in this chaotic jumble of events and movement that the stranger next to Jim gets shot. I think there's no way they are going to break down that wall – and even if they do, there are two more security walls to get through before they reach the inner sanctum. Some of the fighters gesture to two bodies lying on the ground. They have blankets thrown over them but we can make out the Gaddafi green military uniforms peeking out. Snipers.

We rig up the Began to do a live broadcast. The row of homes between us and the compound wall acts as a great safety barrier. You can hear the boom of rockets coming in from the Gaddafi side but the Opposition fighters are on a mission and just keep firing, firing, firing. They keep coming up to update us on their progress. I interview one of them who speaks good English and says he's a dentist when he's not fighting revolutions. We are 'live' into the Kay Burley afternoon programme and a small crowd has gathered round the dentist to hear what he's got to say. He's talking a big game. 'We're going to break into the compound today, maybe in the next few hours. We're going to hunt Gaddafi down. We're going to find him,' he shouts. 'We've already broken through one of the gates ... I think, is it, yes, it's the North.' The news makes my ears prick up but one word comes to mind. Impossible. He's surely exaggerating. We're at the West Gate and this one looks nowhere near to being broken down. How could they have made so much more substantial progress elsewhere?

At that point, for some unfathomable reason, perhaps because we are just here, interviewing them, watching them fight, the men around us start chanting, 'Sky News! Sky News! Sky News!' It's most bizarre, if not a little disconcerting. I shush them like some school-ma'am and they slink off back to their fighting. We carry on broadcasting. The wall's not coming down but the rockets are landing closer. Bee Badik, the director in London, keeps talking to me via my earpiece, telling me to end the report the minute I feel uncomfortable or unsafe. Then a plume of smoke rises in the background behind me. 'OK, Alex, that's it, we're pulling off you. It's too close,' she says. 'Take cover.'

We decide to go back to the hospital for a breather. We need to get out of this noise and commotion for a bit. It's not hard to get a lift. There seems to be a constant stream of vehicles going up and down these lanes bringing supplies and taking back injured.

Once back, Jim makes us a drink with the hot water from the tap and some tea bags he's saved, adding plenty of sugar. They're like that in the military. Nothing if not resourceful. We need it, though. We're shattered, we're still shocked, and we know the day is not over yet. I ring in to the foreign desk on the sat phone and tell the duty editor, Andy Gales, that we're back and having a quick rest. He says the head of Sky News, John Ryley, wants to talk to me. 'It's going to be a Mumbai-style conversation, isn't it, Galesy?' I say to him. (During the Mumbai terrorist attacks, John and I have an exchange of words as the Taj Hotel is being attacked about the correct distance I and the crew should be from the hotel and the firing.)

John's on the line now: 'Alex, you're doing a great job. The crew are doing a great job, but be careful,' he cautions. 'Don't go so close. I want you all to pull back a little.' I tell him we're all back and having a cup of tea. 'Good for you. That's great.' I say we all want to be in that compound with the rebels when they finally break through. He listens. Pauses. 'Be careful.' He puts me back to Andy, who asks what my plans are now. 'They're just about through into the compound, Andy. We're going back,' I tell him. 'Right. Keep safe and ring us when you get there,' he says. And we set off.

We try a different gate. This time it's the South. Again, packs of fighters are here, pointing everything at the wall and in an excited state. They have already made huge holes in the wall and are continuing to pound away, whooping and shrieking at every piece that falls. We set up to do a live broadcast into the five o'clock evening show. By this time Anna Botting is also in Libya with a separate team and she is presenting the programme from the outskirts of the capital.

There's plenty of action where we are, lots of rocket-firing going on in the background, dozens of fighters rushing to and fro. They are really going for it. But Anna interrupts me to say there's news coming in that the rebels have breached part of the wall and are *inside* the compound. What? So they weren't bluffing. Shit, why didn't we listen? Why didn't we take them more seriously? What are we doing *here*? I tell her on air we are going to try to check it out for ourselves, and tear the earpiece out. 'Christ, they've broken through! We have to move.' The guys are as devastated as me. Damn, damn and more damn, or words to that effect. We have the wrong effing gate. Everyone is of the same mind. We have to get there and get there quickly. It must be the North Gate. From now on we're running. But it seems so is the whole of the city. Cars are rushing around, honking their horns. No one seems to have much of an idea which part of the wall is broken down but the news is out fast and they are celebrating already.

We see a huge wrought-iron gate which is swinging open on its hinges. There are a few rebels wandering around, guns slung over their backs. The garden is littered with debris. The front entrance and what I can make out as the front room look like they have been trashed. The men say it's the home of one of the Colonel's sons. Doesn't look grand enough to me. Do they know what they're talking about? I don't think so. There are no crowds here. In fact we're the only ones. I think we're in the wrong place and I want to get somewhere recognizable which is unmistakably Gaddafi territory.

The rebel we bump into next says he will guide us. 'Stay with me. I will keep you safe,' he says.

I stick to him like glue, sometimes hanging onto his shirt. He is more than six foot tall and has a gun and apparently a pretty good idea of what's happening. He keeps stopping cars and saying hello to other fighters he knows and asking them the quickest way to the North Gate. People are running all over the place now, criss-crossing the roads, running in between the cars, which have rebel flags flying from them, but there's no real flow in any one direction. We turn round the corner and see crowds outside another entrance in the far distance. 'The North Gate?' I shout to the fighters coming towards us. 'No, this is the West side. It's not clear yet. There are many Gaddafi forces there. It's not safe,' comes back the reply. Oh man!

We turn back. I keep looking at my watch. It's half-past five London time. We have half an hour until the six o'clock news. Come on, come on, we have to find it. How difficult can it be? But the compound is huge, with its own network of tunnels under-ground, its own zoo, its own football pitch, plus homes for the Gaddafi family, their workers and their families. There's even a museum in there. Gaddafi has left the remnants of the previous American bombing of Tripoli as a standing relic, a reminder of Western aggression. Our guide is taking us in another direction now. Running, running, running. We're panting. No one is saying much except shouting questions about the North Gate. Where the hell is it? Our rucksacks are banging on our backs with all our equipment inside – the Began, the laptop, the cables, the emer-gency medical kit. We could have done with Andy, I'm thinking. Is he on his way back? Is he stuck in Zawiya? Is he safe? We get to yet another entrance. This has an entirely different feel to it. It is crowded with people and vehicles, many of them rebel military trucks but also scores of civilian cars. Is this it? It certainly looks promising. It's ten to the hour. Come on, don't stop, guys, keep running.

Once again I'm hanging onto the shirt of our guide as he cuts a path through all the people rushing in and rushing out. We step through what looks like the rubble of an exterior wall. I see a little distance away the reporter from the *Sunday Times*, Miles Amore, sitting against a wall. He looks shattered. He has his helmet off. I wonder why but we don't have time to say hello, let alone stop. (I find out later Miles has taken a bullet in his helmet. He's just had a very, very narrow escape.) As many people seem to be rushing out as are rushing in, but many of those leaving are carrying slim black cases. 'Guns,' shouts Jim. They have raided the Gaddafi weapons store. 'What about here then for the live?' says Jim. No, we need to get somewhere recognizable. We press on, through the second security barrier, then the third.

There is open space now, some grass. I can see a tent on fire and then, bingo! There it is. The monument of a golden fist crushing an American fighter jet. It's the symbol of Gaddafi's power, a construction to show the West he will never be cowed. It's the first time I have seen it for myself. It's smaller than I imagined and a fighter holding a rebel flag is trying to climb up it. As I am gaping at the scene, Jim and Garwen are already pulling out cables from the rucksacks, setting up the Began for our live at the top of the six o'clock. There are no Gaddafi forces here, no Gaddafi supporters, no Gaddafis full stop. Less than fifteen hours earlier Saif Gaddafi had addressed crowds here, insisting to the world they were still in power, still had support, would never give up. They're nowhere around now.

There are several faces I recognize. Tareg – the rebel who helped us in Zawiya in March and whom we saw again leading the fightback in Zawiya in August – is one of them. He comes up to me and shakes my hand. 'Good to see you, Alex. We've done it, man. We have done it.' He is the most emotional I have ever seen him. His mother, Linda, his pregnant sister and her 2-year-old daughter were all held by Gaddafi soldiers at gunpoint as they ransacked the family home in Zawiya at the start of the uprising, searching for men and weapons. Tareg has plenty of reasons to celebrate the demise of Colonel Gaddafi's rule. I hold his upper arm. 'My God, I never thought you would,' I say. 'But you have. You have.' 'Interview me,' he says. 'I want my mum to see I am OK.' I promise him yes, but just give me a bit of time. Garwen hands me my earpiece. 'We're through to London,' says Jim.

We bang into Sky's control room with seconds to spare. The six o'clock programme is already on. I can hear the headlines in the background as the Executive Producer, Jamie Woods, greets me. 'Crawfie, well done. Coming to you after the headlines. Ramsay is in the compound too.' Great, so two Sky teams are inside and ready to broadcast live. 'Can you ask him what took them so long to get here?' I ask Jamie. I can't see Jamie but I can imagine him smiling. 'Later, Crawfie, later,' he says. The competition between Stuart Ramsay and me is fierce and legendary in the newsroom. We're good friends. We may work well as a team but the competition defies description.

From then on, we're on air live, watching tumultuous events unfold in front of us again. The fighters are climbing the museum and standing on its roof. Others are firing at the same museum, causing those on top to scuttle downstairs for a bit before returning and jubilantly dancing from their high-rise vantage point again. There is shouting, firing into the air, singing – and much praying. I interview a few of them, including Tareg, who screams into the microphone: 'Where are you now, Gaddafi? Where are you now?' Good question. Where is he?

Then out of the smoke, which is billowing around from the multiple fires, strides an extraordinary-looking figure. He is wearing a white, gold-braided peaked hat that looks astonishingly clean in all this black smoke and dirt. He has a gold chain swinging round his neck and he's holding what looks like a large fly-swatter with a huge gold handle. I call him over. 'Where did you get the hat?' I ask. 'I've just been in Colonel Gaddafi's bedroom,' he says. What?

Mr Hisham Alwindi – the name this shining character gives us – is so excited he can barely believe what he is telling me. 'I went inside his room and I was like, oh my God, I'm in Gaddafi's room. My God!' He says he's going to give the hat to his father, who 'has suffered a lot under Colonel Gaddafi'.

Amid all the firing, the craziness, the pristine hat, he makes an almost prime-ministerial speech calling on Libyans to forget the past, to stand together, even thanking all the countries who have 'stood by us'. He's lovely, I am thinking. What a gracious young man.

(The interview with Mr Alwindi is later remixed into a rap song by an Israeli journalist and musician called Noy Alooshe who has done the same with one of the Colonel's defiant speeches. It is an online hit and about the only part of my Libyan coverage which my children see. The rap is doing the rounds at their school. I am cool for a day.)

I ask Mr Alwindi if he will take us to Gaddafi's bedroom. He is struggling to hold onto his hat. Everyone wants to try it on. He's letting a few fellow rebels put it on and take pictures of themselves with it but there's always an unpleasant tussle to get it back. 'Don't let that go,' I say. 'Yeah, it'll fetch a lot on eBay,' says someone. I think it's Jim. 'No way. I'm never getting rid of this,' says Mr Alwindi.

We pack up the Began and follow him round the corner, stepping over a dead kitten (what's it doing here?). We are all in one line, walking along a wall at the back of the 'museum' created by Gaddafi. We are exposed, with a large area of garden to our left and a cluster of trees which look like a small wood. Whatever it is, there are hostile people hiding there. We can't see them but they see us and start firing. We immediately turn round and run back towards the golden fist. There seems to be firing coming from another part of the compound too, this time beyond the fist. Are there still Gaddafi forces inside the compound? Large numbers of people are running towards the breached wall now to get out. We join them.

As we're all rushing to get out, we see the other Sky crew: chief correspondent Stuart Ramsay, Ed Bayliss, the cameraman, and Tom Rayner, a young but very talented producer. There's a man I don't know but assume is their security. He's introduced as John Morrison, a former military man who turns out to make a mean cup of tea.

Garwen and Jim are running towards them now, shouting: 'Stu! Stu!' and hugging his team. We all know each other very well. Garwen used to be Stuart's cameraman when he was Africa correspondent; Jim worked with him on countless embeds in

Afghanistan. Stuart and I have been rivals as well as friends for more than twenty years. I don't know what's going through the minds of the others but I'm thinking, thank God, the cavalry's arrived. We've done our bit. Isn't it time to hand over the baton now and for us to go home? The other team say they have transport. Their vehicles are waiting outside the compound. Hurrah! Mr Alwindi, who is still with us, says he will guide us out. 'Who's the guy in the Gaddafi hat?' says Stuart. 'Oh, he's our new friend. He's been in Gaddafi's bedroom. Nice souvenir, isn't it?'

It's getting dark now and we're walking and walking but still not completely outside the compound. It's crowded with cars and military vehicles and people thronging all over the place. Then again, out of nowhere, there is the sound of machine-gun fire. The red flashes of tracers are coming towards us. Every fourth or fifth round is loaded with a phosphorus-tipped bullet which glows as it's fired, enabling the person shooting to better line up on his target. They are going everywhere, including in between our legs as we are running. The group of us jump down into a sandy ditch with the tracers following us. I scramble down after the men and we hide there for a few seconds. I see Mr Alwindi scarpering across the empty patch of land we have found ourselves on, shouting: 'Come on, come on, we'll go the back way.'

I shout to the others, and they hesitate. They're thinking, who *is* this strange bloke in the hat? And where is he taking Alex? But they see me following him and are encouraged to trust him. Mr Alwindi has managed to run, duck, scramble and run again without dislodging his prized hat once.

Chapter Fourteen

RUNNING ON EMPTY

Now we're in a race to get out and away from the compound. Come on, guys, come on. It's dark, with just the headlights of vehicles lighting our way. We're a big group now and we're moving quickly, not running, though. There are too many potholes and uneven surfaces to do that very safely, but we're moving with some speed. No one wants to hang around too long here. But it feels so good to be with the others, to be with friends, to know there are others to lean on now and to help us out.

Christ, was that the second or the third time today we have nearly been killed? I can't believe we have survived it all. My emotions are see-sawing. There's still a fair amount of looting going on, people are rushing everywhere, and we need to get as far away from this place as possible right now. The shooting inside has scattered many of the scavenging gangs in an edgy stampede, and we're among them.

Mr Alwindi is not the only one who has emerged from the compound with a stolen gift. There are men cradling brand-new nine-millimetre pistols in smart black cases, others holding shiny, golden versions. Some are just lifting whatever they can get their hands on – ornaments, pot plants, chairs. But the clear preference is to grab a weapon as a souvenir. Every other person seems to be carrying a new-looking black gun case. No one's too certain what's going to happen from now on but the hordes seem to be thinking, defence, defence, defence. It's called insurance. In the new Libya, anyone who is anyone has a weapon.

Mr Alwindi delivers us right to the doors of our transport. There's a short conversation with the driver, which doesn't go well. The Ramsay team driver is from a very well-connected family in Zintan. He's part of the rebel Zintan brigade, so he doesn't know Tripoli much at all. I ask him to take us back to the hospital where we have been staying and which is nearby. The driver flatly refuses. 'No,' he says with a shake of the head. 'That's too dangerous.' It's a very uncompromising and definite no. It immediately irritates me. What?

Come on! The hospital is only a short distance from the compound and close to both Green Square and the Rixos Hotel. The driver has been told by the Zintan fighters that there is much conflict there and he should avoid the area. There's no way he's going anywhere near, especially as he's unfamiliar with the roads. We suddenly have nowhere to go and nowhere to stay.

Mr Alwindi takes one look at this unfolding argument and disappears with a wave of his fly-swatter. He can't hang around. He's taking the Colonel's hat home to show Dad.

'Come with us then,' Stuart says. 'We've a house. It's safe. There's electricity. You can get a shower and we'll come back to the hospital tomorrow when it's light and less dangerous.' All our ears perk up at the mention of a shower. That sounds so good. I'm desperate to be clean. Desperate.

But what about Andy? He should be back from Zawiya and in the hospital by now with our recharged batteries, the extra cables, and those oh-so-important personal items – like a clean T-shirt and knickers. I'm still also rather selfishly thinking Tampax. I bet the others aren't. They would make me feel so much better. 'We can get a message to him through the news desk. They'll let him know you're OK and we'll meet up with him in the morning,' Stuart says. Within seconds we're in the van and off.

The roads are chaotic, noisy and busy. The driver keeps stopping to chat to fellow fighters. We don't notice at first because we're still running on adrenalin from the compound break-in. We're still gasping about how close the tracers were. But, after half an hour of stopping and starting and making very slow progress, I want to lean forward and tap him on the shoulder and say: 'Please, we need to get back. We don't have time for you to catch up with all your old fighting buddies.' I just about stop myself, but I'm having to fight this rudeness and impatience.

The Ramsay team house is situated in the rural outskirts of Tripoli. It seems and is miles away from the centre of the city. It takes us ages to get there. I'm feeling anxious. I don't like being so far away from the heart of the action. And does this Zintan fighter not know we have work to do tonight? I'm very irritated he wouldn't take us to the hospital. And then, when we finally arrive, the house is in darkness. There's no electricity. Oh man! Where's the power we were promised?

The Ramsay crew know it's not ideal. It's sparse, with not even sofas this time. I can't see very well in this darkness, but it feels like it's only half-built or just been roughly thrown together by a builder in a hurry. It has a kitchenette and two rooms as well as a small roof terrace. But, I keep having to remind myself, at least it's a place to stay and we're with close friends and colleagues. We walk through the doors and feel stronger and safer. We all immediately strip off our flak jackets. We look like we have been walking in the rain. We're all so sweaty and damp. The lack of power means there's no air con or fans blowing to combat the heat.

We're using torches now. Much of the city is like this, with electricity cut off. But there's still some running water and that means there's a chance to wash down properly after days of sleeping, standing and running in the same clothes. It's been worth trekking out all this way just for that. Even before actually having a shower, the thought feels glorious. My mood lightens.

The power flickers back on, thank God. Great, that means at least I can see the soap suds washing away my filth and – important, this – any little insects which might be crawling around on the floor. I wouldn't have cared either way. I just want to get this soaking wet bra and damp shirt off my skin, at least for a little while. Good thing the shirt is brown. The others lend us fresh T-shirts, soap, shampoo and socks.

The shower is an incredible pick-me-up, much more so than I ever imagined. I don't think about anything but getting clean while under the stream of water. I don't think about the man shot through the head in front of us earlier today. I don't think of the brain matter on Jim's shoulder and splattered over Garwen's camera lens. I don't think about being fired upon as we try to get into Gaddafi's bedroom. I don't think of the tracer fire from the .50-cal machine-gun as we're rushing away from the compound. I just think about getting clean. I just want to wipe the grime and dirt and sweat and muck off my body.

I feel truly fantastic when I get out. But I've still got to put on some of my old dirty clothes. There are some items you can't borrow from male colleagues. Nevertheless, my skin is clean and smelling fresh for the first time in ages and it's psychologically a massive boost. Being dirty just wears you down after a while. Garwen seems the same. He has another burst of energy.

The driver's family is breaking the fast next door and cooking furiously. He offers to share some of their food while we are busy working on our reports for that night and the next day. Thank you, thank you. These lads from Zintan aren't so bad after all. My irritation has been washed away with the shower too. The driver arrives with a large metal bowl full of meaty chunks in a brown liquid. We all sit on the floor around it, dipping large chunks of bread and gulping the milky tea. It's our first hot cooked meal for days and it tastes stupendous.

Stuart, Ed and Tom have rigged up the camera on the roof terrace and are broadcasting live. Stuart is soon explaining on air what's been going on inside the compound and the incredible change in fortune for the Gaddafi family, which itself signals a massive shift in power inside the capital. The rebels have been trampling all over his home, ransacking his bedroom, for God's sake. There's no way back from this, is there? And where is he? Where is the Colonel who said he would die on Libyan soil? And where are his troops? Where is the rest of his family?

We know Saif was in this same compound just the night before. He'd had the brass neck to take a group of journalists there to demonstrate how the Gaddafis were still in the capital and still fighting. Now there are rebel fighters trashing his possessions, tearing down his chandeliers, burning his belongings. So where are they hiding? And how did they get out? That's what everyone is asking, including us.

We'd been told about a series of tunnels underneath the compound. Many Libyans talked about them, including those who said they'd worked on their construction. But even on Tuesday – when we were reporting that Saif may have used the tunnels to avoid the Tripoli protesters in order to get in and out of the Rixos the night before – it sounded more like something out of a James Bond film.

Garwen and I edit a report using the pictures he and Jim filmed of the destruction, the celebration and the pillaging near the golden fist inside Bab al-Aziziya. Garwen is telling the others all about the fighter who was shot next to him. 'I can't get the sight of him out of my head,' he says. 'How did we cope with that?' I ask him. I still don't know. Apart from the horror of seeing another human being killed so needlessly in front of us, there's the added thought that that bullet could so easily have entered one of us. In fact, it's incredible it didn't. We talk about it among ourselves a lot. I think the other team must be sick of hearing about it but they say nothing. They know we have to share it with them, get it out.

We can hear the sound of NATO jets overhead for most of the night and they're carrying out a number of bombing raids. The explosions are loud and feel close. Horribly close. We're all shattered, but the banter among the two crews keeps us all going. Everyone is working flat out, but there's still time for some competitive jousting and catching up.

'Fucking hell, couldn't you have left us *some* of the revolution to cover?' Stuart says. He's keen to hear all about the taking of

Green Square, as well as what it was like at our end of the compound. He's feeling a little frustrated because he thinks he's arrived at the story too late and been beaten to it by his arch-competitor, albeit friend. Anyone who knows Stuart will realize just what an understatement 'a little frustrated' is. Talking to him at this stage is like being in the middle of a Quentin Tarantino movie, someone says. There's such a stream of profanities pouring out of him. He's beside himself. He's come straight from his family holiday in Ibiza – straight from beaches, dancing and loud music – so it's a bit of a gear change.

Ramsay has spent much of the previous six months covering events in Libya. He's spent weeks and weeks away from his young family and holed up in the Rixos Hotel, trying to dodge the minders and the regime apparatchiks, to tell the real story of oppression in Libya. He's passionate about the story. He was waiting for this very moment like so many other foreign journalists. Now he feels he's missed out on the denouement and he can't believe his bad luck and rotten timing. He knows we already think we are handing over the baton to him and his team. 'You know you're not going home yet, guys, don't you?' he says to us, more than once. We just smile at him, disbelievingly. Of course we are. It's job done, isn't it? Green Square's been taken, the compound's been invaded. Surely Gaddafi is beaten, isn't he?

Stuart fills us in on a lot of the news which we have missed, telling us that late on Sunday night/Monday morning – when the rebels marched into Tripoli and Green Square – the ITN news crew led by John Ray had headed towards the Rixos, only to be arrested as soon as they walked in. They believed the hotel had been retaken by the rebels. Both Stuart and I know John.

He used to work at Sky with us. Are we really talking about events which happened barely two days ago? Thank God – in so many ways – that we never made it to the Rixos. Poor John. He must be feeling a little frustrated himself. How awful to have made it through the gunfire into Tripoli only to find yourself thwarted by possibly the only Gaddafi forces left in charge in the capital.

The five-star Rixos Hotel has now become a very dangerous place indeed for the journalists inside. There are thirty-five people trapped, representing television channels, newspapers and organizations from around the world (these include Sky, BBC, CNN, Reuters, Fox News, Associated Press and a Chinese television crew.) The AP reporter Dario Lopez-Mills calls it a '£500-a-night prison'. They're now effectively human shields for the renegade Gaddafi men guarding them. They're feeling very, very vulnerable.

The journalists have been held at gunpoint for the past five days. They're been starved of information about what's going on just a short distance away. Most of the hotel staff have fled, leaving just the guards behind. Neither the journalists nor the guards really know what's going on or who is in charge outside. They can hear shooting and explosions and obvious signs of battle all around them. Their Internet access has been blocked, increasing the sense of isolation. They're all becoming increasingly nervous about what's going to happen to them.

Stuart tells us our Sky colleagues Jude and Darren are holding up OK but are understandably getting more and more keen to get out. They're still able to make intermittent calls using their satellite phone, but their guards have accused them of being Western spies and threatened them with execution. Everyone is desperate to get out of this fevered atmosphere.

Even so, the journalists and crews are showing incredible fortitude and bravery. They've managed to explore parts of the hotel, despite being under guard, and they've discovered that Libyan state television used to broadcast from the hotel's basement. So the Libyan television presenter brandishing a gun on air insisting she would defend Colonel Gaddafi to the end was doing that from the Rixos? It seems so. Colonel Gaddafi turned up at least once, unexpectedly. Was he staying at the hotel too? None of us would be surprised at this stage.

They've also found a room which has been used to store copies of computer printouts. They're the email exchanges between the journalists who've been staying in the hotel and their offices across the world. There's been a long-held suspicion among the journalists that the regime was somehow intercepting their mail. This was dismissed as paranoia. It seems everyone underestimated the Colonel, his hunger for power and his appetite to manipulate. There are files and files and files of printouts of every email conversation.

We hear from the office in London that Andy has made it back to the hospital, doing the return leg in the same ambulance which took patients out earlier. He'll stay there until we reunite with him the next day.

It's the early hours by the time we're able to think about sleeping. Most of the men slip into their sleeping bags on the roof of the farmhouse, with some on the floor of the room just off it, alongside the kitchenette. It's still unbelievably hot and there is a chance of a light breeze here. I take the one empty back room, which has a slim mattress.

We manage one or two hours' rest before we're all up again. We have much to do. I suggest the Ramsay team move into 'our' hospital. It feels like our hospital. We've been the only non-medical staff or patients staying there and we're a familiar sight wandering the corridors. The hospital, to my mind, is ideally located for covering the battle in the capital. It is close to Green Square (now renamed Martyrs' Square) and the compound. We all suspect there will be developments today, yet we have no clue what they will be. The teams definitely need to be much nearer the centre and ready to respond.

Garwen, Jim and I are anxious to see Andy again. It seems weird not being with him. We're also – to be honest – all still thinking, hoping that this might be it for us. We've had only about six hours' sleep since Sunday and we're working on automatic now. We know we need to help out with the practicalities for the new team – such as finding somewhere for them to safely stay closer to the centre – but once that's sorted, surely we can start planning our journey home? That's going to take some time anyway.

Sky has a few teams in the area by now, all working round the clock to broadcast the latest news concerning the fast-moving developments. But we're all spread across a huge city, one which is still fragile and insecure. There's the presentation team in the capital, anchored by Anna Botting and produced by Tim Gallagher, who is leading this squad. This allows Sky to 'double anchor' its news coverage. It means the channel will have a presenter anchoring from its London base as well as Anna out in the field – on the ground – presenting the news programmes from currently the most talked-about capital in the world.

The director in London will cut between the two presenters in two capitals, so the viewer will get a comprehensive round-up of events from Tripoli, as well as finding out what's happening around the rest of the world. Anna is the front person, the linchpin who will link the different reports coming in from myself, Stuart and Ian. She will also manage interviews from this spot and co-ordinate the different comments and statements from inside Libya – from the Opposition, from the remnants of the Gaddafi regime and from ordinary Libyans – but also comments and statements coming in from politicians or activists across the globe.

One of Tim's jobs as her producer is to liaise with Sky's British HQ, informing his opposite number in the London studio gallery of any interviews he has arranged in Libya and receiving information back from the producer in London about interviews or comments they have got from, say, Barack Obama in Washington, David Cameron in Downing Street, Nicolas Sarkozy from the Elysée Palace, or any other significant figure. Anna will have to manage linking these all together, moving from one topic or report or interviewee to another – often with just a few seconds' notice and a few words of direction in her earpiece from the director in London.

The presentation team is key to the channel's output. They have to be in as secure a position as is possible in a war zone, one where they can present hours of rolling live coverage in relative safety. The team has managed to find a separate safe house in the west of Tripoli, near a school building and near the rebel command headquarters. Right now it's probably one of the most impregnable places in the city.

One of the reasons this is hugely essential is because they are the least mobile of any of the Sky teams in the field on account of their presentation role. They have with them a satellite dish which they are using to broadcast the best-quality pictures possible in High Definition. Just dismantling the dish takes a certain amount of time and expertise. It is a lot less mobile than the Began. Although engineer Steve Peters is among the quickest and most proficient at this of anyone alive, it means the team is restricted and their movements somewhat limited. On the plus side, it means Sky can broadcast the sharpest pictures possible, compared to the slightly fuzzy productions from the portable Begans operated by the mobile reporter teams (i.e. us, Ramsay and Ian Woods). We can also send edited reports back via the dish that much more quickly compared to the lengthy chugging time it takes via the Began.

The Botting team is on air pretty much most of the time right now because so much is happening. It never lets up. Sky also has Ian Woods and his crew moving round Tripoli, scouting for information. He's travelled in from Zawiya, where he passed by our farmhouse and stayed overnight. Ian and cameraman Richie Vale have moved into the Botting household, which is now full to overflowing. Ian and Richie are heading off to the compound this morning to see what the situation is like on the ground there.

Moving news teams around a war zone is just as much of a military operation as conducting ground troops. It's taking all the resources and energy of the news desk teams back in London to keep on top of events and stay one step ahead. They're working back-to-back shifts as our back-up, support and information conduits. They act as the contact point for everyone out in the field, ensuring they've thought of everything in terms of safety, the news angles and the political developments in Libya and beyond.

Much of their skill is in anticipating what's likely to happen ahead of it actually happening and responding to it as quickly as possible when anything does kick off.

They're also keeping a close eye on all the industry competition. If Al Jazeera is reporting on fresh fighting in the east, then they will pass it on. If Reuters is saying there are Gaddafi snipers in the south of the city, then that's critical information which may affect our movements and they'll also pass that on to us. They're watching a bank of television monitors with pictures and reports coming in from international reporters all over Libya. And they'll be taking calls and emails from politicians, bloggers, activists and regime supporters all at the same time.

Libya isn't the only story they have to deal with. It might be the one dominating the headlines and most of the news bulletins and it's also where most of their staff are based. But they have to keep abreast of what's happening elsewhere too – in Egypt, Yemen, Syria – in case there are developments there which require a response.

When we arrive at the hospital we find Andy wandering around in a stupor in the quadrangle. It turns out he has had a somewhat disturbed night. He was asleep in the showpiece Gaddafi ward when a gang of rebels burst in armed with guns looking for Gaddafi loyalists. He is awoken by a torchlight being shone in his face and loaded guns pointing in the same direction. After much frantic negotiating and explaining he manages to persuade them he is nothing more than a *sihafi* who is waiting for the rest of his team. But he moves downstairs to a tiny empty office on the ground floor just to be on the safe side. There's still limited staff at the hospital, while the patients keep arriving in a relentless stream. There's not even enough floor space for us all to sleep in this office. It's the end of our stay here.

The kind Dr Muhammad is still with us. I ask him if he knows anywhere we can stay, anywhere at all. Just a bit of floor space, that's all we're asking. He goes off to ask around, I think. He doesn't talk much. He just says what's needed. I think he's still terribly tired. I know that feeling. The whole city seems to be suffering from lack of sleep. Garwen and Jim are filming even more of the incoming casualties. I spot Garwen pushing a wheelchair-bound man into the hospital. There aren't even the nurses to fetch drinking water, so Garwen is offering him some.

Stuart and his team are busy working, setting up a live position from outside the hospital. Andy is trying to find the microphone I left in a rebel car the day before. It's a hopeless task. In the meantime I'm left in charge of the remaining equipment piled in this office. I'm told it's an important job. It's actually babysitting. I can't stay awake any longer. I try, but this sudden inertia has rendered me utterly useless. I sit down on the small, two-seater couch and fall asleep. I hear the occasional doctor come in, and one puts a white medical sheet over me. I barely register it.

Dr Muhammad returns. He says he's found somewhere we can stay. This man is a saint. I'm sure of it. He says he's not sure it will be suitable, but perhaps we should have a look. It's about eight minutes' drive away from the hospital. Garwen, Jim, Andy and I set off with him in his car. When we get there he opens the door to not one but three apartments all in the same building. There's even a rooftop space for broadcasting live using our Begans. The apartments belong to his family. His younger brother has been looking after them. Now they're ours. We find them quite suitable.

It is incredible generosity. Astonishing, actually. We cannot believe it. We would have jumped at the offer and been grateful if he'd said we could all camp down on the floor of his living room. Now we have three apartments. They are modern and fully furnished, each flat having its own fridge and cooking area. There are beds – proper beds – with frames and mattresses and sheets. There are two bedrooms in one of the apartments and one in each of the two others. There are sofas and bathrooms too. Oh my gosh. We're getting better accommodation here than if we were in a functioning hotel – and there aren't any of those in the capital right now. The building also has power. It's in an area where electricity has been restored or is being maintained somehow. Even more astonishingly, Dr Muhammad is saying he doesn't want any payment for this. Don't be ridiculous, we all chant. Andy says in his firmest voice that this arrangement is unacceptable, that we can't stay here unless we pay. It's the sort of tone he normally reserves for me when he's asking me to do an online report. I often hear him using the phrase 'this is non-negotiable, Alex', but in this case it's Dr Muhammad on the receiving end.

We rush back to the hospital to tell the others the news. Stuart and his team are still outside, broadcasting. There's been shooting and more fighting, he says. It's coming from the direction of Bab al-Aziziya, the Gaddafi compound. Some Gaddafi men appear to be guarding the entrance to the underground tunnels. Is Ian Woods, our Sky colleague, still there? The London news desk tells us he's had to pull out because of the firing. There seems to be a group of Gaddafi men still holed up inside, near the South Gate.

Garwen goes into action again with his camera – with me following – into the hospital. There is a European television crew there. A French cameraman is sitting on a hospital bed, waiting to be seen by a medic. His hand is pressing a blood-soaked cloth to his throat and chin. 'Oh my God, what's happened?' I ask. 'Do you need any help?' His female colleague is very stressed and tries to shoo me away. 'He can't talk. Leave him, please. Our office knows about it. Thank you.' They've all had a terrible scare. But the cameraman reassures her. 'It's fine,' he says.

He is Bruno Girodon, the husband of the former *Sunday Times* journalist Janine di Giovanni, herself a war veteran but at home now looking after their son Luca. He knows the importance of information and how essential it is in a place like this. He says his crew – who work for France 2 television – were walking next to the compound when shooting broke out. 'There are troops and snipers still all around,' he says.

During the firing a bullet has ricocheted off the road and gone through the skin under Bruno's chin. He's been left with a hairline fracture to his jaw, but the bullet has exited without actually catching a major artery or vein. He has temporary hearing loss too. It was so close. It's astonishingly similar to the incident involving the French blogger in Misrata but with a miraculously different outcome. 'Jesus,' I say, 'just a bit this way or a bit the other way ...' Be quiet, Alex, I'm saying to myself. I think he knows what a close shave that was.

'I know,' Bruno says, shaking his head. He asks if we can help them find some transport. They need to pick up their belongings and leave. They're heading out of Libya. Their office is pulling them. Enough is enough. 'Of course, of course,' I say.

Once bandaged up, Bruno follows and does an interview with Stuart at our live camera position. Stuart knows his wife Janine from various war zones around the world. At the end of it Bruno says: 'God, I hope Janine isn't watching. I haven't told her yet.' Stuart tells him he had better ring soon before someone else tells Janine they've seen her bloodied and shot husband on Sky News. We all laugh, including Bruno, despite his fractured jaw. Sometimes it's the only way you can get through this. You have to have a macabre sense of humour and just push on.

Stuart is again trying to prepare us for the inevitable, trying to break us out of this mindset we've got ourselves into. We've been going round all day today holding invisible plane boarding passes in our hands. 'You know you won't be leaving just yet, don't you?' he says again. 'There's still too much to do. Green Square was not the end.' He's right. We're realizing ourselves, with sinking hearts, that we're not going to get out of Tripoli tonight, maybe not for a few days yet.

For a start, we don't have anyone who will drive us out. An exit from here is going to take some organizing if it's to be done safely. It's far too late in the day today and, anyway, there's a lot of reporting yet to be done. All the Sky teams on the ground in Tripoli are going to be working full throttle to get the whole picture covered. Damn it. We're desperately disappointed as we fight our extreme tiredness. But none of us wants to leave a story in mid-flow. In fact, if we'd been ordered to leave, we'd be resisting. We have to just recharge and then we'll be up and running again.

We hear that the situation is shifting for the journalists in the Rixos. A team from the Red Cross has gone in – white flags waving – to rescue them. All the escapees, including our colleagues, have been taken to the Corinthia Hotel. Their guards either put down their weapons or flee when the 7th Cavalry arrives. John Ray and his ITN crew bolted out of the hotel earlier, through a rear fire exit. They've thumbed a lift and been taken in by people in the neighbourhood who are looking after them. Tom and Andy are trying to work out how to pick up Jude and Darren from the Corinthia. The two of them say they'll stay with the rest of the freed journalists in the Corinthia for at least one night while we come up with a plan to get them.

We wait for a while, arranging transport to get us back to the apartments. There's still such chaos and unpredictability in the city. It's hard to find those who have vehicles, who have fuel, and who are also prepared to drive through these crazily dangerous streets. There's also a feeling of desperation setting in among the residents of Tripoli. Much of the water supply has been cut because pumping is dependent on electricity, which is very intermittent. The shops are shut and businesses closed down. It's been like this for days now and, among the people in the city centre, there is growing panic about how long this situation is going to last. Food and water are scarce. We see people fighting in the street over bottles of water.

We have dwindling rations ourselves and somehow we need to build up a stockpile. We're all starving and thirsty. The temperature stays stubbornly in the forties and everyone is dehydrated. The owner of the small shuttered shop outside the hospital is persuaded to open for a short while, especially while there is a small group of customers outside. If it's safe enough for people to stand around, then it's safe enough to open up. We're lucky because at least we have money. Many of the locals don't even have that because the banks aren't opening. We quickly buy as much as we can carry back to the apartments – water, soft drinks, dried pasta and yet more canned tuna. This seems to be the only food available right now. The Libyans must be a nation of tuna lovers. This is really going to stretch Andy's culinary skills. We can't wait for him to test out our new cooker.

Garwen, Andy, Jim and I set off for the apartments with our stash of food and drink, leaving the others still broadcasting from the hospital. When we get back we find to our dismay that the water has run out. Jim and Garwen climb onto the roof to check the water tanks. They've run dry. One of the neighbours has a well, so we knock on his door and he lets the guys fill up a couple of barrels. On the way back, we find a tiny shop selling spices, sugar and salt out of large metal containers. People are struggling to find bread, milk, water and flour, yet the specialist spice man is open. It's bizarre. We buy a selection to spice up the tuna pasta. That'll put fire in our bellies.

Jim and Andy are cooking up a storm of a meal with huge, army-sized portions of chilli tuna pasta. We are on the floor with tiredness by the time the other team return. They must be shattered too, but somehow you feel it more when you stop and rest. At least that's what I tell them. It's so much more tiring doing nothing. That does not go down quite as well as the chilli tuna pasta. The other team continue broadcasting from our position on the roof and start work on an edit for the morning. Tom Rayner has somehow managed to get all their belongings from their previous safe house out of town and relocated it to the new apartments.

Garwen, Jim, Andy and I are starting to feel a little guilty now about just how much work the Ramsay team is doing in comparison to our sparse on-air offerings. 'Yes, but we did sort out the accommodation, the food, the water and the tuna pasta,' I say. 'I mean, we'd all be really bloody stuck up shit creek without a paddle if we hadn't done that, wouldn't we?' 'Hmmm, yes,' Stuart says, 'but any bloody chance you could give us a hand with the fucking journalism now?' 'Christ, you're grateful. I don't think you've actually said thanks to us yet,' I reply. The others chuckle. They're used to this good-humoured rivalry.

The two teams sit down together and work out a plan about how we're going to split the coverage and cover the story between us the following morning. We've got some food inside us and a safe place where we can stay for the foreseeable future. Now we're all going to have to find some energy from somewhere and get back to work.

Chapter Fifteen

REVENGE

Thursday, 25 August

We've been out only a short time when we come across the first two dead bodies. I spot them before I see anything else because they're almost immediately outside the South Gate of the Bab al-Aziziya compound, which we've just walked through. They're slightly isolated in the middle of one of two grassy roundabouts just outside the complex. They have their hands tied behind their backs with plastic flex and they're face down on the ground. It's immediately apparent they've been executed. Both the cadaver heads and what I can see of their faces are in a terrible state because of gunshot damage. The temperature is still more than forty degrees and the corpses are bloated, with clouds of flies buzzing round their wounds.

None of their injuries are as shocking as the sight of hands tied behind their backs. It's the helplessness of these men, the utter inability to have done anything but await death, which screams out. Christ, I'm suddenly noticing more of them. Garwen's not saying a word. He's just moving among the bodies, silently filming this awful scene.

We notice half a dozen more bodies scattered along the same grassy patch. Most – but not all – have their hands bound. They have the dark skins of sub-Saharan Africans. They look like they could be Gaddafi mercenaries. He recruited mostly from Chad, Niger, Algeria and Sudan. They're wearing no uniforms, only jeans and T-shirts. It's not immediately clear who they are. Burnt vehicles litter the road next to the roundabout. There are all the signs that there's been a fierce battle here. But it's the bodies which stand out among the wreckage. We're just staring at this grotesque scene, trying to work out what's happened, when an ambulance loaded with doctors drives past. They're the doctors we know from Zawiya, the same group of doctors we followed into the hospital, the same senior doctor who insisted we get a place in his ambulance in the front seat.

Their collective demeanour is now so very different. They're quiet and sombre and, like us, they don't like what they're seeing. We exchange muted greetings. None of us knows who killed these men. But if they are mercenaries, or if others even thought they were mercenaries, then this points to a rebel revenge attack. It's horrifying to look at, disgusting and violent. This is war, and war is merciless and brutal and unfair. There are few heroes. Men who were once engineers, metal-workers and farmers are now killers. And someone has tied up these men and fired a bullet through their brains.

The way the bodies are lying – all spread out – makes it appear the killings were not done simultaneously. There is a stretch of grass between each of them. Did some have to watch as their friends and colleagues were executed? We've hardly said more than a few words to the doctors before there's the sound of shooting from the direction of a block of flats on the opposite side of the roundabout. We're on the fringes of the Abu Salim area, a Gaddafi loyalist district. The bullets are coming in our direction, thumping the grassy embankment we're on. Someone is watching us from the flats. We're the new targets. We bolt.

The ambulance with the doctors screeches off and we run blindly away in the direction of the second roundabout, desperately trying to find cover. There are tents and we run towards them. We can see a group of rebel fighters already there, crouching behind them. They're shouting and waving their hands at us: 'Come, come. Snipers, snipers.' We stop, panting. So there are some Gaddafi forces still here and they aren't too far away either.

It goes quiet again. I can see there are many more tents farther along. We start walking round the encampment, slowly and hesitantly at first. Stuart has told me there used to be a camp of pro-Gaddafi loyalists set up at the back of Bab al-Aziziya. He and the other journalists staying at the Rixos several weeks earlier were taken there by the regime to see the Gaddafi supporters protesting about the NATO air strikes. Is this it? It's in the right location, but part of this tented village looks like a makeshift field clinic and, frankly, quite military.

There are about eight – maybe ten – tents on this second roundabout and, as I peek inside the first one, I see about five bodies scattered on the floor. One or two are on mattresses. There are drugs and medicines thrown all over the place. Another body is on a wheeled hospital bed and still has an intravenous drip in his arm. They all have bright green ribbons tied to their wrists. They look like they were patients, but these patients hadn't been able to even crawl off their beds or make it to the front of the tent before being shot and killed. This was quick. International law decrees that these men should have been taken as prisoners of war. All of them. However, if their executioners even knew about international law, they certainly hadn't been sticking to any detail when they rampaged through this encampment.

I'm walking hurriedly round the other tents now. I don't know how much time we'll have before the shooting begins again and we have to leave this area. I want to see what's in these tents. This doesn't look good and it's reeking of both retaliation and revenge. It looks to me like the work of the new power in Tripoli – the rebels. But I want to be sure. I have to be sure before saying anything. So I'm hurrying, and so is Garwen. Jim is keeping a keen lookout from close by. Our transport is parked on the roundabout verge. Andy is staying in it with Dr Muhammad's young brother, Magdi. The young lad is terrified and Andy doesn't want to risk him speeding off in fright if the firing starts again and leaving all of us stranded. He's working hard to calm him.

Garwen and I walk through the tents, one by one. Some seem to be military tents, with stacks of files in boxes and further boxes of ammunition in one corner. I pick up one of the files and flick through. It's written in beautiful, perfect-looking Arabic and has elaborate military maps and battlefield diagrams. The diagrams have been filled in with different colours, again all perfect. Someone took a lot of care with these drawings. I take it with me. I can't read the Arabic, but I want to find someone who can later, when we're out of this place. I wonder whether it will give any insight into the workings of the defeated Gaddafi army.

Outside one of the tents there are the remains of two – maybe three – burnt bodies. Parts of the remains have been utterly incinerated, reduced to black and grey ash. I wouldn't be able to make out they were even human once except, in the mid-section, we can see the bone structure of a hand with fingers and part of what looks like a leg. I'm nervous about going inside the tents now, scared about what I might see. But I can't stop myself either. Behind another tent flap there are yet more bodies. They too are lying in beds. One is on his side in a foetal position. They're wearing green Gaddafi uniforms and there are more green ribbons tied round their wrists. The ribbons are shouting out: We are Gaddafi men. We fought for him and now we've died for him.

It's a nauseating discovery, but not everyone shares our revulsion. Outside, the rag-tag group of rebels on the roundabout are surprised – even slightly amused – at our dismay, our shock. Was it only days ago that the residents of Tripoli were welcoming these people into their city as heroes? But battle and years of repression have hardened the hearts of these young men.

'These are Gaddafi's men. They are the black mercenaries he paid to kill us,' one says. They deserved it, is the overwhelming message. This is war. And this is the revenge of the victors.

Some of the rebels are trying to convince us these men died in action, during battle. It's a lie, and a ridiculous lie at that. How does a man who's been fighting end up with his hands tied behind his back and a bullet through his head? I'm angry at their nonchalance, their teenage dismissiveness, their view that these lives were cheap and somehow didn't count.

One of the fighters is setting fire to the string of tents on the first roundabout and soon a substantial part of the camp has burst into flames. The forensic evidence shrivels.

The bespoke, adapted vehicles of the Misrata rebels are turning up at the intersection of two roundabouts. They're massing again, preparing to enter the pro-Gaddafi neighbourhood of Abu Salim. We can hear the constant noise of mortars and the whistle of sniper fire. The explosions and firing are coming from the direction of Abu Salim, just a quarter of a mile away. The Misrata brigade believe the resistance is strong because they are shielding a 'big person' – possibly one of the Gaddafi sons, maybe the Colonel himself.

There's the edge of a large wood at the far end of the double roundabout from where we are, among the now burning tents. It's near where we saw the first two bodies. On the other side of the wood is the Rixos Hotel, but the road alongside it is impassable at the moment as shots are ringing out every few seconds. The rebels seem to be entering Abu Salim from several different directions. As we move down the road – watching the rebel vehicles stack up behind each other – I can see two tanks parked alongside a wall. One is hidden under a tree, presumably to avoid detection by NATO jets. Another is farther along the same wall and has been covered with branches and foliage. The wall is the perimeter of a large residential area with rows and rows of houses and apartments banked up against it. I wonder about the mindset of anyone who can position these huge military murdering machines close to where hundreds of men, women and children are living.

We get talking to a group of rebels on the back of a pick-up with an anti-aircraft gun welded on the rear. I ask one if we can go with them when they move in. He smiles. 'I can't take you, Alex. It's too dangerous.' I climb onto the back of the truck, next to him. 'Please, we need to see what's going on down there,' I say. The driver is beginning to move off slowly. He bangs on the back. 'Stop!' Then he turns to me. 'Listen, I can never live with myself if something happened to you,' he says. 'I'm sorry. Please understand. In my country I have to look after you. I'm sorry.' I stare at him for a few seconds, wondering if I can change his mind, if I should continue the persuasion. But I know I can't. It's pointless. I jump off.

The pick-up drives away with him shouting: 'I'll tell you what happened when I get back.' Damn it. That's not how television reporting – any reporting – works. I glance up and look at Garwen, who has the look of a man who thinks *that* was possibly one truck ride too many anyway.

A number of fighters are making their way on foot down one of the main roads alongside the Abu Salim district. We can just see blocks of flats over a perimeter wall which is about four feet high. I can see a few people scurrying between the flats. They look like civilians. Occasionally, I spot faces at the windows.

This is a pro-Gaddafi area and the rebels seem to be looking for an excuse to shoot anyone and anything. Some of them are just firing wildly into the apartment blocks, aiming at windows. 'What are you shooting at?' I ask between the bursts of firing. 'Gaddafi,' they say.

Gaddafi? Really, Gaddafi? Are they saying that because they mean Gaddafi *men* or an actual Gaddafi family member, or even Muammar himself? Could he still be here? Surely not. But the rebels seem to think that's a strong possibility.

The French magazine *Paris Match* has already reported that Gaddafi has evaded capture from a private house in central Tripoli a night or two ago. They say they got the information from a 'credible source'. Now the city is awash with rumours and it's hard to separate fact from fiction or wishful thinking for that matter. Right now they think Colonel Gaddafi is being shielded by loyalists here among these residential buildings of Abu Salim. They're determined to smoke him out and hunt him down if he is.

The dictator has been heard talking on a loyalist television channel, urging his supporters to carry on the fight. 'Don't leave Tripoli for the rats,' he's saying. 'Fight them and kill them.' By now there are hundreds of rebels spreading out among these homes. They're wearing jeans – some are in shorts – and they're firing anti-aircraft guns and rockets. Some have sniper guns themselves, probably liberated from the compound the night before.

We continually see dead bodies – on the side of the road, in gullies, underneath the bridges, on the concrete banks, in dry river beds. In this heat they're putrefying quickly and the stench of rotting flesh means we're not given to close inspection of these mangled corpses. It's difficult to establish whether they're rebel fighters, Gaddafi forces, immigrant workers or Libyan civilians. Many of the bodies are in a terrible state. Most of them are in civilian clothing, but at least one is dressed in a green hospital gown.

We are moving along on foot with the rebels, who have been bolstered by troops in vehicles. There is the constant sound of heavy fighting now in parts of Abu Salim. We hear explosions and the repetitive noise of heavy machine-gun fire. It's impossible to know whether the Colonel himself is here, but, judging from the gunfire coming from these apartments, there is, at the very least, a fairly large group of his soldiers or loyalists concealed among the residents.

Prisoners have been taken, but there are more enemy out there and the rebels intend to flush them out. The fire station has been ransacked, looted and sent up in flames, and a further number of Gaddafi mercenaries have been caught. The NTC has offered a substantial reward – said to be around £1 million – for the capture or killing of Colonel Gaddafi. Wanted: dead or alive. The Opposition believe Libya cannot really step into the sunlight until the people know the former dictator is dead or in prison. He could conceivably still be in the capital. But rebel columns are also closing in on Sirte, Gaddafi's birthplace. He still has a kernel of support.

There's so much happening now all over the capital. We hear the rebels are storming the infamous Abu Salim prison, the most notorious in all of Libya, smashing the locks of cells with sledgehammers and freeing all the prisoners. Pictures are being posted on YouTube of these dramatic moments. Among those released is an American journalist, Matthew van Dyke, who has been held for the past six months in solitary confinement. He looks terribly gaunt and pale and so much older than his thirty-two years. Pictures of him at the start of the uprising in March show him young and full-faced. He looks confident and alert. Now he's battered and worn and his clothes are hanging off him. He telephones his mother to let her know he is safe and being looked after by the rebels. 'I was in solitary confinement the whole time, with nothing to do but look at the wall,' he tells reporters. 'I would rather they [the guards] had just taken me out and beaten me, even every day, than go through the solitary confinement, because what it does psychologically is astonishing. I had no idea that the brain could work in the ways it did in my case.' He says he was mistaken for an American spy or a member of the CIA. He feared he would be cut off from the outside world for decades until rebels broke open his prison cell.

Now we're treading carefully as there's still more shooting. It's coming towards us. We duck behind a concrete central reservation as the bullets whistle past. We're cowering, trying to squash ourselves into as small a bundle as possible. It's not a failsafe defence against a bullet, but it makes us feel better.

I realize – to my horror – that in the scramble to find cover we have found ourselves shoulder to shoulder with one of the rebel snipers flouting a brand-new sniper gun. Christ, I don't want to be sitting right next to the sniper. He's the one man the Gaddafi soldiers will have in their cross-hairs. The rebel sniper fires accurately enough at his opposite number in the flats that he stops return fire and allows the band of rebels we're with to move farther in.

There must be about 1,000 rebels now involved in the gun battle. They're sandwiching the apartment blocks. We retreat a little and try to set up a live broadcast. I can hear Stuart Ramsay on air at the same time. He's reporting from the other side of the apartments, near the wood outside the Rixos. The fighting is so fierce in that area that Stuart and Ed have been pinned down. They've had to take cover and leave the camera recording the action live.

The hunt for the leader is fuelled even further when we hear that Moussa Ibrahim, Gaddafi's most high-profile spokesman, has telephoned the Associated Press agency to say the Colonel is safely in hiding and leading the battle. Ibrahim says the leader's morale is high. 'All our leader's family are fine,' he says. That's more than can be said for us. There are bullets flying in from everywhere and there's smoke coming out of several adjacent buildings.

We're also having terrible trouble with the Began, which seems to have decided it's weary too and not going to work very productively today. We keep rigging it up, getting a signal, waiting to go on air, and then the signal drops out seconds after we start broadcasting. It happens about three times.

The executive producer in the gallery is John Dowden, who is known for his patience. He's the father of six children and so well used to dealing with unpredictability and mayhem. This, though, is testing even John's composure. There's nothing worse in television terms than cutting short a programme that is already being successfully broadcast only to see both the picture and audio falter and fail within seconds. I think the most I manage to say before the Began's satellite signal drops out is about thirty seconds' worth of: 'There's battling, there's firing, they're searching street by street, room by room ...' It's frustrating in the extreme.

By connecting to London I do hear the occasional snippet of news through my earpiece. The Ramsay team is with the Zintan fighters and they've discovered a huge cache of weapons and ammunition buried in the woods at the back of the Rixos. It's enormous, at least six deep pits full of bullets, shells and rockets. Yet more weapons for the rebels to fight with. The team have also found at least five black men with their arms tied behind their backs and apparently executed.

Stuart is reporting that there seem to be large defections of Gaddafi forces to the rebel camps. The rebel leadership is saying its fighters have also discovered large stockpiles of medicine and food hoarded by the regime in Tripoli. The humanitarian crisis in the hospitals should now be dramatically eased.

The news desk in London says the British Defence Secretary, Liam Fox, has been telling reporters that NATO intelligence and reconnaissance systems are trying to hunt down Gaddafi. This is contradicted by the Pentagon in Washington. An official there says NATO is just conducting surveillance over Tripoli to ensure that civilians are protected from attack.

The rebels seem to be under the impression that their Western allies are using spy planes to intercept communications between loyalists and this has stoked even further the rebels' belief that

Gaddafi has not left the capital. A statement from a senior US defence council official has been given to Sky saying all the signs are Gaddafi is still in Tripoli, but there's no confirmation he's in that block of flats. The British foreign secretary, William Hague, is being quoted saying it is 'very important' Gaddafi is caught so the Libyan people know there's no chance of his returning.

Many of the NTC leaders are moving to Tripoli today. Sections of the capital might still be in flames and engaged in violent assault, but the leadership is staking its claim politically.

We're now crouching behind one of the abandoned tanks, along with a number of other journalists and photographers. There are small pockets of rebels in front of us, still firing randomly into the apartment blocks. They're out of control now. Their guns are going off wildly. They don't seem to be receiving much in the way of orders and they are certainly not giving much thought or care to where their bullets are landing. There's screaming and shouting and we realize one of the rebels has shot a fellow fighter. Hang on, there are more. No, it's not just one. It looks like three – maybe four – rebels have been hit by mistake. They're being carried by distraught friends, men who are shouting for ambulances and shouting at the others to stop firing. The friends are crying and yelling angrily at the stupidity of the other fighters around them as they load their blood-ied comrades into the back of an ambulance. We can tell immediately there's no hope for these fighters. They're already dead.

It's getting crazy around here. And it looks like it could get crazier. We have to get back to edit a report for the evening programme. Our driver Magdi has been getting increasingly jumpy about staying here much longer. Where is he? We can't find him at first. We've been so focused on trying to do a live, trying not to get hit by a maniacal rebel, trying to determine whether Gaddafi really is in the apartments, that we've lost sight of our young driver. Andy has told him to hide behind a concrete wall covered in foliage. And he has stuck to those instructions religiously.

We're now keen to get back to *our* block of flats. We find Magdi and, back at the apartment, we pile inside and tear off the flak jackets. The adrenalin has shaken us out of our stupor, which is just as well as there's lots to do yet. Garwen starts loading the pictures into the computer in preparation for the edit. Jim is getting some food and tea for us all. Andy is busy talking to London. 'There are still reports that Gaddafi is surrounded and in flats near Abu Salim,' he says. I go on air by telephone, giving my assessment based on what we've just seen – which is, who can possibly know? I'm telling them about the chaos, the mistaken shootings, the considerable confusion.

Stuart is still out at Abu Salim, cornered by the battling. He too is reporting he thinks it very unlikely that Gaddafi is in the flats. Andy has more pressing problems to worry about. We're hearing about considerable fighting going on near the Corinthia Hotel and he has to try to get our two colleagues Jude and Darren out of there. He sets off with the increasingly reluctant but ever sweet Magdi.

Garwen and I push on, preparing a report for that evening's news. There is so much developing and changing all the time, it's a considerable challenge for us all to keep on top of events. We hear Andy arriving back with Jude and Darren. He says he didn't notice any shooting. Well, that's good. Garwen and I give them a great welcome hug. They look delighted to be among friends. They're desperate to tell us what they went through while trapped in the Rixos. And what a story they have to tell.

They talk of being threatened with execution three times, how their guards were convinced they were spies working for NATO, how the armed Gaddafi men were urged to shoot them through the legs so they couldn't run away. It sounds terrifying. They look exhausted although exhilarated at being free. They explain how they were so starved of information they had no real idea who was doing the shooting, or how many guards remained outside the hotel or on the rooftop.

Our report has already gone on air during the evening programme *Sky News at Five* by the time the Ramsay team return after dark. They're very skittish and wired up from all the fighting, but there's little time for rest. They're the evening on-air live team and will be broadcasting all night with commentary to supplement our edited report.

We can hardly function any more. Around the team flat it's almost formation collapsing. Jude and Darren take the bed in the top flat. The Ramsay team are 'live' on the roof and we leave them to it. We're in the middle apartment. Andy's been taking up floor space in my room – the only bedroom – but I manage to persuade him to move outside, to the seating area. This way there is a door between me and his dreadful snoring. He takes the suggestion quite well, without any obvious offence. I had offered to let him have the bed, but it was a proposal aired with little conviction and even less sincerity. Safe in the knowledge that neither Andy nor the other guys will take me up on the offer, I repeat it. It's delivered in the tone of a woman prepared to mud-wrestle to keep her mattress. Jim and Garwen are on the L-shaped sofa. Our eyes do not stay open for long.

Chapter Sixteen

FAREWELL TO 'NEW' LIBYA

Friday–Saturday, 26–7 August

I'm sitting in the Sky safe house in Tripoli, in front of a camera and talking. Situation normal. But this is different. A different approach for a different audience and, to be honest, I'm a little nervous. That might seem a bit odd, crazy even, after all we've been through over the past few days, weeks and months, but it's true.

I'm speaking to the guests at the MediaGuardian Edinburgh International Television Festival – an eclectic audience of television's brightest, most influential, most enquiring, most senior, most junior and most questioning folk. It's an event I've never been to, but I know it's a big deal in the television realm. It showcases the industry's movers and shakers – the controversial and the powerful – as well as the 'little' people, the workers, like myself. Indeed, the *Guardian* describes it as an event where 'any researcher can just walk in and pick a fight with the BBC Director-General'.

Those who've been asked to speak in the past include television writers, producers, directors and programme-makers, as well as senior management figures like Greg Dyke, John Birt, Mark Thompson, and Rupert and James Murdoch. You get the picture. It's a big deal. I know this because my Sky bosses have been ringing me in Tripoli to find out what I'm going to say and to try to give me moral support. I'd let this appointment drift to the back of my mind during all the fighting, the attempts to stay alive – but now the day is upon us. There's no avoiding it any more.

I'd mentioned the festival talk in passing to the team during the many hours we'd spent getting into Libya. They're aware of this speaking arrangement and my nerves surrounding it. The original plan was for me to deliver a speech of about forty-five minutes. God! A speech? Nearly an hour long. Come Saturday, 27 August, I've no speech prepared. I'd been half-hoping the organizers were going to realize I was in Libya and find someone else, someone who could deliver an hour-long speech without referring to notes, someone more used to it perhaps.

Sky's associate editor, Simon Bucks, has tried to focus my mind on what I'm going to say. He's helped me draft some notes and ideas weeks ago. Thank you, Bucksy. Thank you a thousand times over. He's so often been my guide, my adviser, my mentor, the voice of reason – all these roles coupled with terrific news judgement. John Ryley has also helped, sending me ideas and trying to prepare me for what they tell me will be a notable occasion in my journalistic life.

The invitation was extended to me months ago, before Libya looked like falling to the rebels, before I was setting off for Zawiya again, before Gaddafi went on the run. Now everything we prepared back in London in the summer seems a little out of date and, anyway, I haven't fashioned it into anything resembling the sort of speech I'd like to deliver.

Andy has thought of a way through this particular minefield. He's suggested to the London office that maybe the way to do the whole thing is by satellite link – from Tripoli. The daunting speech element would be removed, to be replaced by a more manageable interview format. It's the only way we can achieve my participation at the festival at this late stage. I'm much relieved at this idea. I'm much more comfortable with the thought of just responding into the camera.

The chair in Scotland doing the questioning is the BBC presenter Jon Sopel, who is a friend I trained with at the BBC. Even better. It feels more like a chat with a mate and much more in my comfort zone.

We travel across Tripoli to get to the safe house where the satellite dish is housed. It's the first time we've seen the Anna Botting team. There's much hugging and hand-shaking all round. They all look very sunburnt and everyone has stubble – Anna obviously excluded. She's managing to appear extremely fresh, despite the heat and the lack of washing facilities. I'm making her look even better. I'm still wearing the same T-shirt I had on when we set off from Zawiya a week ago. I'm not wearing a scrap of make-up. But I know where my cosmetics bag is – in the back of the car we said goodbye to outside the Khamis Brigade headquarters last Sunday. I look incredibly tired and I feel it. We're all exhausted. Anna lends me some of her make-up and sits with me murmuring encouraging noises. 'Oh yes, much better. So much nicer.' She's being very liberal with the truth. I plaster it on my face and it does make me feel a little better, a little more confident. This stuff does do what it says on the tin.

I persuade the guys to sit outside with me to lend moral support. I'm already thinking that if I get any opportunity whatsoever I'm going to bring them into the interview. I grab a few quick words with Jon Sopel beforehand to test the sound is working and they can actually see us in Scotland and I let him know this is my plan. He agrees. He wanted to hear from them anyway.

Next thing, we're on air. Mike Inglis is the man behind the camera. I've briefed him about the guys coming on so he can adjust the shot. He's kind and I feel reassured by him. Tim G is hiding behind one of the house pillars, monitoring the feed into Scotland. If the signal goes down, he'll be the one who has to sort out the mess. Steve Peters is working his wizardry with the satellite dish, although at this stage I'm wishing the picture wasn't quite so crystal clear and perhaps a bit more fuzzy like the Began. That way no one would be able to see my notable features: tired, red eyes and unkempt hair.

Anyway, it's too late now. We're on air. I start by making a joke about how I've been made up to look this wretched and dishevelled, but I can't see the audience and I can't hear them either. Damn, I should have steered clear of trying to be a comedienne, especially in a very unamusing place like Tripoli. Jon asks me about getting into Green Square, providing the cue to bring in the lads, who are sitting on the garden wall next to me.

Me: 'Can I bring them on, Jon, because we couldn't have done it without all the team? Do you want to have a look at them? Come on, these guys are amazing. This is Andy, Cat Sat as we called him, this is Garwen, one of the cameramen, Jim Foster, the other cameraman. These are the guys that made it happen. As my ex-Foreign Editor Adrian Wells used to say, you're just the singer in the band. Well, this is the band.' I can hear the crowd – which we can't see – clapping noisily and enthusiastically as they spot the whole team for the first time. None of them, of course, can hear anything as I am the only one wearing an earpiece. They're all standing awkwardly around me as I tell them about the reaction back in Edinburgh.

The interview whizzes by, with Jon asking me a range of questions covering a variety of topics, including being a working mum and war correspondent, getting into Green Square first, and our experiences in Zawiya in March.

It's a huge relief to have it over with. As the guys hear me say thank you to Jon and Mike relaxes over the camera, they realize it's over and start clapping. We've made it through everything – even this final ordeal of the MediaGuardian Edinburgh International Television Festival. It's time to think about going home.

There is a big problem with the transport. We were all hoping to share the vehicles which were taking the other team out led by Ian Woods, but he has gone on ahead with Jude and Darren. They're anxious about being caught up in firing and it's definitely better to leave early while most of the fighters from both sides are sleeping off their Ramadan meals. We're going to have to wait a bit longer while we find alternative ways of getting away from here. If we can only get to Zawiya, then our friends there will be able to help us.

I sit down on the sofa and immediately fall into a deep sleep. About an hour or two later I'm woken by Stuart. 'Oh my God, you have got to see this,' he says. He takes me into the kitchen, where he and Ed are trying to edit. On the monitor is a picture of charred bodies, most burnt beyond recognition. They look barely human but they are human. There are human skulls, there are the finger bones, there are femurs. The corpses are still burning, smoke rising from them. After ten days of seeing gruesome sight after gruesome sight, this is yet another one. Will it never stop? Ed's camera lens moves along the floor, showing body after body after body. 'They were killed by the Khamis Brigade,' Stuart says.

His team has just returned from scouting the south-east of Tripoli. They've encountered some fierce fighting near a warehouse. The locals tell them it was being used as a temporary prison by the brigade and run by the Colonel's much-feared son Khamis. Once the firing has tailed off, they've been urged by the residents to look in the warehouse. As they're approaching they can sense the stench. The locals are pressing scarves and cloth to their mouths and noses to try to block out the awful smell.

Stuart has spoken to the residents, one of whom says he was a recent prisoner in the warehouse himself. He tells them that they were detained by the Khamis Brigade and accused of supporting the rebels. Some of them had been held for months, with limited food and water despite the fierce summer heat. He somehow managed to escape when the soldiers began shooting at them and throwing grenades.

I look at the pictures and immediately feel we should not be leaving Libya. There's so much more to do, so much more to uncover, so much more still evolving. We're hearing that the rebel forces and armed civilians are rounding up thousands of black Libyans and migrants from sub-Saharan Africa, accusing them of fighting for Gaddafi. They're being held in makeshift jails across the capital. Stuart and his team have seen many being hauled in by the Opposition fighters. Virtually all of them maintain they're innocent migrant workers. There's nothing to suggest they're lying, but that's not stopping the rebels from punching, kicking and, in some cases, just summarily shooting them. Every immigrant is now seen as the enemy and years of pent-up resentment against the Gaddafi regime is being visited on these poor souls.

We want to contribute towards the team effort, but we know we just don't have the energy. We're not going to be much good to anyone and, right now, we're itching to leave.

Andy somehow manages to persuade two men to take us to Zawiya, where we have fuel stored. That in itself is enough to tempt them to make the journey. Being paid in fuel? It's got to be worth it. No one knows what the road is like, but we're hearing through the journalists' grapevine that others have made the trip and their journey was uneventful. That doesn't mean it will be the same for us, but it's the only way out.

We say goodbye to the others. It's always tough leaving a story which is still live. Normally we'd have to be levered out of here, but we're all truly spent. In our tired minds we can see home, our families, soothing baths, crunchy salads, and a cold glass of wine at the end of the very long road we're about to embark on.

I don't really notice the drive to Zawiya. It's spent in a haze, slumbering in the back of the van. My head is colliding with the back seat, also a passenger window, as we fly over bumps and potholes. The others are drifting in and out of sleep too, judging by the contortions of their necks and their open mouths.

By the time we arrive in Zawiya it's dark but we notice a change instantly. There is power. There are streets lights on and even some stalls open. I see three men sitting outside what looks like a café, watching a television which has been pinned on the wall. They're watching news about Libya. There's nothing else anyone is interested in right now. What a change in just a few days. It's almost normal.

Ahmida is there to meet us, along with Abdul al-Zaq. What would we have done without these guys? They've been so protective of us, so caring, so generous with their time. We head off to the house, where we give the drivers their fuel reward and send them back on their way to Tripoli. We pack Ahmida's cars with our luggage as the house owner now wants his property back. It's another sign of the change in Zawiya. His family is due back any time soon. Zawiya is now considered safe enough to return home to. Things are moving so quickly.

Ahmida takes us to another house which again seems half-built. It has no power, but a room for us to camp on the floor. We're not here long. We're up before dawn to make the long drive to the Tunisian border and Djerba. We use head torches to have showers and use some of our fuel to power a little gas ring. It heats up the pot noodles, which are getting lonely in our food stores.

As we near the Tunisian border we see streams of people, their vehicles piled high with goods, heading back *into* Libya. There's also a little rebel souvenir stall already selling flags, key rings, hats, T-shirts – all in the Opposition tricolour of red, green and black. Before only the brave and the fighters dared wave this flag. Now everyone wants one.

Our mobile phones start to ping into action as we're crossing the border into Tunisia. Normality at last, or at least signs of it. My friend of more than twenty years, Di Porter – who is not a journalist but an interior designer – is bizarrely the first person to contact me.

I'm still in a sort of drunken, sleepy state – still bouncing around the car – when she somehow manages to get through. I don't even really realize at this point that the phones are back in action. It startles us all. We've got used to being in a communication-free zone.

Di tells me there's an article in the *Sunday Times* by columnist India Knight. She's collapsing in giggles at the other end of the phone, obviously with the paper out in front of her. 'She says she's got a massive schoolgirl crush on you, Crawfie.' Di's howling with laughter. 'She says you must have gigantic balls of titanium which must be the reason you're only filmed from the waist up. It's hilarious.' I must admit, it does sound very funny. India Knight is a funny woman. Wish I could write like that.

We don't realize it yet but there's been quite a media storm following our ride into Tripoli, based primarily on two things. First, it was Sky in the vanguard and not the state broadcaster, the BBC. Second, of the four journalists on the back of the rebel pick-up truck, one of them was not only a woman but, above all things, a mother. Not just a mother of one or two but, blimey, four children. I mean, *four* children! Good grief. Has she not heard of contraception? Does she not realize how irresponsible she's being by reporting from the back of a truck in a war zone? Whatever next.

John Ryley calls me to find out if we are safely out of Libya and says: 'I don't think you realize what an impact the coverage has had.' He's right. We've no idea whatsoever.

Thursday, 20 October
My family has just landed in Cape Town on the South African coast. It's a school break and we're taking a few days to visit our old friends Amanda and Bruce Walker. We've just got back from the

airport and pulled up our chairs at a beautiful open-air restaurant in Newlands to enjoy lunch when Kate Shaw from the Viney (literary) Agency rings me. 'Gaddafi's dead,' she says. 'Go, go,' says Rick. 'What? I can't believe you,' says Frankie.

I spend the next twelve hours trying to get back to Johannesburg in an effort to catch an international flight and get to Tripoli. I am desperate to be there, desperate to see the Libyan reaction, desperate to find out what happened, desperate to piece together the last moments of this man who has ruled the country so ruthlessly for forty-two years.

Garwen is equally fired up. He's rushing back from Durban, where he's been with his family. I spend hours in Cape Town airport as my flight's delayed, watching mobile phone footage of a bedraggled, bloodied old man being pushed and shoved around by an angry mob with guns on the bonnet of a pick-up truck in Sirte. Despite the shaky nature and poor quality of the footage, the man looks unmistakably like Colonel Gaddafi. The 69-year-old dictator is dazed, barely conscious, and pleading for his life. He has blood around his chest and face. He's surrounded by a crowd and, over the constant screaming, there is shooting. You can hear someone shouting: 'Keep him alive.' The crowd is pushing and shoving to get near him, get a piece of him. Gaddafi can be heard asking one of them: 'What did I ever do to you? Do you know right from wrong?' and 'Don't shoot! Don't shoot!'

Somehow the person who is taking the mobile phone pictures pushes his way to the front and his camera catches Gaddafi being dragged off the vehicle and pulled along the ground. He's not human to them any more. He's not their Brother Leader, he's not a grandfather and father. He's just a piece of meat. He's still alive at this point but wounded, probably fatally. It looks like he has gunshot wounds to his leg and back but he's also been beaten badly. Blood is pouring from his head. We see him touching his head. He looks at his hand covered with blood. He can't believe this. It is a profoundly disturbing series of film clips, barbaric in nature. This is mob rule. Pure savagery. The next footage which emerges shows him dead and being dragged through the streets in nearby Misrata.

Every television screen in the airport is running this footage continuously and the waiting passengers, me included, are watching with a mixture of fascination and complete horror.

I never make it to Tripoli this time. My location and the length of time it's going to take to make the journey mean a number of my colleagues are going to get to the key locations before me. I am horribly disappointed. I feel like I have missed out on a dramatic twist in Libyan history which has all the hallmarks of a Shakespearean tragedy. I am fascinated by what happened to Gaddafi and now eager to see what happens in the country from here on in. But I can't persuade my bosses to send me. They're just not having any of it.

We may never know exactly what happened to Colonel Gaddafi in the last few hours leading up to his horrific ending, but this is what has been pieced together by eye-witnesses. He had been hiding in his home town of Sirte, the last centre of resistance after eight months of fighting. But, as the rebels closed in, he had tried to escape in a convoy of about 100 vehicles. Where he was heading is unclear – maybe Niger, but probably Bani Walid, just south of Tripoli. He didn't get very far before the convoy was spotted by NATO. A US Predator drone and a French Rafale jet bombed it, destroying about a dozen cars and killing around fifty loyalist fighters. A spokesman for NATO said in a statement: 'At the time of the strike we did not know that Gaddafi was in the convoy. These armed vehicles were leaving Sirte at high speed and were attempting to force their way around the outskirts of the city. The vehicles were carrying a substantial amount of weapons and ammunition, posing a significant threat to the local civilian population. The convoy was engaged by a NATO aircraft to reduce the threat.'

The air attack splintered the convoy into several groups, which fled, some on foot. Gaddafi managed to hide with a small group of his bodyguards inside two nearby storm drains or sewers, leaving a trail of blood which was spotted and followed by Opposition fighters. By this stage, Gaddafi already had injuries in both his legs and possibly his abdomen. The first mobile phone footage uploaded on the Internet shows him being dragged from these drains before we finally see him shirtless and bloody on the ground. The actual moment of death doesn't appear to have been filmed. The NTC at first says he was shot in a crossfire – but it looks more like he was summarily executed in the head or the stomach. Other footage emerges of his son Mo'atissim. He is seen sitting and smoking before there is an announcement that he too has died.

By Friday – the day after – both bodies are put on display in Misrata, in a freezer room normally used to store perishable supermarket goods. Hundreds upon hundreds line up to see for themselves that the Brother Leader is finally gone. Some take photographs of themselves with the dead dictator on their mobile phones. People even upload pictures onto Facebook showing themselves in the freezer with the two dead bodies. It's as though the two men have forfeited all human right to dignity even in death.

Friday, 18 November

Less than a month later the Colonel's most high-profile son, Saif al-Islam, is captured. This time the NTC is determined to take him alive. He is taken, alongside several bodyguards, near the town of Obari in Libya's southern desert. His guards have been trying to smuggle him out to Niger. The Libyans are determined he will stand trial in his own country despite a warrant for his arrest by the International Criminal Court. Saif has already told the ICC he is innocent of the crimes against humanity of which he is accused.

Libya has rid itself of the Gaddafi mafia. After more than four decades of being ruled by a tyrant who bought up foreign mercenaries to fire on his own people, suppressed free speech, kept his population poor and terrorized, they are free to start over.

But it has a long way to go before it can claim to be democratic – and it has an awful lot of challenges ahead.

Perhaps the final words on Libya's future should go to Mr Alwindi. Remember him? He's the young guy who walked into Colonel Gaddafi's bedroom and claimed his hat. 'Libyans are not afraid of anyone any more,' he says, 'so I am generally optimistic, but there're also a lot of bad things going on here – corruption and Gaddafi-ism.' Interestingly, he uses the word 'Gaddafi-ism'. Remnants of the old era still exist, are still manipulating, still working. Gaddafi himself may have been erased but his thinking, his modus operandi, his supporters, or what's left of them, are still out there in some numbers. We've even seen the 'retaking' of Bani Walid, with the green flag of Gaddafi being raised there in the months after the fall of the regime.

Many people feel suspicious of certain members of the National Transitional Council. They feel they are weak and not knowledgeable about politics. There are a huge number of weapons now across the country, with just about everyone owning a gun or several guns. The militia who gave up their jobs, livelihoods and families to take to the streets and fight are now demanding stakes in any future government. They don't want to lay down their arms because once they do they feel they will lose the hard-won 'power' they fought for. Men who were previously unemployed have become heroes following the battles. The whole power base in this huge country has shifted. Families and whole communities have had to adapt to the war. They may have changed allegiances to survive, settled old scores out of revenge, or are waiting to. Tribes who have existed for four decades under one structure and one set of rules and one power base are now having to rethink and realign. And, of course, there are still the elections to be held. For more than forty years the country has existed with no notable political parties or a political structure or mechanism. Before elections are even held, the NTC – supposedly the good guys – are talking of the possibility of using violence to quell the counter-revolution in places like Bani Walid. Has the revolution turned full circle? It's certainly nowhere near over yet.

Mr Alwindi still has the Colonel's hat. He's been offered huge amounts of money to sell it. But he and his father are not interested. 'This hat is priceless,' he says. 'It means a lot to me and to those who gave their lives for the freedom of Libya.'

He's waiting for a museum – a secure museum – in which they plan to display the hat. 'It might take two to three years before a safe place can be found,' Mr Alwindi says. It might do, Mr Alwindi, it might do.

ACKNOWLEDGEMENTS

I still can't quite believe that all we witnessed and lived out in these pages happened in such a short period, less than a year. I have tried my best to be as accurate as possible in remembering what happened as seen through my eyes.

I really couldn't have experienced – and perhaps more importantly, got through – what is outlined in this book without my hugely supportive family. They are my grounding. Thanks doesn't quite cut it. My daughter Frankie said: 'Will Dad's name be on the book as well or will you be taking all the credit?' So on the button as always. Whatever credit there may be goes to Richard as an all-round sounding board and home editor.

Oceans of thanks to all my children – Nat, Frankie, Maddy and Flo – to whom I have managed to bequeath my complete lack of patience and who I think got quite good at Fruit Ninja during my scribblings. I hope you think it's been worth it.

It has never been a solo journey and nothing would have been possible without the team of fellow witnesses who – luckily for me – were with me all the way. I can't say enough to thank them and frankly I am proud to count such stonking human beings and incredible professionals like them as my great friends. Thanks to you all for your wisdom, friendship and humour over so many years – Martin Smith, Garwen McLuckie, Jim Foster, Stuart Ramsay, Neville Lazarus, Tim Miller and Andy Marsh.

They filled in my memory gaps, acted as thoughtful prompts and have generally been tremendously encouraging. Grateful thanks too for the excellent pictures and extensive notes provided by Neville, and for the pictures provided by both Neville and Tom Rayner. Thanks also to John Ryley, who encouraged me to write this book, and then gave me the space and time to make it happen.

But none of this would have been possible without those Libyans who showed so much courage and kindness to strangers – Dr M, Dr Salah Rodwan, our brave driver Dr Mohammed and his brother, and many, many more whose names, I'm afraid to say, I never knew but who took many risks to save us, help us, protect us. I hope this book provides some testimony to the courage and humanity so many showed in the face of brutality and fear.